BILLIARDS

THE OFFICIAL RULES & RECORDS BOOK

1998

BCA RULES COMMITTEE
Jerry Briesath, Chair; Randy Goettlicher,
Robert Jewett, John Lewis, Tony LiBurdi, Vicki Paski, Richard Rhorer

BCA STATISTICS/RECORDS COMMITTEE
Michael Shamos, Chair; Robert Byrne, John Lewis

Published By
BILLIARD CONGRESS OF AMERICA
910 23rd Avenue
Coralville, Iowa 52241-1221
(319) 351-2112
fax: (319) 351-7767
fax on demand: (319) 337-4701
web: http://www.bca-pool.com
e-mail: bca@netins.net

ISBN 1-878493-08-6
ISSN 1047-244

FOREWORD

by Don Shimel, President and CEO

This commemorative edition of Billiards: The Official Rules and Records Book celebrates the 50th anniversary of the Billiard Congress of America. For a half-century, the BCA has promoted and supported the sport of billiards and the billiard industry. At no time has the outlook for our sport looked more favorable. Nearly 45 million people in the United States play pool. The BCA organized the largest billiards trade show in the world (*the BCA International Trade Expo*), and hosted the first-ever World Billiard Congress, which brought together the heads of billiards federations from around the globe to advance our sport onto to the Olympic stage.

This edition of the rule book features an historical look. Old-fashioned fonts convey a sense of history, not only of the BCA, but also of our wonderful, centuries-old sport. The cover shows antique billiard equipment painstakingly restored to pristine condition. Our sincere thanks go to Mark and Connie Stellinga for permission to photograph these rare artifacts from their magnificent collection.

In addition to the rules of the games with which you're familiar, this edition also sports the rules of several games of yesteryear to allow players to step back in time. This year's book also contains a comprehensive narrative on the BCA's history by noted historian and scholar Mike Shamos. The BCA is deeply grateful to Mr. Shamos for his stalwart efforts in searching through mountains of data to highlight half a century of significant events that shaped the thriving sport and industry of today. Mr. Shamos also wrote the condensed history of billiards chapter.

Photographs of past BCA Presidents pay tribute to those who have built this organization into its current status as the leader in the billiard industry throughout the world. I am humbled and honored to have been part of this group. The rules and records in this commemorative edition have been updated, and reformatted to provide you with the most accurate, reader-friendly rule book ever. BCA staff members Sandra Weber, Jason Akst and John Lewis have contributed huge amounts of time and effort to this year's book and we thank them for their efforts.

As the BCA celebrates its golden anniversary year, you can be sure that we will keep our eyes squarely on the horizon, even as we celebrate the achievements of the past. Join with us in commemorating the last fifty years, and continue to support our endeavors for the next fifty as well. I hope you find this book helpful and entertaining.

MISSION STATEMENT OF THE BILLIARD CONGRESS OF AMERICA

The mission of the BCA is to govern and/or promote competition and recreational participation in the sport of pocket billiards in the United States by establishing and disseminating information on game rules, instruction, equipment specifications and business operations.

In cooperation with the BCA recognized amateur, professional and world governing organizations that promote and sanction tournament and league competition, the BCA shall strive to increase awareness of and participation in the sport to all people. Working with all integers worldwide, BCA will perform its functions on a non-profit basis with the highest ethical standards and fair treatment of its members and the entire billiards community.

RECOGNITION OF CONTRIBUTIONS

The BCA would like to especially thank the following individuals and organizations for their invaluable contributions to the 1998 Official Rules and Records Book:

Tom Rossman
Mike Shamos
Mark and Connie Stellinga

MAJOR AMENDMENTS IN THE 1998 BCA RULES AND RECORDS BOOK

The entire "Tournament Results and Records" section has been updated in all categories.

The rules of Bank Pool have been slightly amended.

BCA equipment specifications have been substantially modified.

iii

ABOUT THE BOOK

Estimated values of the antique items depicted on the cover and elsewhere are from the collection of Mark and Connie Stellinga of Coralville, Iowa, and are not published for two reasons. As Mr. Stellinga notes, the selling cost of antiquities is always between the buyer and the seller, and also, many of these items are so rare that placing a value on them is difficult because there is nothing with which to compare the item.

SHAKER BOTTLE

The shaker bottle is used for bottle pool and pea pool *(rules on pg. 111 & 137 respectively)*. Early bottles such as this one are made of leather. This is a Brunswick "Bulldog" bottle. The bulldog - a popular image during the Victorian Period - was embossed on the bottle. This bottle dates to the early 1900s and is approximately 4 ½" tall. The "peas" are marble-sized.

TROPHY

This ornate, silver-plated trophy is typical of a national championship-level prize ca. 1890. It was never awarded, because there is no inscription on the trophy. From the Brunswick-Balke-Collender Co. *(BBC)*, this trophy is art noveau style and is approximately 16" tall.

MATCH SAFE

Early matches had a nasty habit of spontaneously combusting, often causing serious burns. This "match safe," beautifully detailed with a billiard scene, is solid sterling silver and has a striking plate on the bottom. Its origin is uncertain, and the safe dates to approximately 1890. It is approximately 2" tall, 1 ½" wide, and ⁵/₁₆" deep.

TABLE

This BBC table, "Cabinet Model 2," is believed to be the only one in existence. Built in 1894-1896, the exquisite craftsmanship features a built-in ball and cue storage area. The cue "drawer" is 60" deep and can hold a dozen full-length cues. This model was sold with a special top that could convert the pool table to a dining room table. The wood is oak, and the table has been completely restored.

CLOCK

This "time and price register" by the J.E. Came Co. of Boston, is a forerunner of modern table time computers. The ornate wood and ivory inlays of this chronograph, dating to the turn of the century, made this an expensive item for its time, costing over $15 then.

CARDS

These "Old Judge & Gypsy-Queen Cigarettes" cards are similar to baseball cards included with chewing gum. The idea was to make the tobacco products more appealing to the billiards enthusiast by also offering collectible items. This set of six cards date to approximately 1890 and are 1 ¼" wide and 2 ½" tall. Lithography is by Goodwin & Co., New York.

RACK

This 1890s "cue cupboard" has two chalk reservoirs, three scorekeeping apparatuses, and special compartments for pea pool players to store their numbers in so as to prevent cheating. This beautiful rack is made by the BBC Co. and is approximately 7' tall, 5' wide, and 20" deep, made of oak.

BALLS

The origin of this set of ivory billiard balls is unknown, but it's likely the Hyatt company produced them for Brunswick. The balls date to the 1880s.

BCA LOGO

The BCA 50th anniversary logo found on the title page and back cover is the winning entry from a recent contest to solicit the best ideas from pool lovers around the world. The winning entry is designed by Laura Campbell and Steve Grodt of R-C Designs International, Irvine, CA.

Publisher: Billiard Congress of America (BCA), Coralville, IA USA
Editor: Jason Akst, BCA
Cover and Book Design: Sandra Weber, BCA
Photography: Mike Schlotterback, French Studios Inc., Marion, Iowa
Internal Photographs: BCA archives, Luby Publishing Co., Stellinga Collection
Printing: Moore Graphic Services, Minneapolis, MN USA

TABLE OF CONTENTS

History of the Billiard Congress of America 1-22
A Brief History of the Noble Game of Billiards 23-28
BCA Equipment Specifications 29-31
Glossary of Billiard Terms 32-48
Instructional Playing Tips 49-64
Rules for Tournament Play 65-69
Instructions for Referees 70-75
General Rules of Pocket Billiards 76-84
Rules for Wheelchair Competition 85

Tournament Pocket Billiard Games
    Eight-Ball (World Standardized Rules) 86
    Nine-Ball (World Standardized Rules) 90
    14.1 Continuous (World Standardized Rules) 93
    Seven-Ball 97
    Ten-Ball 99
    Rotation 101
    Bank Pool 102
    One Pocket 105

Other Popular Pocket Billiard Games
    Baseball Pocket Billiards 108
    Basic Pocket Billiards 110
    Bottle Pool 111
    Bowlliards 114
    Bumper Pool 116
    Cowboy 118
    Cribbage 120
    Cut-Throat 123
    Equal Offense 125
    Internet Equal Offense 127
    Fifteen Ball 128
    Forty-One 129
    Honolulu 132
    Line-Up 134
    Mr. and Mrs. 135
    Pea (Kelly) Pool 137
    Poker Pocket Billiards 139

Six Ball 142
Games of Yesteryear 144

Snooker Games
International Snooker 150
American Snooker 169
Golf 173

General Rules of Carom Billiards
Cushion Caroms 182
Four-Ball Caroms 183
Straight Rail 185
USBA Three-Cushion Rules 186

The Diamond System 191-196

Billiard Congress of America Hall of Fame 197-209

Tournament Results & Records

Amateur
BCA North American Eight-Ball Champions 210
BCA North American Amateur Nine-Ball Champions 213
BCA National Junior Champions 214
BCA National League Recognized State Championships 215
BCA Sanctioned Tournaments 216
ACU-I Pocket Billiard Champions 219

Professional
U.S. Open 14.1 Champions 222
U.S. Open 14.1 Records 222
Pocket Billiard Champions 223
WPA World 9-Ball Champions 229
Pro Tour Champions 230
National Three Cushion Champions 231
World Three Cushion Champions 232
Snooker Champions 235

BCA Tournament Sanctioning Information 237
BCA Membership Information 238
BCA Presidents Photos 240

History of the
Billiard Congress of America

by Mike Shamos

At age 50, the Billiard Congress of America *(BCA)* is the longest continuously operating billiard association in U.S. history. Many such organizations have existed; some survived for several decades, others for only a few years. The BCA is by far the strongest and most effective the country has ever seen.

I was honored to be asked to write a summary of BCA history for its 50th anniversary. While I had a general notion, as do most people in the industry, of the BCA's accomplishments over the years, I had no idea how much it has really done for the game at all levels, reaching young to old, amateur and professional, solo cuemaker to multinational table manufacturer.

In a nutshell, the history of the BCA chronicles a victory over the forces that tended to repress the game, such as a decline in participation, the closing of pool rooms, and even overt hostility from politicians and zoning officials. The BCA's record, though not without difficulty and missteps, is one of massive contribution and innovation that has been a pleasure to research and document.

BEFORE THE BCA

The word "congress" means "coming together." In the U.S., of course, the word also implies "official" because it is the name given to our legislature in the Constitution. The first time billiard authorities in this country came together for an official purpose was in 1863, when a Billiard Congress was held to establish the rules for the first American championship tournament, won by Dudley Kavanagh. The Congress was not a permanent body; it consisted of player representatives and tournament officials and met when needed to set rules and resolve disputes. But it had official status because of the reputations of its participants, which included the most famous players of the day.

Our first permanent billiard organization was formed, appropriately enough, by the father of American billiards himself, Michael Phelan. In

1865, he established the American Billiard Players Association "for supervision of the interest of billiards, the encouragement and advancement of players, and the general welfare of the billiard profession at large," a fine credo even today. *(In this article, the word "billiards" is used in its generic sense to mean all cue sports; the technical distinction between pool and billiard games is not observed.)*

In the 1860's, the two largest billiard manufacturers in the country were Phelan & Collender and J. M. Brunswick & Co. As an owner of the former, Michael Phelan had a vested interest in the health of the game and the industry surrounding it. He thus began the close connection between organizations and manufacturers that survives to the present time.

Within a year, Phelan's group had a rival. In 1866, the Association of State and Provincial Billiard Champions of America was created. There was a natural rivalry between the two entities, and neither grew powerful enough to claim to represent the entire profession. Over the next 120 years, numerous organizations were spawned to serve particular needs that were not being fulfilled by any existing group. In some cases these arose out of envy, turf battles, spite or other unwholesome sentiment. In others, new bodies were formed out of legitimate need when the existing establishment failed to perform its proper function.

For those who believe that the acrimonious dispute between the BCA and the Professional Billiards Tour *(PBT)* of the early 1990's was unprecedented, it missed that distinction by nearly a hundred years. During the late decades of the 19th century, amateur sports in the United States was under the stern jurisdiction of the Amateur Athletic Union *(AAU)*. It appeared to billiard players that the AAU was prejudiced in favor of more active sports such as fencing and track and field. This dissatisfaction led in 1899 to the formation at the Waldorf Hotel in New York of the National Association of Amateur Billiard Players *(NAABP)*, a body designed to meet the particular needs of carom players as opposed to those of amateur sportsmen in general. The announced goal of the NAABP was "to guard and maintain the purity and integrity of amateur billiards, to protect the interests and conserve the rights of amateur billiard players."

The AAU saw the move as a threat to its dominance of amateur athletics and retaliated with sanctions now recognized as common in such circumstances. NAABP members were declared ineligible for AAU events, their titles were not recognized, and threats were made against clubs that hosted NAABP events. However, the NAABP offered players what the AAU had not — attention to their needs. By 1903, the NAABP had become the governing body of amateur billiards, a role it maintained until 1929.

The rise of pool after Ralph Greenleaf won the national title in 1919 created a different void that the NAABP was unable to fill. Being an amateur body, it had nothing to offer professional pool players, so in the early 1920's the National Billiard Association of America *(NBAA or, more often, the NBA)* was created. For the next 20 years, the NBA ran promotional activities designed to bring more young people into the game.

The industry's first trade association was formed in 1940, the Billiard and Bowling Institute of America *(BBIA)*. Its composition reflected the close association between billiards and bowling that exists in the U.S. but is absent in most other countries. The BBIA still operates today, and for many years was crucial to the BCA's survival by supplying needed funds and support.

In 1941, the NBA was reorganized as the Billiard Association of America *(BAA)* after a group of dissident players led by former champion Bennie Allen, formed a rival, the Professional Pocket Billiard Players Association, in a power struggle. Immediately afterwards, WWII struck. Although pool was an extremely popular recreation in military bases, and famous players toured the camps giving exhibitions, professional pool for all practical purposes went into in suspended animation. Manufacturers such as Brunswick converted some production facilities over to defense work, and tournaments virtually ceased. There was only one world pool tournament held the entire time the U.S. was at war.

FORMATION OF THE BCA

The principal accomplishment of the BAA was the publication in 1945 of the Official Rule Book. No rules had appeared since a small pamphlet was issued by the BBC Company in 1925 that contained just a brief summary of each game. The BAA rule book, by contrast, was comprehensive and its format was adopted verbatim by the BCA and has remained largely unchanged in layout ever since. The BAA also entered into a relationship with the Boys Clubs of America to sponsor an annual pool tournament. But the game languished after the war. No sponsors could be found to revive the annual world 14.1 tournament, so the title had to be decided by challenge matches, an inherently unfair structure since up and coming young players had virtually no opportunity to be accepted as challengers. The BAA was unsuccessful in promoting the game.

In 1947, a group of manufacturers decided to form a new organization to be known as the National Billiard Council to unify all elements of the billiard community, including players, proprietors, dealers and manufacturers. Its board of directors was populated by luminaries who were needed to establish ties with other groups, including Porter Butts, Director of the Association of College Unions (*ACU*), which had sponsored intercollegiate billiard competition since 1934, Walter M. Hall, Director of the Boys Clubs of America; V. K. Brown, Chicago's Director of Recreation; Jack Warner, Chairman of Warner Brothers Studios; Governor Walgreen of the State of Washington; Wilson P. Foss, the wealthy Chairman of Traprock Corporation and a former amateur balkline champion; Federal judge Francis Baker of Indianapolis; and commentator Lowell Thomas. John Canelli was the executive secretary responsible for drafting a charter.

The NBC was incorporated as a non-profit organization in Toledo, Ohio in 1948. Of its initial budget of $5,000, half came from the BBC Company and half from the BBIA. Its role was advisory only, however. It was not a governing or sanctioning body. It did, however, serve as a clearinghouse for disseminating information, resolving disputes and addressing problems at all levels from municipal to national.

Tournament activities, which had been funded and dominated by the BBC Company for decades, including Boys Clubs events, room tournaments, city championships, sectional qualifiers and national and world competition, were regarded as too expensive to be taken over by the new organization, so they were left in the hands of BBC. The NBC thought it inadvisable for tournaments to appear to be controlled by a single manufacturer. A group that included Benjamin Nartzik, owner of the National Billiard Chalk Company, John Canelli, Pierre Wilhem, Fred Schmidt of A. E. Schmidt, William Lawson, H. B. MacCready and John Gibbons suggested creating an arm known as the Billiard Congress of America that would have the authority to sanction tournaments and award prizes and trophies. The private arrangement was that BBC would continue to fund the tournaments, the BBIA would contribute as much money as it could for activities, and BBC would, over and above its tournament budget, match all BBIA money dollar-for-dollar.

The first meeting of the BCA was held at the Stevens Hotel on March 23, 1948 with Benjamin Nartzik as Chairman. That date is considered the birth of the BCA. It was to have 13 directors, three appointed by BBC, three by the BBIA, three proprietor representatives and the remainder from the NBC. This structure was a milestone — no previous organization had combined such groups together. The NBC was to provide space for the BCA at its offices in Toledo. During the 1950s it makes little sense to draw a distinction between the NBC and the BCA. They had substantially the same board members and shared the same address. The function of the BCA was to provide a visible presence independent of any manufacturer. The NBC role was to solicit manufacturers to provide funds for BCA activities. Thus they were closely connected but both groups were careful to apportion responsibilities appropriately. In the remaining history, no distinction is drawn between them.

The early vision of the BCA founders was to have the organization serve as the game's governing body and bring together all of its various constituencies, from players to manufacturers. It would be a true "coming together" that would justify use of the word "congress." But a governing body in sports is not like a governmental unit. It derives its power by consent of the sport's participants rather than statute. For the BCA to achieve recognition as a governing body, its goals and methods had to satisfy not only the BCA members but also the various elements of the billiard community who were not members.

The first visible accomplishment of the BCA proper was the revival of annual national and world tournaments. The first such pocket tournament in seven years was held in February 1949 at the Navy Pier in Chicago. It was a two-week extravaganza that featured national pocket and three-cushion competition followed immediately by two world tournaments. The BCA used the occasion to call a special meeting to include top players who were in town for the tournaments. The meeting, held appropriately enough at the Congress Hotel, included such players as Charles C. Peterson, Willie Hoppe, Willie Mosconi, Danny McGoorty, Joe Chamaco, Juan Navarra, Irving Crane, Andrew Ponzi, Jimmy Caras, Bennie Allen, George Chenier, Charles McElligott and Onofrio Lauri. All were of top rank, many were former champions and six were eventually inducted into the BCA Hall of Fame. The list rehabilitates to some extent the reputation of McGoorty, who is often thought of as a dissolute player because of his portrayal (through his own quoted words) in Robert Byrne's "McGoorty: The Story of a Billiard Bum." McGoorty, it is not well known, was devoted to billiards and participated in the organizational activities of the BCA.

The players informed the BCA that tournament purses were low when compared with those in other sports (a situation that has still not changed) and that holding pool and three-cushion tournaments in the same venue at the same time was frenetic and confusing. They also suggested holding events in larger arenas and charging admission! The idea of selling tickets instead of giving them away was not new; billiard tournaments had charged admission for a hundred years. But in 1949 the game's popularity was uncertain because of the seven-year tournaments hiatus and the organizers were afraid of scaring away spectators, so no charge was imposed, which naturally lowered the prize fund. The players encouraged support for amateur tournaments and decried the lack of publicity for professional events.

The NBC proceeded to implement many of the proposals communicated

5

by the BCA. Three-cushion and pool qualifying tournaments were to be held in 25-40 cities at an entry fee of $5. The winners would move on to sectional tournaments in which the first prize would be $300. The sectional winners would go to the Nationals, which carried a first prize of $1,000. The World tournament would consist of the top three National finishers and the previous year's World champion in double round-robin format for a top prize of $2,000 and the World title. By the end of 1949, 46 tournaments had been held in 28 cities along with 11 sectional events, and the BCA experienced early success.

Charles McElligott, a national-class three-cushion player and respected referee, was engaged as tournament organizer at a salary of $300-400 per month. Mr. McElligott was provided with a stenographic assistant whose salary was $4,000 per year, not much less than McElligott's. The moribund BAA was disbanded and its previous responsibilities handed over to the BCA. Measures were also considered to combat local ordinances restricting minors from patronizing billiard rooms. It was paradoxical for the BCA to support competition among Boys Clubs if the participants themselves were barred from pool rooms. At the NBC's meeting in Dayton, Ohio in November 1949, discussion was held on establishment of a Hall of Fame, an effort that took almost 20 more years to bring to fruition.

THE 1950's

The 1950's were a decade of soul-searching in American billiards. It was clear that the postwar years would not be kind to the game. Men who had played before the war learned new trades while in the service and returned to a country burgeoning with employment opportunities. The days of spending the afternoon in a pool hall were over, and rooms began to close rapidly. It was therefore essential to promote the games in colleges and maintain an active tournament program.

The first BCA event at which admission was charged was the world pool tournament in Chicago in February 1950. A prime seat cost 60 cents. The ticket revenue slightly more than covered the expenses of decorating the arena.

At this time, with the 1952 Olympics approaching, the subject was raised of the inclusion of billiards. However, at the time it was believed that the International Olympic Committee wanted to reduce, not increase, the number of competitive events.

The 1950 BCA budget was approximately $64,000, of which over half was spent on tournaments, college programs received $5,000, the Boys Clubs

6

about $4,000, and the remainder going to salaries and expenses. The tournament program was extremely successful, with 54 cities participating. City tournaments attracted 500 players and the intercollegiate events 300, while the Boys Clubs produced over 9,600 participants. Charlie Peterson started a tour of the nation's colleges, while Columbia Pictures planned to distribute a film on the life of Willie Hoppe.

Income from tournaments increased the 1951 budget by more than 33%, and refinements were adopted to raise spectator satisfaction. Ticket prices were increased to $1. To ensure the presence of top stars in the world championship, four players were to be seeded. These contestants would not have to participate in the preliminary national tournament. The result, possibly unanticipated, was that the national title declined in importance. Clarence "Sunshine" Anderson, a well-known room operator and trick-shot artist, was hired to give college exhibitions.

We will see that one of the BCA's strengths has been its ability to cope with adversity. In May 1952, the BBC Company informed the BCA that it was reducing its annual contribution from $55,000 (over 60% of the entire budget) to $35,000. It was only with difficulty that the BBIA was persuaded to maintain its participation at $20,000. The BCA could only respond by cutting operations and severely reducing any activity that did not produce revenue. The college program budget was cut from over $7,000 down to $500, just enough to pay for trophies. The Boys Club tournaments were revised to reduce costs. Because the world tournaments produced a significant surplus, extra effort was invested to make them successful. Masako Katsura, the first woman to enter world three-cushion competition, was voted a special travel budget of $500 to make the trip from Japan. (She finished sixth out of 11, right in the middle of the field.) Seeding was so important that the names of specific players to be seeded in both the pocket and three-cushion tournaments at the world, national and sectional levels were voted on by the BCA board.

The BCA financial situation worsened again in 1954, when BBC reduced its support to $10,000 and the BBIA did likewise. Ed Radon, who supervised the college programs, announced that he would waive his annual salary of $5,000, a truly heroic gesture. The directors refused to allow him to work for nothing, but did agree to reduce his compensation. Even with Radon's sacrifice, the operating budget would only be about $15,000, far short of the amount necessary to stage world tournaments, and the BCA reluctantly announced that none would be held.

The consequences of this decision were far-reaching but unavoidable. Willie Hoppe, the world's most recognized billiard figure, retired after winning the 1952 three-cushion title. Interest in the game waned after Ray Kilgore, an excellent but nearly unknown player, won in 1953. Lowell Thomas, probably unhappy about the direction things were headed, resigned as a BCA director. The result of interrupting the sequence of world three-cushion tournaments was the death of world professional three-cushion competition. After an unsanctioned tournament in Buenos Aires in 1954, professional events ceased until the formation of the Billiard Worldcup Association *(BWA)*, a European organization, in the 1980s. World amateur competition, which had been run by the Union Mondiale de Billard *(UMB)* since 1928, rose in importance, particularly after Raymond Ceulemans' first world three-cushion victory in 1963.

The situation was almost as bleak for pool. Irving Crane protested the BCA decision not to hold a 1954 world tournament, but to no avail. Without money, no alternative was possible. An unsanctioned competition was held at Allinger's in Philadelphia, won by Luther Lassiter. Most BCA stalwarts stayed away, but Crane played by way of protest. While BCA tournaments resumed in 1955 and 1956, the damage had been done. After Willie Mosconi, the dominant player of the era, retired in 1956 after suffering a stroke, the BCA did not hold another straight pool tournament for 10 years.

For the remainder of the decade, the BCA channeled most of its support to the Boys Club and the ACU, which expanded to become the ACU-I, Association of College Unions-International. To hold down costs, collegiate finalists were selected based on points-per-inning average rather than through sectional qualifiers. This method was unsatisfactory because of differences in playing conditions at the different colleges, so the ACU-I divided the country into 15 regions and restored sectional events. With so many regions, travel expenses could be kept low since the players did not have to journey very far to compete.

Intercollegiate billiard competition, which rarely received much press, was very important to the continued health of the game. As college enrollments increased, most potential young stars found themselves on campus. Without the opportunity to play pool competitively, many of them would have turned to other sports. Among the well-known players who were winners of the ACU-I national pool title were billiard historian and instructor William Hendricks *(1964)*, professionals Dan Louie *(1973-74)* and Max Eberle *(1993-94)*, writer-instructor Bob Jewett *(1975)* and BCA Hall of Famer Nick Varner *(1969-70)*.

With BCA support, ACU-I competition was critical to the growth of women's billiards. A women's collegiate division was established in 1942. Its

8

ranks produced many later BCA U.S. Open entrants, such as San Lynn Merrick, Donna Ries and Julie Fitzpatrick. WPBA touring pro Cathy Vanover *(then Petrowski)* was the national winner in 1989.

The 1950's closed out with a further decline in the BCA budget. BBC, experiencing financial problems, reduced its contribution to $8,000. The BCA was forced to consider revising its college program to cut costs even further. While home table sales were encouraging, pool rooms were still closing, which had the effect of reducing the later demand for home tables because of declining participation in the game.

THE 1960's

The 1960's saw both feast and famine for billiards. In 1960, the BBC Company, once so large that it owned its own forests and sawmills to supply lumber for tables and cues, was nearly bankrupt, a victim of billiards' postwar decline. At the time, however, Brunswick was one of the world's most famous trademarks. Thus when BBC was saved by merger that year, the new entity named itself Brunswick Corporation, a multinational powerhouse involved in a wide range of sports products. Billiards ceased to be its principal focus, which meant that its financial contribution to the game would continue to decline. Revenue was made up through publication of a pamphlet called "How to Play Pool," of which 133,000 were printed, and through a revision of the Rule Book.

The BCA Official Rule Book is one of the organization's most enduring legacies. Without standardized rules, the game would be chaotic. Innumerable arguments would result, and performances of different players could not be compared. A game without official rules is barely deserving of respect, let alone a world championship. The first edition gave detailed rules for 27 different games. By codifying even the lesser-played variations, such as Line-Up and Bottle Pool, the BCA has invested these games with a permanence they might not have achieved on their own. The Rule Book also contained listings of former champions, photographs of great players, and results of tournaments that occurred throughout the year, thus providing a bridge between the present and the past. At the same time, it provided regular income, since no one felt comfortable playing with an out-of-date edition. Therefore, every time the BCA issued a new edition it expected a substantial distribution.

In 1960, all BCA decision-making was in the hands of the board of directors. Separate committees had not been established, so even such matters as game rules were brought before the full board. That year it

9

considered a thorny problem in American Snooker, a variant of adapted for American tables. The question was what should be done after a foul. In British snooker, a player who was left snookered after a foul could request that any balls preventing him from contacting the required object ball be "lifted," that is, temporarily removed from the table and replaced after his stroke. Lifting is cumbersome, since it requires moving balls and marking their positions. Difficulties arise if the spot from which a ball was lift becomes occupied by another all during the shot. The proposal, which was passed unanimously, was to allow the incoming player after a foul, whether he was snookered or not, to accept the balls in position or pass the shot back to the opponent. Lifting was thus eliminated from American Snooker and this rule has not changed in the last 38 years.

In 1961, moviegoers were electrified by Paul Newman's superb and totally believable performance in "The Hustler," a top-notch film treatment of the 1959 novel by Walter Tevis. The billiard landscape in the United States changed overnight, which sent the BCA off in a new direction. People who had not touched a cue in years suddenly found the urge to play again, but were confronted by a nation depleted of pool rooms. There were few places to go, even fewer they cared to patronize. For the first time in decades there was a boom in new room construction, and potential proprietors needed help with equipment, operations, publicity and licensing.

The BCA, with its budget at a low point, was not prepared for such good news, but immediately began to demonstrate the resilience that has contributed to its long life. Another 150,000 copies of "How to Play Pool" were printed to bring in revenue quickly. Two more booklets for proprietors were published, one dealing with league play and tournaments and the other with how to manage a billiard room.

Participation in college programs and ACU-I tournaments increased by over 60% in the year since "The Hustler" was released. Attendance was higher and the board was surprised to learn that a national publication devoted a two-page spread to the championship finals.

With a huge number of players active again in straight pool and an enthusiastic country anxious for a new champion, it was embarrassing not to have any world or national title competition being held in the U.S. The BCA was still not in a position to sponsor professional events, so in 1963 it sanctioned the Billiard Room Proprietor's Association of America (BRPAA) to organize a world pool championship, which was held annually until 1968. The BRPAA, formed in 1961 to conduct tournaments, has about 800 paying members.

Benjamin Nartzik, who had served faithfully as President for 16 years, fell ill in May 1963 and died on June 30. Financial pressures had caused both the NBC and the BCA to default on their obligation to pay corporate fees to the State of Ohio. It was deemed necessary by the board to transfer the assets of both entities into a single merged corporation in a different state, so on July 31, 1963, just one month after Nartzik's death, the BCA reincorporated in Illinois. William Sheffer replaced Nartzik as President and Don Neer took over for John Canelli as Secretary/Treasurer.

One of the first acts of the reorganized association was to establish a format for straight pool league play. To prevent runouts and save time, games were to consist of 15 innings only, with a player being allowed to score a maximum of 14 points in any one inning. Contests were three games, with one point being awarded for each victory and one extra point for high ball total. This format was suitable for handicapping through a system developed by future Hall of Fame member Lou Butera.

In 1964, Joe Farhat and future Executive Secretary Bob Froeschle were sent on a fact-fining mission to an unsanctioned straight pool tournament in Las Vegas to determine whether there would be interest in having the BCA sponsor a professional tournament once again. The answer was resoundingly positive, so the BCA set about planning for its U.S. Open series.

Establishing a truly open tournament was a controversial idea. For many years, world tournaments operated strictly on an invitational basis. Players who caused "trouble," such as asking for more money, were taught a lesson by not being invited back the next year. In 1936, a sectional method of selection was introduced. Most players were invited, but several slots were reserved for winners of sectional tournaments around the country. This fell somewhat short of open competitions, since the sectional qualifiers themselves were controlled and only one competitor from each region advanced to the world tournament, which was a single or double round-robin, severely limiting the number of entrants. The BCA U.S. Open, by contrast, was to be fully open and in double elimination format could easily accommodate twice as many players as any prior world tournament.

In 1964 the first "BCA Bulletin" appeared, the forerunner of the "BCA Break," a newsletter for members. With its renewed energy, the BCA began a variety of important projects, such as developing a sanctioning policy, preparing specifications, lobbying for favorable laws and ordinances governing pool rooms, and serving the needs of proprietors.

By 1965, the BCA's income was nearly $100,000, which allowed it to undertake more ambitious tasks. William Gunklach, Jr. of National Billiard

Manufacturing became the third President. The next year was a turning point for the BCA in many ways. Under Gunklach's leadership, a Proprietors' Management Clinic and show were held with 65 registrants and 10 exhibitors, providing just a hint of what would later become the BCA Trade Expo. Any early version of the present College of Pool Knowledge was conducted by Willie Mosconi and Jimmy Caras. Any student who completed the one-day course successfully became a registered BCA Instructor. This was the precursor to the present BCA Certified Instructor program.

The first annual BCA U.S. Open straight pool tournament in 1966 was a rousing success. Irving Crane won the $2,500 first prize and set a new high run record in sanctioned play of 150 and out. It still stands as a U.S. Open record. Hall of Famer Dallas West began his unbroken string of Open appearances that is also still a record. At the Sherman House Hotel, site of the tournament, the BCA Hall of Fame finally came into existence with the induction of Ralph Greenleaf, Willie Hoppe and Charles C. Peterson, all posthumously.

Irving Crane's historic 150-and-out run at the first BCA U.S. Open in 1966.

In 1967, a women's division was added to the U.S. Open, won by Dorothy Wise in the first of her five consecutive victories. The men's prize, which went to Jimmy Caras, was $3,000 while Wise only received $500, but the event was a milestone since it was the first women's professional pool tournament held since 1935. Without the ACU-I and U.S. Open women's divisions, it is doubtful whether women's professional pool would even exist today.

A major but little-known BCA accomplishment in 1967 caused a profound change in pool worldwide. In a significant revision to the Rule Book, official rules for Nine-Ball were added for the first time. Responsibility for the rules no longer lay with the board, but was handed over to a committee chaired by Bob Froeschle and members Willie Mosconi, Jimmy Caras, Joe Balsis, Don Tozer, Dan Cahill and Joe Farhat. Nine-Ball had been played since the 1920's and was extremely popular, but regarded mostly as a gambling game at which only unofficial tournaments were held and for which no published rules existed. It was featured in "The Hustler," on which Mosconi was the technical adviser, and since 1961 it had been played at the Jansco Brothers Hustler's Tournaments in Johnston

City, Illinois. Denying the game a place in the Rule Book was counterpro-ductive and wouldn't stop people from playing it, so a single page was added summarizing the rules. Even this small gesture, though, served as official BCA recognition of the game and paved the way for sanctioned tournaments.

In 1968, the first Hall of Fame dinner was held to honor inductees Jacob Schaefer, Sr., Jake Schaefer, Jr. and Willie Mosconi. This took place at the Jack Tarr Hotel in Lansing, Michigan in conjunction with the U.S. Open tournament. A three-cushion division had been added to the Open, and Larry *("Boston Shorty")* Johnson won the first title. The BCA instituted a Player of the Year prize for men and a Woman of the Year prize for women. U.S. Open winner Joe Balsis was awarded $2,500 by the A. E. Schmidt Company over and above his Open purse. Dorothy Wise, winner in the women's division of the Open, received an additional $1,000 as Woman of the Year. Herman Rambow was elected to the Hall of Fame, the only cuemaker to be so honored.

THE 1970's

By the end of the 1960's, BCA revenue was up and the game was popular again, so it was to be a surprise that American billiards was facing the longest drought in its history. Political protests of the late '60s caused many people to rethink basic values in areas diverse as the proper role of government to self-improvement and personal health. In the leisure field, active sports such as tennis and aerobics replaced more sedentary ones. It was no longer acceptable in some quarters to indulge in "frivolous" activities like pool and there was pressure for young people to spend their time helping others or bettering themselves. During the 1970's the number of pool rooms dropped precipitously. Many of the modern rooms that had opened in the aftermath of "The Hustler" were forced to close. They were neither fish nor fowl — decor calculated to appeal to mom and the family did not attract the hard-core player who formed the bulk of the proprietors' clientele. When these rooms could no longer draw family business they failed, which affected sales of tables, cues, cloth, chalk and every other accessory.

The BCA began the 1970's with 22 manufacturers, 108 proprietors, 56 ACU-I colleges and 250 individual members, an insignificant number. Jim Wilhem of Saunier-Wilhem was now President and Don Neer had resigned as Secretary/Treasurer. News on other fronts was even worse. The National Sporting Goods Association was chosen to manage the BCA, which could not even afford to pay its own staff because of a downturn in revenue. The BCA furnishings were valued at $2,900.50, consisting mostly of a Royal

Electric typewriter and three filing cabinets. I mention this depressing fact not to denigrate the organization but to marvel at the persistence of the directors and their love for billiards at a time when it would have been easy to close the doors. Remarkably, the BCA remained committed to holding the U.S. Open.

In 1970, Steve Mizerak began his run of four consecutive U.S. Open victories. While an excellent player, his previous high finish in title competition was third place in the BRPAA world tournament at the Hotel Commodore in New York in 1968. After his string of Open wins, Mizerak was a marketable property, which led to his selection as spokesman for Miller beer.

The BCA minutes for 1971 reflect that the only positive news came from the sale of the Rule Book. Despite Mizerak's repeat as Open winner, the Player of the Year award went to Irving Crane, while Dorothy Wise repeated on the women's side.

In 1972, the BBIA informed the BCA that it would no longer make a guaranteed financial contribution, but might do so on a volunteer basis, funds permitting. Charles Bailey was named President and Fred Herzog of the NSGA became Managing Director. The U.S. Olympic Committee sent a letter to the BCA stating that to achieve Olympic recognition, a sport must be practiced in at least 40 countries on three continents and its international federation must have at least 40 nations as members but must not control both amateur and professional competition. It was clear that billiards was far from satisfying these requirements.

A high point of 1972 was the victory of Jean Balukas in the U.S. Open at age 13. She first entered the tournament in 1968 at age 9 and finished fifth. She was fourth in 1970 and third in 1971, but starting in 1972 reeled off seven straight wins, a record for both men and women.

The story of Balukas and Mizerak helped the BCA secure television coverage of the U.S. Open in 1973, which added $5,000 to the BCA treasury. At this time the BCA took up the difficult problem of equipment specifications. In any organization whose members are manufacturers, equipment specifications are contentious.

Jean Balukas captures the 1972 U.S. Open.

The manufacturers that meet them say "aye," while the ones who don't meet them are opposed. The agreed specification was a slate bed at least one inch thick, three slabs with two metal pin dowels and mounted on a hardwood lumber frame of minimum thickness $^{13}/_{16}$" and covered with a direction cloth.

Pabst Brewing and Brunswick sponsored a tournament in 1973 at the University of Iowa that featured the top players from the U.S. Open, including Joe Balsis, Cisero Murphy, Irving Crane, Dorothy Wise and Jean Balukas. When over 3,000 people attended every session, it was decided to expand the event to four colleges the next year.

By 1974, the presidency of the BCA was decided by annual election, a far cry from the Nartzik days of service until death. Mike Geiger took over as President and was succeeded the next year by Kim Gandy. Gandy began the year with a deficit of $19,000 but had the BCA in the black by 1978. While publicity was good, sponsors were scarce. Pabst and Brunswick withdrew their support for straight pool tournaments. The BCA then decided that its future could be found in Eight-Ball, and so added Eight-Ball leagues and established an National Amateur Eight-Ball tournament that lost money.

The transition to Eight-Ball was important, since straight pool was rapidly losing popularity. The game of Equal Offense was introduced in 1976. Aside from the U.S. open, however, the BCA was not promoting any professional tournaments and even proposed to suspend the U.S. Open. The male players were unhappy that they did not enjoy their former level of support, and formed the Professional Pool Players Association (PPPA). Relations between the BCA and the PPPA were not cordial, and a long era of alienation between the BCA and male professional players began. The players observed correctly that the BCA was not in a position to promote professional events, which it interpreted as a lack of moral support. No one faulted the pros for looking out for their own interests, but in retrospect the same could as easily have been done under the BCA umbrella as outside it.

By contrast, the Women's Professional Alliance (WPBA), now the Women's Professional Billiard Association, launched its own annual Nine-Ball tournament in 1977 to complement the straight pool portion of the U.S. Open. The BCA was slow to recognize the potential of Nine-Ball as a competitive, spectator and television event, which was a factor in spurring the professional to proceed on their own.

Paul Lucchesi was President in 1977 and the U.S. Open tournament was suspended in favor of amateur pool, leaving the professionals without a BCA-sanctioned title event. The BCA North American Eight-Ball Championships began with an open men's singles division. Efforts were made to combine the BCA Hall of Fame with the Bowling Hall of Fame, but this overture was rebuffed. In 1978, Jim Wilhem became the first person to serve non-consecutive terms in that role and a ladies' singles division was added to the national Eight-Ball tournament. In 1979, team Eight-Ball events were added to the national amateur tournament and a school for referees was conducted by Red Jones and Conrad Burkman. At the end of the decade, organized pool was struggling and was about to enter its bleakest period.

THE 1980's

The '80s were a transitional decade for pool. The condition of the game started off horribly, then got steadily worse until 1986, when the film version of "The Color of Money" appeared. Within a year, the renaissance had begun, with even greater strength than the revival caused by "The Hustler" 25 years earlier.

In 1980, after a disagreement with the NSGA over BCA management, the BCA selected Bob Froeschle as its Managing Director and relocated from Chicago to Iowa City. Up to that time, the need for an industry trade exposition had been satisfied by the annual NGSA show. In 1981, however, the billiard exhibitors, instead of being located together, were dispersed all over the exhibit hall. The BCA directors decided that the billiard industry needed its own trade show and named Paul Huebler, Dave Maidment and Charlie Robertson to a committee to look into the possibility. Huebler was named BCA President.

The U.S. Open was revived in 1983 and the modern form of the College of Pool Knowledge was established. That year, the BCA also produced its first instructional videotape, "Consistency is the Name of the Game." Frank Zdy of Continental Productions was engaged to produce a trade exposition the following year in return for a percentage of the gross revenue.

The billiard industry finally came into its own in 1984 with the advent of the BCA Trade Expo at the Tarrant County Convention Center in Fort Worth, Texas. The floor area of 50,000 square feet accommodated 187 booth spaces visited by about 1,500 attendees. It was obvious from the beginning that the show was a huge success. It provided a forum for everyone connected with the industry to meet, renew acquaintances, review new products and, most important, do business. Furthermore, in American commerce, an industry has a hard time commanding respect unless it is able to put on a trade show. With the Expo came sponsor recognition and a vying among cities to serve as host for future shows. The BCA became a hot property.

In 1984 the BCA was not able to mount another U.S. Open. The turning of the organization away from professional pool and more toward amateur competition convinced the men professionals that they needed an organization of their own that would look out for their interests and formed the Men's Professional Billiard Association *(MPBA)*. The goals of the BCA and MPBA were consistent; each was interested in seeing more professional tournaments, and no overt conflict was perceived. Ten years later the situation would be different.

The second Trade Expo in 1985, again in Fort Worth, was even more successful. The number of exhibitors and booth spaces was up by 20%. In 1986 the event expanded by another 20% and had outgrown its convention facility in just three years. The North American Eight-Ball Championships, held in conjunction with the Trade Expo, added a senior men's division and attracted 191 men, 128 women, 41 seniors, 100 men's teams and 55 women's teams.

The 1986 release of "The Color of Money" was a galvanizing event for the billiard industry, whose fortunes have risen with each passing year since then. Many explanations have been offered for the rebirth, ranging from the youthful appeal of Tom Cruise to complex sociological theories. It cannot have hurt that Paul Newman won an Academy award for his portrayal of a now-wiser Eddie Felson. What is clear is that the fundamental nature of the game and its players is now different. Pool is a fully coeducational activity that hardly bears a trace of the stigma that burdened the game even during the 1960's. Room owners today are more likely to have partners in the restaurant or entertainment business, with solid investment advisors watching the bottom line. Slack time in rooms is now filled with players from corporate leagues and private receptions. Most telling of all, makers of non-pool products are happy to use pool in their advertising campaigns, a sure sign that the game is thoroughly accepted across American society.

The 1987 Trade Expo occupied 40% more space in Louisville than it had in Fort Worth. At the induction of Erwin Rudolph into the Hall of Fame at the end of the Expo, all the living Hall of Fame members were present for a banquet at which each was presented with a gold watch and a jacket in recognition of their status.

The BCA was beginning to enjoy the aftermath of "The Color of Money." It accepted its first Japanese voting member and hired its first public relations firm, Roberts & Co., to handle publicity. The Expo provided a fertile source of revenue, and it appeared that as long as the show continued to be held the BCA would never again suffer the financial reverses it experienced in the 1970s.

In 1988, Mark Cord was hired as Assistant Director to Bob Froeschle, who had indicated that he would shortly be retiring. The Expo grew to 90,000 square feet and 330 booth spaces. At the general meeting, attended by more than 250 people, it was decided to expand the board to 18 members instead of the previous nine to allow for better representation of different constituencies, including proprietors, retailers, players and manufacturers. Recalling the success of the pamphlet that helped it survive during the 1960's, the BCA produced a new one, "How to Play Pool Right," written by George Fels and Alvin Blick.

In 1989, the BCA was able to hold the 14th U.S. Open tournament after a gap of six years. It was won for the first time by a foreigner, Oliver Ortmann, who beat Steve Mizerak in a 200-point final. On the amateur side, a men's junior division was added to the Eight-Ball event, won by prodigy Chan Witt who died tragically in an automobile accident a few years later. On the retirement of Bob Froeschle, Mark Cord became Managing Director. The Trade Expo grew to almost 400 booth spaces in 100,000 square feet, the largest ever, and the BCA hired a full-time public relations director.

At the end of the decade, the BCA was running a full plate of tournaments, including the North American Eight-Ball Championships, with men's and women's individual, senior and team divisions and a junior

The 1997 BCA North American 8-Ball Championships drew more than 7,000 entrants and prize money topped $500,000.

individual division, along with the U.S. Open straight pool competition. John Lewis was brought in to assist with these efforts. However, there were no BCA professional Nine-Ball events, an omission that was to cause the organization a good deal of trouble in the 1990's.

THE 1990's

This is the first decade since the 1920's in which billiards continued to rise in popularity each year without any downturn, and the international surge in pool continued. The BCA became a member of the World Pool-Billiard Association (WPA) and gave up the right to sanction world title tournaments without WPA approval. This was a remarkable and foresighted cession of power. For almost 120 years the U.S. had wielded the authority, as in baseball, to refer to its own pool, balkline and three-cushion events as bestowing on the winner the "world" title. This was to be no more, but in return the BCA was able to take its proper place in the world billiard community.

In 1990, the World Confederation of Billiard Sports was formed to serve as the worldwide supervisory organization that would satisfy the standards of the International Olympic Committee if cue sports were to have any hope of gaining a berth in the Olympics. In harmony with these international moves, the BCA developed a stylish new logo. It also extended a hand toward ever-younger players, expanding its junior amateur competition to two divisions, one for ages 15-18 and one for 14 and under.

On the promotional front, the BCA produced its first television commercial, "Pool, the Game of the '90s" and a video for proprietors titled "A Sport Whose Time Has Come." It did come. In 1991, associate membership *(the proprietor's category)* was up 288% over 1990. Recognizing the coed nature of the game, the BCA added a Scotch Doubles division to the North American Eight-Ball Tournament. The BCA Billiard Education Foundation *(BEF)* was created to promote higher education for people associated with billiards. Contributions to the BEF have increased every year since then. Just two years later, the BEF was able to distribute $75,000 in scholarships and prizes. The BCA budget was now a hundred times larger than it was just a decade earlier.

The absence of BCA professional competition strained relations with the MPBA. In 1991, the MPBA formed the Professional Billiards Tour Association *(PBTA, now the PBT)* was formed to establish a regular circuit of professional tournaments. It installed Don Mackey as Commissioner and nearly immediately hostilities erupted between the PBTA and the BCA. Mackey charged that the BCA, far from being the governing body of American billiards, was the governing body of nothing but was merely a trade association. The PBTA, he asserted, was the governing body of men's professional billiards. At the other end of the spectrum, the Women's Professional Billiard Association *(WPBA)* had a peaceable relationship with the BCA. Not only was it a member of the BCA, it was recognized by the BCA as the governing body of women's professional billiards. The PBTA could easily have achieved the same status. Mackey, however, announced his intention to force the BCA to disband, and the dispute smoldered for five years. In 1996, the PBT quietly became a BCA member, and in 1997 it renounced its claim as a governing body. While the disagreement raged, however, professional pool suffered. Sponsors were not easy to attract into an atmosphere of conflict, and what was the significance of a tournament sanction from an organization whose authority was disputed?

In 1992, an extensive Certified Instructor Program was introduced to bring rigor to an area that was previously unstructured. The program has grown rapidly and now encompasses more than 100 instructors in the U.S. and five foreign countries at the Recognized, Certified, Advanced and Master Instructor levels.

Mark Cord left in 1993 to become Executive Director of the Women's Professional Billiard Association (WPBA), which was running its successful Classic Tour. He was replaced for the next two years by Bruce Maurer The U.S. Open was revived for a 16th time, now sanctioned by the WPA. The BCA entered the computer age by providing its members with software for tournament and league management. An era passed with the death of Willie Mosconi, whose lifelong contributions to billiards included world championship play, ceaseless exhibitions, book writing, work with the Boys Club, short films, movie credits, an autobiography and service to the BCA. Mosconi was remembered at the 1994 Hall of Fame banquet and the Mosconi Memorial Scholarships were established for regional winners of the ACU-I tournaments.

Dimension was added to the amateur events through a men's and women's Master division and Nine-Ball and artistic pool (*a form of trick shot competition*) at both the adult and junior levels. As far as the professional game, the last U.S. Open straight pool tournament was held in 1993 and is unlikely to take place again unless straight pool increases in popularity. A PBTA boycott of the event did not help matters, and it is ironic that the PBTA may have contributed to the death of a game at which its own members were the best players in the world.

In 1994, Bruce Cottew, a former Army officer and city manager, replaced Bruce Maurer as Executive Director. The BCA went on-line and began accepting electronic mail. Cottew's approach has been to put the BCA on solid financial footing while greatly expanding its reach. One of the issues he reviewed was the BCA's principal income source, the Trade Expo, a study that eventually led to selection of a new producer.

In 1996, Fran Crimi of New York became the only woman BCA Certified Master Instructor in the world. Reflecting the game's increasing international character, the BCA Rule Book was published in Spanish and German editions. This effort will be instrumental in establishing the BCA as the principal source of official rules, even though it has agreed to adopt the World Standardized Rules. It also provides the opportunity for the BCA to promote its tournaments and activities worldwide by including them in the Rule Book.

Staying wired in 1996, the BCA set up an Internet home page at www.bca-pool.com. Staff expansion caused the organization to outgrow its office space in Iowa City, so it moved to 6,000 square-foot premises in nearby Coralville. The BCA Break went to a four-color process and increased its frequency from four to six issues per year. Jason Akst was brought in as Marketing and Public Relations Director, Ted Welter as Deputy Executive Director and Bruce Baker was given responsibility for League and Certified Instructor matters.

The 1997 BCA International Trade Expo covered 186,000 square feet, and a record 838 booths were in attendance.

The BCA's Trade Expo contract with Frank Zdy expired and the 1997 Expo was put on by the William T. Glasgow agency of Chicago. Zdy's role in the establishment and expansion of the Expo was pivotal, however, and should not be forgotten in exuberance over the 1997 show in Las Vegas. Zdy developed and refined the format, and was responsible for a string of successes from 1984-1996. His last show was more than four times the size of his first, and the Trade Expo has been the salvation of the BCA. That said, the 1997 Expo was the largest ever. Held in conjunction with the first World Billiard Congress, buyers from more than 1,200 companies fanned out over 863 booth spaces. The finals of an Italian Five-Pin tournament was held on the show floor and carried by Italian television. A couple even got married at the Brunswick booth, figuring that Las Vegas was the perfect place for such a ceremony. The Congress drew about 100 delegates from 50 national federations, and the proceedings were translated simultaneously into Italian, Spanish, Japanese and Mandarin Chinese.

By year's end, under the direction of Steve Kahl, the BCA had launched its All American Tour, a traveling system of amateur tournaments throughout the country to promote increased participation and an enhanced level of tournament direction and sportsmanship in amateur play.

Living Legends are BCA Hall of Famers, from left: Dallas West, Ray Martin, Lou Butera, Jean Balukas, Steve Mizerak, Jimmy Caras, and 1997 co-inductee Arthur "Babe" Cranfield. Ruth McGinnis, who died in 1974, was also inducted in 1997. Partially obscured from view are Nick Varner and Jimmy Moore.

SUMMARY

In reviewing the above chronology, it is easy to measure the BCA accomplishments. Among the most important is that it remained in existence and stayed dedicated to the game during the most difficult of times. Without an umbrella association to hold together the various constituents of the game, organized billiards might well have vanished in the United States. If I may be permitted to add a personal touch to this BCA history, here is my top ten list of the BCA's achievements during its first 50 years. The ordering is based on an assessment of their long-term significance for billiards.

1. BCA Rule Book.

2. BCA U.S. Open.

3. BCA Hall of Fame.

4. BCA International Trade Expo.

5. Support for the ACU-I and Boys Club.

6. World Tournament Sponsorship 1948-1968.

7. BCA North American Eight-Ball Championships.

8. BCA National Junior Championships.

9. BCA Certified Instructor Program.

10. Joining the World Pool-Billiard Association.

Mike Shamos is Chairperson of the BCA Statistics and Records Committee, a member of the Hall of Fame Committee and a BCA Certified Instructor.

1 © 1997 Michael Ian Shamos. The author gratefully acknowledges the assistance of John Lewis, BCA Program and league Director, and Jason Akst, BCA Marketing and Public Relations Director, in the preparation of this article.

A BRIEF HISTORY OF THE NOBLE GAME OF BILLIARDS

by Mike Shamos

The history of billiards is long and very rich. The game has been played by kings and commoners, presidents, mental patients, ladies, gentlemen, and hustlers alike. It evolved from a lawn game similar to the croquet played sometime during the 15th century in Northern Europe and probably in France. Play was moved indoors to a wooden table with green cloth to simulate grass, and a simple border was placed around the edges. The balls were shoved, rather than struck, with wooden sticks called "maces." The term "billiard" is derived from French, either from the word "billart," one of the wooden sticks, or "bille," a ball.

The game was originally played with two balls on a six-pocket table with a hoop similar to a croquet wicket and an upright stick used as a target. During the 18th century, the hoop and target gradually disappeared, leaving only the balls and pockets. Most of our information about early billiards comes from accounts of playing by royalty and other nobles. It has been known as the "Noble Game of Billiards" since the early 1800's, but there is evidence that people from all walks of life have played the game since its inception. In 1600, the game was familiar enough to the public that Shakespeare mentioned it in *Antony and Cleopatra*. Seventy-five years later, the first book of billiard rules remarked of England that there were "few Towns of note therein which hath not a publick Billiard-Table."

The cue stick was developed in the late 1600's. When the ball lay near a rail, the mace was very inconvenient to use because of its large head. In such a case, the players would turn the mace around and use its handle to strike the ball. The handle was called a "queue"— meaning "tail"— from which we get the word "cue." For a long time only men were allowed to use the cue; women were forced to use the mace because it was felt they were more likely to rip the cloth with the sharper cue.

Tables originally had flat vertical walls for rails and their only function was to keep the balls from falling off. They resembled river banks and even used to be called "banks." Players discovered that balls could bounce off the rails and began deliberately aiming at them. Thus a "bank shot" is one in which a ball is made to rebound from a cushion as part of the shot.

Billiard equipment improved rapidly in England after 1800, largely because of the Industrial Revolution. Chalk was used to increase friction between the ball and the cue stick even before cues had tips. The leather cue tip, with which a player can apply side-spin to the ball, was perfected by 1823. Visitors from England showed Americans how to use spin, which explains why it is called "English" in the United States but nowhere else. *(The British themselves refer to it as "side.")* The two-piece cue arrived in 1829. Slate became popular as a material for table beds around 1835. Goodyear discovered vulcanization of rubber in 1839 and by 1845 it was used to make billiard cushions. By 1850, the billiard table had essentially evolved into its current form.

The dominant billiard game in Britain from about 1770 until the 1920's was English Billiards, played with three balls and six pockets on a large rectangular table. A two-to-one ratio of length to width became standard in the 18th century. Before then, there were no fixed table dimensions. The British billiard tradition is carried on today primarily through the game of Snooker, a complex and colorful game combining offensive and defensive aspects and played on the same equipment as English Billiards but with 22 balls instead of three. The British appetite for Snooker is approached only by the American passion for baseball; it is possible to see a Snooker competition every day in Britain.

BILLIARDS IN THE UNITED STATES

How billiards came to America has not been positively established. There are tales that it was brought to St. Augustine by the Spaniards in the 1580's but research has failed to reveal any trace of the game there. More likely it was brought over by Dutch and English settlers. A number of American cabinetmakers in the 1700's turned out exquisite billiard tables, although in small quantities. Nevertheless, the game did spread throughout the Colonies. Even George Washington was reported to have won a match in 1748. By 1830, despite primitive equipment, public rooms devoted entirely to billiards appeared. The most famous of them was Bassford's, a New York room that catered to stockbrokers. Here a number of American versions of billiards were developed, including Pin Pool, played with small wooden targets like miniature bowling pins, and Fifteen-Ball Pool, described later.

The American billiard industry and the incredible rise in popularity of the game are due to Michael Phelan, the father of American billiards. Phelan emigrated from Ireland and in 1850 wrote the first American book on the game. He was influential in devising rules and setting standards of behavior. An inventor, he added diamonds to the table to assist in aiming, and developed new table and cushion designs. He was also the first American billiard columnist. On January 1, 1859, the first of his weekly articles appeared in *Leslie's Illustrated Weekly*. A few months later, Phelan won $15,000 in Detroit at the first important stake match held in the United States. He was a tireless promoter of the game and created the manufacturing company of Phelan and Collender. In 1884 the company merged with its chief competitor, J.M. Brunswick & Balke, to form the Brunswick-Balke-Collender Company, which tightly controlled all aspects of the game until the 1950's. Its successor, Brunswick Billiards, is still the largest American manufacturer.

The dominant American billiard game until the 1870's was American Four-Ball Billiards, usually played on a large *(11 or 12-foot)*, four-pocket table with four balls — two white and two red. It was a direct extension of English Billiards. Points were scored by pocketing balls, scratching the cue ball, or by making caroms on two or three balls. A "carom" is the act of hitting two object balls with the cue ball in one stroke. With so many balls, there were many different ways of scoring and it was possible to make up to 13 points on a single shot. American Four-Ball produced two offspring, both of which surpassed it in popularity by the late 1870's. One, simple caroms played with three balls on a pocketless table, is sometimes known as "Straight Rail," the forerunner of all carom games. The other popular game was American Fifteen-Ball Pool, the predecessor of modern pocket billiards.

The word "pool" means a collective bet, or ante. Many non-billiard games, such as poker, involve a pool but it was to pocket billiards that the name became attached. The term "poolroom" now means a place where pool is played, but in the 19th century a poolroom was a betting parlor for horse racing. Pool tables were installed so patrons could pass the time between races. The two became connected in the public mind, but the unsavory connotation of "poolroom" came from the betting that took place there, not from billiards.

Fifteen-Ball Pool was played with 15 object balls, numbered 1 through 15. For sinking a ball, the player received a number of points equal to the value of the ball. The sum of the ball values in a rack is 120, so the first player who received more than half the total, or 61, was the winner. This game, also called "61-Pool," was used in the first American championship pool tournament held in 1878 and won by Cyrille Dion, a Canadian. In 1888, it was thought more fair to count the number of balls pocketed by a player and not their numerical value. Thus, Continuous Pool replaced Fifteen-Ball Pool as the championship game. The player who sank the last ball of a rack would break the next rack and his point total would be kept "continuously" from one rack to the next.

Eight-Ball was invented shortly after 1900; Straight Pool followed in 1910. Nine-Ball seems to have developed around 1920. One-Pocket has ancestors that are older than any of these; the idea of the game was described in 1775 and complete rules for a British form appeared in 1869.

From 1878 until 1956, pool and billiard championship tournaments were held almost annually, with one-on-one challenge matches filling the remaining months. At times, including during the Civil War, billiard results received wider coverage than war news. Players were so renowned that cigarette cards were issued featuring them. The BCA Hall of Fame honors many players from this era, including Jacob Schaefer, Sr. and his son, Jake Jr., Frank Taberski, Alfredo De Oro, and Johnny Layton. The first half of this century was the era of the billiard personality. In 1906, Willie Hoppe, at the age 18, established the supremacy of American players by beating Maurice Vignaux of France at balkline. Balkline is a version of carom billiards with lines drawn on the table to form rectangles. When both object balls lie in the same rectangle, the number of shots that can be made is restricted. This makes the game much harder because the player must cause one of the balls to leave the rectangle, and hopefully return. When balkline lost its popularity during the 1930's, Hoppe began a new career in three-cushion billiards which he dominated until he retired in 1952. Hoppe was a true American legend — a boy of humble roots whose talent was discovered early, a world champion as a teenager, and a gentleman who held profes-sional titles for almost 50 years. One newspaper reported that under his manipulation, the balls moved "as if under a magic spell." To many fans, billiards meant Hoppe.

While the term "billiards" refers to all the games played on a billiard table, with or without pockets, some people take billiards to mean carom games only and use pool for pocket games. Carom games, particularly balkline, dominated public attention until 1919, when Ralph Greenleaf's pool playing captured the nation's attention. For the next 20 years he gave up the title on only a few occasions. Through the 1930's, both pool and billiards, particularly three-cushion billiards, shared the spotlight. In 1941 the Mosconi era began and carom games declined in importance. Pool went to war several times as a popular recreation for the troops. Professional players toured military posts giving exhibitions; some even worked in the defense industry. But the game had more trouble emerging from World War II than it had getting into it. Returning soldiers were in a mood to buy houses and build careers, and the charm of an afternoon spent at the pool table was a thing of the past. Room after room closed quietly and by the end of the 1950's it looked as though the game might pass into oblivion. Willie Mosconi, who won or successfully defended the pocket billiard title 19 times, retired as champion in 1956.

Billiards was revived by two electrifying events, one in 1961, the other in 1986. The first was the release of the movie, "The Hustler," based on the novel by Walter Tevis. The black-and-white film depicted the dark life of a pool hustler with Paul Newman in the title role. The sound of clicking balls sent America into a billiard frenzy. New rooms opened all over the country and for the remainder of the 60's pool flourished until social concerns, the Vietnam War, and a desire for outdoor coeducational activities led to a decline in billiard interest. By 1985, there were only two public rooms left in Manhattan, down from several thousand during the 1930's. In 1986, "The Color of Money," the sequel to "The Hustler" with Paul Newman in the same role and Tom Cruise as a an up-and-coming professional, brought the excitement of pool to a new generation. The result was the opening of "upscale" rooms catering to people whose senses would have been offended by the old rooms if they had ever seen them. This trend began slowly in 1987 and has since surged, even resulting in a public stock offering in 1991 by Jillian's, a Boston-based room chain.

While the game has had its heroes since the early 1800's, it has had to wage a constant battle for respectability. Poolrooms were often the target of politicians and legislators alike, eager to show their ability to purge immorality from their communities. Even today, obtaining a billiard license can require compliance with antiquated regulations. In the 1920's, the poolroom was an environment in which men gathered to loiter, smoke, fight, bet, and play. The rooms of the 1990's bear no resemblance to those of earlier times. The new rooms have a cachet approaching that of chic restaurants and night clubs. They offer quality equipment, expert instruction, and the chance for people to meet socially for a friendly evening. Being totally without stigma, these rooms are responsible for introducing an entire new audience to the game and are resulting in the greatest surge in billiard interest in the United States in over a century.

WOMEN IN BILLIARDS

Until very recently, billiards was completely dominated by men. The atmosphere of the poolroom was very forbidding and women had trouble being accepted there. Nonetheless, women have been enthusiastic players since the game was brought up from the ground in the 15th century. For over 200 years, women of fashion have played. Since the 1890's, there has always been at least one prominent female professional on the scene, from May Kaarlus, a spectacular turn-of-the-century trick-shot artist, to Ruth McGinnis, who toured with Willie Mosconi in the 1930's and could beat most men, to Dorothy Wise, winner of the first five U.S. Open tournaments for women, and Jean Balukas, who took the next seven. Today there are enough women professionals to merit a separate organization, the WPBA, to solicit commercial sponsorship and organize tournaments. It is very difficult for a woman to develop billiard skill because male players, her family, and friends usually do not support her efforts and it is not easy to find experienced women instructors or coaches. As this situation changes, we can expect women to equal men in ability and take the game to even greater heights.

Mike Shamos is the Curator of The Billiard Archive,
a nonprofit organization set up to preserve the game's history.

BCA
EQUIPMENT SPECIFICATIONS

TABLE SIZES:

3 ½' x 7', 4' x 8', and 4 ½' x 9' with the Play Area measuring twice as long as it is wide (± ⅛") from the cloth covered nose of the cushion rubber to the opposite cushion rubber. 4 ½' x 9' tables with a Play Area of 50" x 100" are the recognized size for professional tournament play.

TABLE BED HEIGHT:

The table bed playing surface, when measured from the bottom of the table leg, will be 29 ¼" minimum to 31" maximum.

POCKET OPENINGS & MEASUREMENTS (CLOTH COVERED RAILS):

Pocket openings are measured from tip to tip of the opposing cushion noses where direction changes into the pocket. This is called the mouth.

Corner Pocket: Mouth .... Between 4 ⅞" minimum to 5 ⅛" maximum
Side Pocket: Mouth .... Between 5 ⅜" minimum to 5 ⅝" maximum

The angle at the corner pocket entrance on each side of the pocket is 142° (±1°). The angle at the side pocket entrance on each side of the pocket is 103° (± 2°).

Vertical Pocket Angle: .... 12° minimum to 15° maximum.

Shelf: The shelf is measured from the center of the imaginary line that goes from one side of the mouth to the other where the nose of the cushion changes direction to the center of the vertical cut of the slate pocket radius.

Corner Pocket: ....1 ⅝" minimum to 1 ⅞" maximum
Side Pocket: .... 0" minimum to ⅜" maximum

Drop Point Slate Radius: The pocket radius measured from the vertical cut of the slate to the playing surface.

Drop Point Slate Radius .... ⅛" radius min. to ¼" radius max.

PLAYING BED:

The playing surface must be capable, either by its own strength or a combination of its strength and that of the table base frame, of maintaining an overall flatness within ± .020" lengthwise and ± .010" across the width. Further, this surface should have an additional deflection not to exceed .030" when loaded with a concentrated static force of 200 pounds at its center. All slate joints must be in the same plane within .005" after leveling and shimming. The bed must be covered with a billiard fabric, the major portion of which is made of wool, with proper tension to avoid unwanted ball roll-off. It is recommended that professional tournament size tables have a three-piece set of slate with a minimum thickness of 1" and a wooden frame of at least ¾" attached to slate. BCA will sanction tournament play on home and coin operated tables with one-piece slate providing the Play Area requirements are met. All playing surfaces must be solidly secured to base frame with screws or bolts.

CUSHION:

Cushions should react so that they conform under controlled conditions to the three cushion angles prescribed in the "diamond" (or site) system showing in the diagram on page 191 of Billiards: The Official Rules and Records Book to ± 1 ball width. The speed of the table cushions should be such that placement of a ball on the head spot, shooting through the foot spot, using center ball english, with a level cue and firm stroke, the ball must travel a minimum of 4 to 4 ½ lengths of the table without jumping.

POOL BALL SPECIFICATIONS:

Molded and finished in a perfect sphere in the following weight and diameter:

Pocket Billiard Balls

    Weight: 5 ½ to 6 oz. .... *Diameter: 2 ¼"
*Diameter tolerance of (plus or minus) .005"

POOL CUE SPECIFICATIONS:

    Player may bring a maximum of 3 cue sticks to a match

    Width of tip: .... 9 mm minimum / 14 mm maximum

    Weight: .... no minimum / 25 oz. maximum

    Length: .... 40 inches minimum / no maximum

Ferrule, if of a metal material, may not be more than 1 inch in length.

The cue tip on any stick used to perform a legal jump shot must be composed of either a leather or synthetic leather material.

Foot Rail

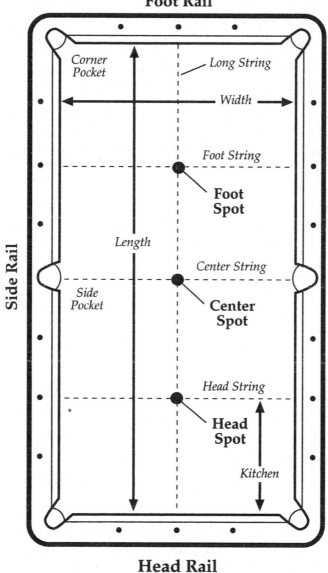

Corner Pocket

Long String

Width

Foot String

Foot Spot

Length

Center String

Center Spot

Side Pocket

Head String

Head Spot

Kitchen

Side Rail

Head Rail

Diagram 1

GLOSSARY OF BILLIARD TERMS

The following glossary contains the billiard terms and definitions essential to the utilization of the rules of games provided in this book. In addition to the definitions of these terms, there are also references to equipment, accessories, and phrases commonly used by billiard players.

Each definition begins with the term in bold face type, followed by italicized parenthetical notation of the game variation or classification in which the term is used or to which it primarily applies.

Where a diagram or other supplemental information is available elsewhere in this book, it is referenced parenthetically following the definition.

ANGLED
(Snooker, pocket games) When the corner of a pocket prevents a player shooting the cue ball directly at an object ball. *(See corner-hooked.)*

ANGLE SHOT
(Pocket games) A shot that requires the cue ball to drive the object ball other than straight ahead. *(See cut shot.)*

APEX OF TRIANGLE
(Pocket games) The position in the grouping of object balls that is on the foot spot; the front ball position of the pyramid or rack.

AROUND THE TABLE
(Carom games) Describes shots in which the cue ball contacts three or more cushions, usually including the two short cushions, in an effort to score.

BALANCE POINT
(General) The point on a cue at which it would remain level if held by a single support, usually about 18" from the butt end of the cue.

BALL IN HAND
(Pocket games) See cue ball in hand.

BALL ON
(Snooker) A colored *(non-red)* ball a player intends to legally pocket; same as on ball.

BANK SHOT
(Pocket games) A shot in which the object ball is driven to one or more cushions before it is pocketed; incidental contact as a ball moves along and adjacent to a cushion does not qualify as a cushion or bank. It is not an obvious shot and must be called in games requiring called shots. *(See kick shot.)*

BAULK
(Snooker) The intervening space between the bottom cushion and the baulk-line.

BAULK-LINE
(Snooker) A straight line drawn 29" from the face of the bottom cushion and parallel to it.

BED OF TABLE
(General) The flat, cloth-covered surface of the table within the cushions; the playing area exclusive of the cushions.

BILLIARD
(Carom games) A count or score; a successful shot.

BLIND DRAW
(General) A method used to determine pairings or bracketing of players in tournaments that assures random placement or pairing of contestants.

BOTTLE
(Pocket games) A specially shaped leather or plastic container used in various games. *(Also called the shake bottle.)*

BOTTOM CUSHION
(Snooker) The cushion located at the head of a snooker table — closest to the half circle.

BREAK
(Pocket games) See open break and opening break shot.

BREAK
(Snooker) Total scored in one inning.

BREAKING VIOLATION
(Pocket games) A violation of special rules which apply only to the opening break shot of certain games. Unless specified in individual game rules, a breaking violation is not a foul.

BRIDGE
(General) The hand configuration that holds and guides the shaft-end of the cue during play. *(See mechanical bridge.)*

BURST
(Forty-One Pocket Billiards) Scoring a total of more than 41 points.

BUTT OF CUE
(General) The larger end of a cue, opposite the tip. On a two-piece cue, the butt extends up to the joint.

CALL SHOT

(Pocket games) Requirement that a player designate, in advance of each shot, the ball to be made and the pocket into which it will be made. In calling the shot, it is NEVER necessary to indicate details such as the number of cushions, banks, kisses, caroms, etc. The rules of "Bank Pool" are an exception.

CALLED BALL

(Pocket games) The ball the player has designated to be pocketed on a shot.

CALLED POCKET

(Pocket games) The pocket which a player has designated a ball to be shot.

CAROM

(General) To bounce off or glance off an object ball or cushion; a shot in which the cue ball bounces off one ball into another is termed a carom.

CAROM, SCORING

(General) Contact by the cue ball with object balls, the bottle or cushions in such a way that a legal score is made, according to specific game rules.

CENTER SPOT

(General) The exact center point of a table's playing surface.

CHALK

(General) A dry, slightly abrasive substance that is applied to the cue tip to help assure a nonslip contact between the cue tip and the cue ball.

CHUCK NURSE

(Straight Rail Billiards) A scoring technique used when one object ball rests against the cushion and the second object ball is to one side of the first ball and away from the cushion. Cue ball strikes the object ball at the cushion so that the cue ball just comes back to touch *(carom)* the second object ball without moving it out of position for a similar subsequent shot.

CLEAN BANK

(Bank Pocket Billiards) A shot in which the object ball being played does not touch any other object balls *(i.e., no kisses, no combinations).*

CLEAR BALL

(Carom games) The all-white ball, devoid of any markings, used in carom games. *(See spot ball.)*

COMBINATION

(Pocket games) Shot in which the cue ball first strikes a ball other than the one to be pocketed, with the ball initially contacted in turn striking one or more other balls in an effort to score.

COMBINATION ON
(Pocket games) Two or more balls positioned in such a way that a ball can be driven into a called pocket with a combination shot, often called a "dead combo" or an "on combo."

COMBINATION ON
(Snooker) See plant.

CONTACT POINT
(General) The precise point of contact between the cue ball and the object ball when the cue ball strikes the object ball. *(See Instructional Playing Tips.)*

CORNER-HOOKED
(Pocket games, Snooker) When the corner of a pocket prevents shooting the cue ball in a straight path directly to an object ball, the cue ball is corner-hooked; same as angled.

COUNT
(General) A score; a successful shot.

COUNT, THE
(General) The running score at any point during a player's inning in games where numerous points are scored successively.

CROSS CORNER
(Pocket games) Term used to describe a bank shot that will rebound from a cushion and into a corner pocket.

CROSS SIDE
(Pocket games) Term used to describe a bank shot that will rebound from a side cushion and into a side pocket.

CROSS TABLE SHOT
(Carom games) Shot in which scoring is accomplished by driving the cue ball across the table between the long cushions.

CROTCH
(Carom games) The corner area of a carom table in straight-rail billiards in which a player may score no more than three successive counts with the balls before driving at least one object ball out of the area. The four crotches are defined as those spaces within crotch lines drawn between the first diamond on the end rail to the second diamond on the side rail.

CRUTCH
(General) Slang term for the mechanical bridge.

CUE
(General) Tapered device, usually wooden, used to strike the cue ball to execute carom or pocket billiard shots. *(Also called "cue stick.")*

CUE BALL
(General) The white, unnumbered ball that is always struck by the cue during play.

CUE BALL IN HAND
(Pocket games) Cue ball may be put into play anywhere on the playing surface.

CUE BALL IN HAND BEHIND THE HEAD STRING
(Pocket games) Cue ball may be put into play anywhere between the head string and the cushion on the head end of the table not in contact with an object ball. *(See Diagram 1, Pg. 31.)*

CUE BALL IN HAND WITHIN THE D
(Snooker) See cue ball in hand within the half-circle.

CUE BALL IN HAND WITHIN THE HALF-CIRCLE
(Snooker) The cue ball is in hand within the half-circle when it has entered a pocket or has been forced off the table. The base of the cue ball may be placed anywhere within or on the half-circle. It remains in hand until the player strikes the cue ball with the top of the cue or a foul is committed while the ball is on the table.

CUE TIP
(General) A piece of specially processed leather or other fibrous or pliable material attached to the shaft end of the cue that contacts the cue ball when the shot is executed.

CUSHION
(General) The cloth-covered rubber which borders the inside of the rails on carom and pocket billiard tables; together the cushions form the outer perimeter of the basic playing surface.

CUT SHOT
(Pocket games) A shot in which the cue ball contacts the object ball to one side or the other of full center, thus driving it in a direction other than that of the initial cue ball path. *(See Instructional Playing Tips.)*

D
(Snooker) An area, semicircular in shape, with the straight side formed by the line drawn between the spot for the yellow and the spot for the green measured 29 inches out from the face of the bottom cushion *(sometimes referred to as the baulk-line)* and the semicircle is determined by the size of the table being used. *(See Diagram 30, Page 151.)*

DEAD BALL

(Pocket games) A cue ball stroked in such a manner that virtually all of the speed and/or spin of the cue ball is transferred to the object ball, the cue ball retaining very little or none after contact.

DEAD BALL SHOT

(Pocket games) A shot in which a dead ball stroke is employed; often called a kill shot, because of the relative lack of cue ball motion after contact with the object ball.

DEAD COMBINATION

(Pocket games) See combination on.

DIAMONDS

(General) Inlays or markings on the table rails that are used as reference or target points. The diamonds are essential for the utilization of numerous mathematical systems employed by carom and pocket games players. *(See The Diamond System.)*

DRAW SHOT

(General) A shot in which the cue ball is struck below center, and the resulting back spin causes the cue ball to return towards the player after full contact with an object ball.

DROP POCKETS

(Pocket games) Type of pockets with no automatic return of the balls to the foot end of the table; balls must be removed manually.

DOUBLE ELIMINATION

(General) A tournament format in which a player is not eliminated until he has sustained two match losses.

DOUBLE HIT

(General) A shot on which the cue ball is struck twice by the cue tip on the same stroke. *(See General Rules of Pocket Billiards, Carom Billiards.)*

DOUBLE ROUND ROBIN

(General) A tournament format in which each contestant in a field plays each of the other players twice.

ENGLISH

(General) Side spin applied to the cue ball by striking it off center; used to alter the natural roll of the cue ball and/or the object ball.

FEATHER SHOT

(General) A shot in which the cue ball barely touches or grazes the object ball; an extremely thin cut.

FERRULE

(General) A piece of protective material *(usually plastic, horn, or metal)* at the end of the cue shaft, onto which the cue tip is attached.

FOLLOW SHOT

(General) A shot in which the cue ball is struck above center and the resulting forward spin causes the cue ball to roll forward after contact with an object ball.

FOLLOW-THROUGH

(General) The movement of the cue after contact with the cue ball through the area previously occupied by the cue ball. *(See Instructional Playing Tips.)*

FOOT OF TABLE

(General) The end of a carom or pocket billiard table at which the balls are racked or positioned at the start of a game.

FOOT SPOT

(General) The point on the foot end of the table where imaginary lines drawn between the center diamonds of the short rails and the second diamonds of the long rails intersect. *(See Diagram 1, Pg. 31.)*

FOOT STRING

(General) A line on the foot end of the table between the second diamonds of the long rails, passing through the foot spot. *(See Diagram 1, Pg. 31.)* The foot string is never drawn on the table, and has no use in play.

FORCE

(General) The power applied on the stroke to the cue ball, which may result in distortion and altering of natural angles and action of the ball.

FORCE FOLLOW

(General) A follow shot with extreme overspin applied to the cue ball, with the term generally used in reference to shots in which the cue ball is shot directly at and then "through" an object ball, with a pronounced hesitation or stop before the overspin propels the cue ball forward in the general direction of the stroke.

FOUL

(General) An infraction of the rules of play, as defined in either the general or the specific game rules. *(Not all rule infractions are fouls.)* Fouls result in a penalty, and are also dependent on specific game rules.

FOUL STROKE

(General) A stroke on which a foul takes place.

FRAME

(Snooker) The equivalent of one game in snooker.

FREE BALL

(Snooker) After a foul, if the cue ball is snookered, the referee shall state "Free Ball." If the non-offending player takes the next stroke he may nominate any ball as on, and for this stroke, such ball shall be regarded as, and acquire the value of, the ball on. *(See International Snooker rules.)*

FREE BREAK

(Pocket games) An opening break shot in which a wide spread of the object balls may be achieved without penalty or risk. Free breaks are detailed in individual games rules.

FROZEN

(General) A ball touching another ball or cushion.

FULL BALL

(General) Contact of the cue ball with an object ball at a contact point on a line joining the centers of the cue ball and object ball. *(See Instructional Playing Tips.)*

GAME

The course of play that starts when the referee has finished racking the balls, and ends at the conclusion of a legal shot which pockets the last required ball. In 14.1 Continuous, a game lasts several racks.

GAME BALL

(General) The ball which, if pocketed legally, would produce victory in a game.

GATHER SHOT

(Carom games) A shot on which appropriate technique and speed are employed to drive one or more balls away from the other(s) in such a manner that when the stroke is complete, the balls have come back together closely enough to present a comparatively easy scoring opportunity for the next shot.

GRIP

(General) The manner in which the butt of the cue is held in the hand. *(See Instructional Playing Tips.)*

GULLY TABLE

(Pocket games) A table with pockets and a return system that delivers the balls as they are pocketed to a collection bin on the foot end of the table.

HANDICAPPING

(General) Modifications in the scoring and/or rules of games to enable players of differing abilities to compete on more even terms.

HEAD OF TABLE

(General) The end of a carom or pocket billiard table from which the opening break is performed; the end normally marked with the manufacturer's nameplate.

HEAD SPOT

(General) The point on the head of the table where imaginary lines drawn between the center diamonds of the short rails and the second diamonds of the long rails intersect. *(See Diagram 1, Pg. 31.)*

HEAD STRING

(General) A line on the head end of the table between the second diamonds of the long rails, passing through the head spot. *(See Diagram 1, Pg. 31.)*

HICKEY

(Snooker Golf) Any foul.

HIGH RUN

(14.1 Continuous) During a specified segment of play, the greatest number of balls scored in one turn *(inning)* at the table.

HOLD

(General) English which stops the cue ball from continuing the course of natural roll it would take after having been driven in a certain direction.

INNING

(General) A turn at the table by a player, and which may last for several racks in some pocket games.

IN HAND

(Pocket games) See cue ball in hand.

IN HAND BEHIND THE HEAD STRING

(Pocket games) See cue ball in hand behind the head string.

IN-OFF

(Snooker) A losing hazard; that is, when the cue ball enters a pocket. The snooker equivalent of a scratch.

IN THE RACK

(14.1 Continuous) A ball that would interfere with the reracking of the object balls in 14.1 Continuous that extend past one rack.

JAW

(Pocket games) The slanted part of the cushion that is cut at an angle to form the opening from the bed of the table into the pocket.

JAWED BALL

(Pocket games) Generally refers to a ball that fails to drop because it bounces back and forth against the jaws of a pocket.

JOINT

(General) On two-piece cues, the screw-and-thread device, approximately midway in the cue, that permits it to be separated into two sections.

JUMP SHOT

(General) A shot in which the cue ball or object ball is caused to rise off the bed of the table.

JUMPED BALL

(General) A ball that has left and remained off the playing surface as the result of a stroke or a ball that is stroked in a manner which causes it to jump over another ball.

KEY BALL

(14.1 Continuous) The 14th ball of each rack; called the key ball because it is so critical in obtaining position for the all important first *(or break)* shot of each reracking of the balls.

KICK SHOT

(General) A shot in which the cue ball banks off a cushion(s) prior to making contact with an object ball or scoring.

KILL SHOT

(Pocket games) See dead ball shot.

KISS

(General) Contact between balls. *(See kiss shot.)*

KISS SHOT

(Pocket games) A shot in which more than one contact with object balls is made by the cue ball; for example, the cue ball might kiss from one object ball into another to score the latter ball. Shots in which object balls carom off one or more other object balls to be pocketed. *(Also called carom shots.)*

KISS-OUT

(General) Accidental contact between balls that causes a shot to fail.

KITCHEN

(Pocket games) A slang term used to describe the area of the table between the head string and the cushion on the head end of the table. *(Also called the area above the head string.)*

LAG

(Carom games) A shot in which the cue ball is shot three or more cushions before contacting the object balls.

LAG FOR BREAK

(General) Procedure used to determine starting player of game. Each player shoots a ball from behind the head string to the foot cushion, attempting to return the ball as closely as possible to the head cushion. *(See General Rules of Pocket Billiards, Carom Billiards.)*

LEAVE

(Pocket games) The position of the balls after a player's shot.

LONG

(General) Usually refers to a ball which, due to english and speed, travels a path with wider angles than those that are standard for such a ball if struck with natural english and moderate speed.

LONG STRING

(Pocket games) A line drawn from the center of the foot cushion to the foot spot *(and beyond if necessary)* on which balls are spotted.

LOSING HAZARD

(Snooker) Occurs when the cue ball is pocketed after contact with an object ball.

LOT

(General) Procedures used, not involving billiard skills, to determine starting player or order of play. Common methods used are flipping coins, drawing straws, drawing cards, or drawing peas or pills.

MASSÉ SHOT

(General) A shot in which extreme spin is applied to the cue ball by elevating the cue butt at an angle with the bed of the table of anywhere between 30 and 90 degrees. The cue ball usually takes a curved path, with more curve resulting from increasing cue stick elevation.

MATCH

The course of play that starts when the players are ready to lag and ends when the deciding game ends.

MECHANICAL BRIDGE

(General) A grooved device mounted on a handle providing support for the shaft of the cue during shots difficult to reach with a normal bridge hand. Also called a crutch or rake.

MISCUE

(General) A stroke which results in the cue tip contact with cue ball being faulty. Usually the cue tip slides off the cue ball without full transmission of the desired stroke. The stroke usually results in a sharp sound and

discoloration of the tip and/or the cue ball at the point of contact.

MISS
(General) Failure to execute a completed shot.

MISS
(Snooker) The call the referee makes in snooker if it is judged the player has not endeavored to the best of his ability to hit the ball on. *(See the rules for International Snooker.)*

NATURAL
(Carom games) A shot with only natural angle and stroke required for successful execution; a simple or easily visualized, and accomplished, scoring opportunity.

NATURAL ENGLISH
(General) Moderate side-spin applied to the cue ball that favors the direction of the cue ball path, giving the cue ball a natural roll and a bit more speed than a center hit.

NATURAL ROLL
(General) Movement of the cue ball with no english applied.

NIP DRAW
(General) A short, sharp stroke, employed when a normal draw stroke would result in a foul due to drawing the cue ball back into the cue tip.

NURSES
(Carom games) Techniques whereby the balls are kept close to the cushions and each other, creating a succession of relatively easy scoring opportunities.

OBJECT BALLS
(General) The balls other than the cue ball on a shot.

OBJECT BALL, THE
(Pocket games) The particular object ball being played on a shot.

ON BALL
(Snooker) See ball on.

OPEN BREAK
(Pocket games) The requirement in certain games that a player must drive a minimum of four object balls out of the rack to the cushions in order for the shot to be legal.

OPENING BREAK SHOT
(General) The first shot of a game.

PEAS
(Pocket games) Small plastic or wooden balls numbered 1 through 15 or 16, use defined in specific game rules. *(Called pills.)*

PILLS
(Pocket games) See peas.

PLANT
(Snooker) A position of two or more red balls that allows a ball to be driven into a pocket with a combination shot.

POSITION
(General) The placement of the cue ball on each shot relative to the next planned shot. Also called "shape."

POT
(Snooker) The pocketing of an object ball.

POWDER
(General) Talc or other fine, powdery substance used to facilitate free, easy movement of the cue shaft through the bridge.

POWER DRAW SHOT
(General) Extreme draw applied to the cue ball. *(See force draw.)*

PUSH SHOT
(General) A shot in which the cue tip maintains contact with the cue ball beyond the split second allowed for a normal and legally stroked shot.

PYRAMID
(Pocket games) Positioning of the object balls in a triangular grouping *(with the front apex ball on the foot spot)*, used to begin many pocket billiard games.

PYRAMID SPOT
(Snooker) The same as the pink spot. The spot is marked midway between the center spot and the face of the top cushion.

RACE
(General) Predetermined number of games necessary to win a match or set of games. For example, a match that is the best 11 out of 21 games is called a race to 11, and ends when one player has won 11 games.

RACK
The triangular equipment used for gathering the balls into the formation required by the game being played.

RAILS

(General) The top surface of the table, not covered by cloth, from which the cushions protrude toward the playing surface. The head and foot rails are the short rails on those ends of the table; the right and left rails are the long rails, dictated by standing at the head end of the table and facing the foot end.

RED BALL

(Carom games) The red-colored object ball. *(Also the name of a particular 3-cushion billiard game.)*

REST

(Snooker) The mechanical bridge.

REVERSE ENGLISH

(General) Side-spin applied to the cue ball, that favors the opposite direction of the natural cue ball path, i.e., inside english.

ROUND ROBIN

(General) A tournament format in which each contestant plays each of the other players once.

RUNNING ENGLISH

(General) Side-spin applied to the cue ball which causes it to rebound from a cushion at a narrower angle and at a faster speed than it would if struck at the same speed and direction without english.

RUN

(General) The total of consecutive scores, points or counts made by a player in one inning. The term is also used to indicate the total number of full short-rack games won without a missed shot in a match or tournament.

SAFETY

(General) Defensive positioning of the balls so as to minimize the opponent's chances to score. *(The nature and rules concerning safety play are decidedly different in specific games; see individual game rules regarding safety play.)* A player's inning usually ends after a safety play.

SCRATCH

(Carom games) To score a point largely by accident, due to an unanticipated kiss, unplanned time-shot, etc.

SCRATCH

(Pocket games) The cue ball goes into a pocket on a stroke.

SEEDING

(General) Predetermined initial pairings or advanced positioning of players in a field of tournament competition.

SET

(General) A subdivision of a match, usually consisting of a number of games. For example, a match might be best 3 of 5 sets with each set a race to 7 games.

SHAFT

(General) The thinner part of a cue, on which the cue tip is attached. On a two-piece cue, the shaft extends from the cue tip to the joint.

SHAKE BOTTLE

(Pocket games) See bottle.

SHOT

An action that begins at the instant the cue tip contacts the cue ball, and ends when all balls in play stop rolling and spinning.

SHOT CLOCK

(General) Any timing device used to gauge the time limit in which a player is allowed to play a shot. The timing device must have at least the functions of a stop watch: reset to zero, start, and stop. A simple wrist watch without timing functions is not sufficient.

SHORT

(General) Usually refers to a ball which, due to english and stroke, travels a path closer to perpendicular to the rail than those for a ball struck without english.

SHORT-RACK

(Pocket games) Games which utilize fewer than 15 countable object balls.

SINGLE ELIMINATION

(General) A tournament format in which a single loss eliminates a player from the competition.

SNAKE

(Carom games) A shot in which the use of english causes the cue ball to make three or more cushion contacts, though utilizing only two different cushions. Also called a double-the-rail shot.

SNOOKERED

(Snooker) The condition of incoming player's cue ball position when he cannot shoot in a straight line and contact all portions of an on ball directly facing the cue ball *(because of balls not "on" that block the path)*.

SPLIT DOUBLE ELIMINATION

(General) A modification of the double elimination tournament format, in which the field is divided into sections, with one player emerging from

each of the sections to compete for the championship, in a single show-down match for the championship.

SPLIT HIT

A shot in which it cannot be determined which object ball(s) the cue ball contacted first, due to the close proximity of the object balls.

SPOT

(General) The thin, circular piece of cloth or paper glued onto the cloth to indicate the spot locality (i.e., head spot, center spot, foot spot); also an expression to describe a handicap.

SPOT BALL

(Carom games) The white ball differentiated from the clear by one or more markings; usually spots, dots or circles.

SPOT SHOT

(Pocket games) Player shoots a ball on the foot spot with the cue ball in hand behind the head string.

SPOTTING BALLS

(General) Replacing balls to the table in positions as dictated by specific game rules.

STANCE

(General) The position of the body during shooting. *(See Instructional Playing Tips.)*

STOP SHOT

(Pocket games) A shot in which the cue ball stops immediately upon striking the object ball.

STRIKER

(Snooker) The player who is about to shoot and has yet to complete his inning.

STROKE

(General) The movement of the cue as a shot is executed. *(See Instructional Playing Tips.)*

SUCCESSIVE FOULS

(Pocket games) Fouls made on consecutive strokes by the same player, also called consecutive fouls.

TABLE IN POSITION

(General) Term used to indicate that the object balls remain unmoved following a shot.

THROW SHOT
(Pocket games)

1.   A shot in which english alters the path of the object ball.

2.   A combination shot of frozen or near frozen balls in which the rubbing of the first ball across the second ball pulls the shot away from the line joining the centers of the two balls.

TIME SHOT
(General) A shot in which the cue ball *(most often)* moves another ball into a different position and then continues on to meet one of the moved balls for a score.

TOP CUSHION
(Snooker) The cushion located at the foot of a snooker table — closest to the black spot.

TRIANGLE
(Pocket games) The triangular device used to place the balls in position for the start of most games.

YELLOW BALL
(Carom games) In international competition, the spot ball has been replaced by a yellow ball without any markings.

INSTRUCTIONAL PLAYING TIPS

By Jerry Briesath and Richard Rhorer

There are many variations of the game of billiards, but the fundamentals of good billiard playing are inherent in every format of the sport. This section deals with these fundamentals.

CUE SELECTION: Try several cues and start with the one that feels most comfortable to you. It is difficult for a beginning pool player to know which weight cue to get. Keep in mind that most professional pool players use a cue that weighs between 18 and 20 ounces. The shaft size of a cue mainly has to do with personal preference and the size of your fingers. Shaft sizes for pool cues basically run between 12 to 14 millimeters. Most professional pool players play with a shaft size of 12½ to 13½ mm.

PROPER GRIP OF A CUE: Hold cue lightly with thumb and first three fingers (*Fig. 1*). When the cue is gripped properly, it should not touch the palm of your hand (*Fig. 2*). It is very important to maintain a light grip on the cue at all times. Gripping the cue too tightly while stroking through the cue ball is a common mistake that must be corrected.

Figure 1   Figure 2

WHERE TO GRIP THE CUE: When you are bent over in your shooting position and the cue tip is almost touching the cue ball, the shooting hand should be directly under the elbow. It is okay to have the shooting hand an inch or two ahead of the elbow at impact. It is never recommended to have the shooting hand behind the elbow at impact (*Fig. 3*).

Figure 3

The following Instructions and Illustrations are for Right-Handed Players.

CUE STANCE: Face the shot. Before you even bend over to shoot, there is a lineup of three points—the chin, the cue ball and the exact place you want the cue ball to go. Turn your body slightly to the right without your chin leaving the point of lineup. Bend over at the waist, put your bridge hand down 7 to 10 inches from the cue ball so that your chin is 2 to 8 inches directly above the cue stick. Adjust your feet to distribute your body weight approximately 50/50 (*as shown in Fig. 4*). A generally accepted stance when you are in your shooting position is to have the tip of the right toe directly under the line of the cue and the left toe slightly to the left side of the line of the cue. This should allow a 4 to 6 inch gap between the hip and the cue for freedom of movement.

Figure 4

Figure 5

A common mistake made by beginners in their shooting position is to have the shoulders and chest facing the cue ball. A preferred technique is to turn the left shoulder out in front and the right shoulder back, thus turning the chest more to the right. This makes a better body alignment (*Fig. 5*).

Figure 6

Figure 7

Bridges: One of the most overlooked fundamentals of the game is a solid bridge. The difference between a good player and a mediocre player can often be traced to the bridge or their bridges. Nothing is of greater importance in billiard play. If the shot you are executing is to be accurate, your bridge must be natural, yet give firm guidance to the cue. Adapt the following formulas for your correct bridges. There are two basic bridges – an open bridge and a closed bridge.

Open Bridge: An open bridge is one formed by placing the hand firmly on the table, cupping the hand, pressing the thumb against the forefinger forming a "V" (*Fig. 6*). The cue

Figure 8

Figure 9

is now placed on the "V" *(Fig. 7)*. To adjust the height of the bridge, simply pull the fingers toward you to raise the bridge *(Fig. 8)*, or pushing the fingers away to lower the bridge *(Fig. 9)*. This allows you to strike the cue ball high, medium or low while maintaining a solid bridge. This bridge is recommended for beginners. Professionals use this bridge on many shots that don't require a lot of power or cue ball spin.

Figure 10

Stretch Shots: When stretching out for a shot where a long bridge is required *(12 inches or more)*, it is important to use an open bridge. Keep the backswing and follow-through very short and use minimum speed *(Fig. 10)*.

Figure 12

Figure 12

Figure 13

Closed Bridge: Place your entire bridge hand flat on the table. The heel of your hand should be down firmly *(Fig. 11)*. Bend your forefinger so that its tip touches your thumb, thus forming a loop *(Fig. 12)*. Place the cue tip in the loop formed by forefinger and thumb, resting the cue against the inner groove of these two fingers. Extend the cue through the loop formed by the above. Now pull your forefinger firmly against the cue, but with the loop just loose enough so that you can stroke the cue back and forth easily. As you do the above, keep your middle, ring and small fingers spread out and firmly pressed against the table. They form the bridge tripod which must be firm yet natural. You have the correct bridge when the cue passes through easily, accurately and with firm guidance and support.

51

The bridge length is the distance between the loop of the forefinger and the cue ball on a closed bridge or the thumb and the cue ball on an open bridge. Most professional pool players use a bridge length of 7 to 10 inches. Whether you use an open or closed bridge, the heel of your hand should be firmly on the table at all times. The bridge hand must not move while you are striking the ball.

Figure 14

Bridge for Follow Shot: Using a Standard Bridge, elevate the tripod fingers slightly. Keep cue level (*Fig. 13*).

Figure 15   Figure 16

Bridge for Draw Shot: Using a Standard Bridge, lower the tripod fingers until your thumb rests on the bed of the table. Keep the cue level (*Fig. 14*).

Rail Bridges: If the cue ball is four inches or more away from the rail, set your bridge hand on the rail. Place your thumb under the index finger (*Fig. 15*). Put the cue on the rail against the thumb, and bring your forefinger over the shaft (*Fig. 16*). Keep your cue as level as possible when stroking your

Figure 17

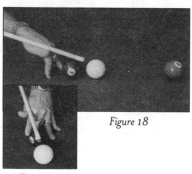

Figure 18

Figure 19

shot. If the cue ball is closer than 4 inches to the rail, place the cue between the thumb and forefinger. Place the other three fingers on the rail (*Fig. 17*).

Bridge for Over Ball Shot: When it is necessary to shoot over an object ball in order to stroke the cue ball, the following bridge should be used. Bracing all four of your fingers on the bed of the table behind the obstructing object ball(s), raise the hand as high as necessary and place the cue on the support made by your index finger joint and the thumb (*Fig. 18 and 19*). This is an uncomfortable bridge, but a necessary one and should be practiced.

Mechanical Brideges: If a shot is beyond reach with any of the above mentioned bridges, a mechanical bridge should be employed. Don't sacrifice a shot because you cannot use the mechanical bridge; it is very easy. Set the bridge on the table 6 to 8 inches from the cue ball. Place your hand on the bridge. Place the shaft of your cue in the notch at the front part of the bridge. *(Use higher notch for "follow," lower notch for "draw" or "stop.")* Place your thumb under the base of the cue and your four fingers over the top of the cue. Your elbow will be sticking out to the side as you stroke; the bridge will be to the left if you are right-handed. Be sure to lay the bridge flat on the table if possible *(Fig. 20)* and secure it with your left hand. Now use the same system as for any other shot.

Figure 20

LEARNING A STROKE: Remember, "Practice doesn't make Perfect; *Perfect Practice* makes Perfect." A stroke is a throwing motion. A good throwing motion starts with a slow backswing with a smooth acceleration through the cue ball. A common mistake by amateur and beginning players is to drop the elbow while stroking through the cue ball. It's important to note that the *throwing* motion must take place only in that part of the arm below the elbow. The less the elbow moves up and down, the more precise the stroke. It should be a pendulum swing from the elbow down.

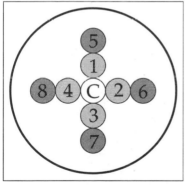

Diagram 2

CUEING THE BALL: For the beginning player, it is important to adjust the bridge so that the cue tip strikes the cue ball a little above center, never to the left or right, while learning accuracy and speed control. As skill level progresses, it will be necessary to learn to strike the cue ball at other places — higher, lower, left, right, etc.

The most important things to learn after a player has progressed past the beginner stage are (1) how to make the cue ball follow, (2) how to stop the cue ball on a straight-in shot and (3) how to make the cue ball draw or reverse direction off the object ball. *(See Dia. 2 for further details.)* The smoother the stroke, the lower or higher the cue ball may be struck without miscuing. Most good players can strike the cue ball almost two full tips off center without miscuing.

Keep in mind that extreme spin requires a very good stroke and smooth delivery. When following the cue ball, the higher the tip strikes the cue ball the more overspin imparted to the cue ball; likewise for pool there is one stroke. You use the same stroke to follow the ball as you do to stop or draw the cue ball.

A common mistake people make when they want to stop or draw the cue ball, is they think they have to *jab* or hit the cue ball and stop the cue tip immediately on impact with the cue ball or even hit the cue ball and pull the stick back. That is not the way to stop or draw the cue ball. To make the cue ball stop, you must put enough back spin on it by shooting

Figure 22

below center to cause it to arrive at the object ball with no spin. The cloth is always trying to rub the backspin off the cue ball. The farther the cue ball is from the object ball, the lower or harder you must shoot to cause the cue ball to stop or come back. *(Dia. 2 shows positions 1-4 and also 5-8, extreme spin.)* When using backspin on the cue ball, it is important to understand the concept that the backspin you put on the cue ball is caused by the tremendous friction the chalk creates between the tip and the cue ball. You must understand that the cue stick imparts backspin to the cue ball as you *throw* it 4 to 6 inches through the lower part of the cue ball. *(Fig. 22 shows how the cue stick follows through 4 to 6 inches after contact with the object ball.)*

HITTING THE OBJECT BALL: The first thing the pocket billiard player must learn is that his eyes should be on the object ball as he executes the shot. During the aiming process his eyes go back and forth between the cue ball and the object ball. When you are ready to pocket the object ball, your eyes are on the object ball.

To shoot a ball into a pocket, the simplest way to determine your point of impact on the object ball is to draw an imaginary line from the center of the pocket

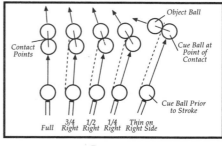

Diagram 3

that bisects the object ball. Where this line extends through the object ball is your contact point. It is the point at which the edge of the cue ball must contact the edge of the object ball. You must aim so that these two contact points will meet *(Dia. 3)*.

POINT OF AIM, POINT OF IMPACT: In Figure 24 and 25, you can see there is a white dot on the object ball. This mark is where the cue ball must contact the object ball in order to pocket the ball. The white dot is called the

54

Point of Impact. The white dot on the table is the Point of Aim. No matter where the cue ball is, the cue stick and the center of the cue ball are aimed at the Point of Aim in order to contact the Point of Impact on the object ball.

Figure 24

A keen eye and judgement are important here. Your skill in hitting the Point of Aim will determine your status in pocket billiard circles. Once again there is no better experience than practice. Accomplish this phase by placing your cue ball close to the object ball, then gradually increase the distance between the two balls. Time and practice will increase your accuracy in striking the cue ball correctly and hitting the object ball where you aim, thus driving it to the exact target area desired.

LEARNING A GOOD SHOOTING SYSTEM: The first thing you have to remember when you play pool is that you don't control the balls. All you control is your body and your cue. What the balls do is only a result of how well your body moves the cue. There are two things you have to get out of the way before you can shoot any shot. You have to make sure the cue is aiming straight and you have to make sure your arm can move the cue straight back and forth the full length of your bridge (*7 to 10 inches*).

Figure 25

A good practice technique for this is to place the cue ball on the spot and shoot it down the table into a corner pocket. Be sure to get your stance and aim correct. Then take a couple of smooth, slow warm-up swings the full length of the bridge. Stop at the cue ball and check your aim by letting your eyes go down the line of the cue to the target and back a couple of times. If the aim looks perfect, lock your eyes on the target, then after a slow backswing, "throw" the cue smoothly 4 to 6 inches through the cue ball directly over the dot. If after executing the shot, the cue is to the left or right of the dot, repeat this system until you can shoot the ball into the pocket and the cue finishes its motion 4 to 6 inches straight ahead and directly over the dot. It is *imperative* that your head remain perfectly still during the shot. This is an important practice to help develope your accuracy and stroke.

The warm-up swings should be slow and smooth in both directions, training the arm to make the cue go straight. After every two or three warm-up strokes, be sure to stop at the cue ball and check your aim. If it looks perfect, take a smooth backswing, and then accelerate 4 to 6 inches

55

through the cue ball at any speed you want to shoot. It's very important that you always maintain the same slow backswing no matter how hard you accelerate through the ball. Never go back faster just because you want to shoot harder. It's just like throwing a ball; to be accurate, you go back slowly, then you throw hard.

It is important to learn to stroke through the ball at all speeds. Although you have more control at slower speeds, sometimes position play will require you to shoot a ball harder. Keep in mind—slow backswing, accelerate forward.

ENGLISH (Left or Right)

When we talk about *english*, we are generally referring to left or right spin on the cue ball. By putting left or right spin on the cue ball, you immediately do three things that can cause you to miss a shot. Beginning with right hand english, when you strike the cue ball on the right hand side, the cue ball (1) immediately deflects off the tip to the left of the line of the cue stick. As the cue ball proceeds down the table, it may (2) curve back to the right just a little bit. It will never curve back as much as it deflects unless you elevate the cue, which we're not going to talk about here. With a level cue and right hand english on the ball, it will first deflect to the left. It might curve back a little to the right depending on the distance. The third thing is that the english might *throw* the object ball. Right hand english can throw the object ball a little to the left of the contact line. The curve back is dependent on the speed and the distance that the cue ball is traveling.

We mention three things that happen when you use right hand english, the deflection immediately off the tip, the curve back to the right and the throwing the object ball to the left. Of these three, the curve is usually very slight. The throwing of the object ball is very slight. The biggest factor in causing people to miss with english is the *deflection* off the cue tip. It is important to remember when using right hand english, aim slightly to the

Diagram 4

right of where you would normally aim on the object ball. When using left hand english, you must aim slightly to the left of where you would normally aim on the object ball.

Left or right hand english is almost never used to pocket an object ball, but rather for playing position on another object ball. The purpose of applying sidespin to the cue ball is to change the angle at which the cue ball comes off a rail after striking the object ball. Always remember, never use english to make balls, only to play position on the next ball. Although english is extremely important in playing position, the pros will tell you the less english you use the less often you get in trouble (Dia. 4).

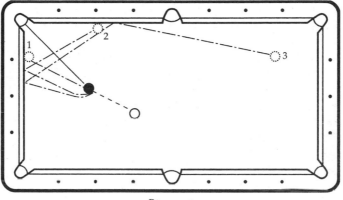

Diagram 5

Follow Shots: Set up the balls as in Diagram 5. By stroking the cue ball between a tip and a tip and a half above center, the cue ball will follow to Position 1. Then, set up the same shot and stroke the cue ball at the same height, add some power and see that the cue ball will end up in Position 2. Now stroke the cue ball again in the same position, but with an even firmer stroke to see the cue ball respond as in Position 3.

Stop Shots: Place the balls on the table as in Diagram 6. Strike the cue ball about a tip below center. Use a smooth stroke and practice stopping the cue ball as it contacts the object ball. Do this a few times to get the feel of how hard you shoot, then practice shooting this same shot a little lower on the cue ball with a little less speed and see if you can still get the same results. Then proceed to Position 2. This time, stroke the cue ball about a tip and a half below center and a little firmer than Position 1. By repeating this practice in a new position, you will learn how much force you need in order to stop the cue ball. Continue this practice with the cue ball in Positions 3 and 4, each time increasing the power of the stroke. If you have any difficulty at a particular position, repeat that practice until it feels comfortable.

Remember, the lower you strike the cue ball, the less power is required to stop the cue ball on contact with the object ball.

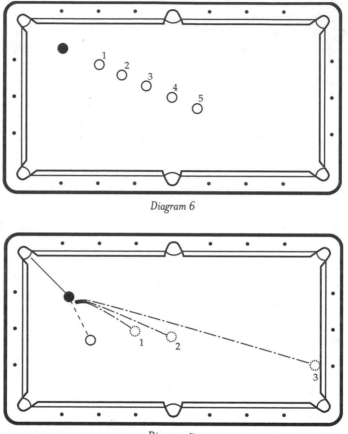

Diagram 6

Diagram 7

Draw Shots: Place the balls as shown in Diagram 7. Notice there is a slight angle in the ball placement so that when you draw the cue ball it will move over to the right slightly and then come back past your cue. The reason for this is so that you can follow through the cue ball 4 to 6 inches to practice a good follow-through on each shot without worrying about the cue ball hitting your cue. With the balls in position, strike the cue ball about a tip and a half below center with a moderate stroke and notice that the cue ball travels a couple of inches to the right of your cue before it travels a short distance down the table to Position 1. By increasing the force of your stroke, you will be able to move the ball farther down the table toward Positions 2 and 3. It is important on all these exercises to be sure the cue tip follows through 4 to 6 inches. If you shoot the cue ball for any stop or draw shot, the cue ball is struck one to one and a half tips below center. When the pendulum motion of the arm is correct, the cue tip will follow through 4 to 6 inches past the cue ball, and continue in a slightly downward motion, ending up touching the cloth.

Position Play: Players are forever trying to play position — that is, making an easy shot and making the cue ball arrive at a place on the table to have another easy shot. The two secrets of playing proper position are (1) memory and (2) speed control. When a beginner is learning to play, he should repeat the same shots over and over. Not only do you watch the object ball being pocketed, but the path of the cue ball after contacting the object ball. If you are continually hitting the cue ball a little above center, the cue ball will always take virtually the same path. Fifty percent of position play is remembering where the cue ball went after that particular shot. The other fifty percent of position play is the speed control of the cue ball.

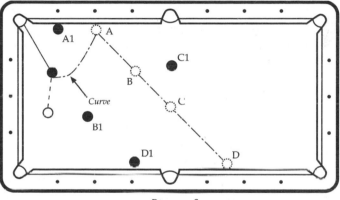

Diagram 8

The most important and easiest way a beginner can learn position is to set up a shot *(as in Diagram 8)*. When you set up a practice shot, mark the cloth with a chalk dot under the object ball and also the cue ball so you start at the same position each time. Pocket the object ball by hitting a little above center and watch where the cue ball hits the first rail and the direction it takes coming off that rail. By shooting this shot several times at different speeds, but striking the cue ball in the same spot each time, you will notice the path of the cue ball will follow in almost the same line each time you shoot. To improve your game, work on playing position on each of the shots in the diagram by varying the speed at which you strike the cue ball.

Now if you set the balls up in the same position and strike the cue ball a little below center, you will notice that the path of the cue ball will be completely different off the object ball. Repeat this several times, until you can make the cue ball go in the same direction, but travel farther down the table depending on the speed of your stroke. After setting up these shots and executing them by hitting the ball a little below center, set them up again and strike the cue ball even farther below center. This is a good exercise to learn the basics of what happens when you shoot the cue ball at different heights and speeds.

Diagram 9

EXERCISES

Follow, Stop and Draw: This exercise is to show you the different ways the cue ball will react when it is cued at different levels. Set up the shot in Diagram 9. The object ball is about a diamond out and directly in line between the two side pockets. The cue ball is at a slight angle toward the diamond past the side pocket. When you hit the cue ball with follow, the cue ball will take a slight curve as shown in the path in the diagram. If you hit the cue ball slightly below center, it will go almost straight down the table. If the cue ball is hit about one and a half tips below center, it will curve back more toward the corner pocket.

Position Exercise: Learning Position Play is learning the easiest way to get the balls off the table. The best way to learn that is an exercise we call 3-Ball, Ball in Hand. This is one of the best exercises to improve your skill level in control and position. Throw three balls on the table. In Diagram 10, we see balls 1, 2 and 3. This numeric order is the easiest way to play off these balls by placing the cue ball as shown. Striking the cue ball above center on the 1-ball, you can see by the path of the cue ball that it will follow into the rail and then head right toward the 2-ball. By going to the rail after pocketing the 1-ball and depending on your speed of stroke, you can end up in any of the three cue ball positions. It is very difficult to make a mistake. This is what pros look for: the easiest way to get position on their next ball. If you

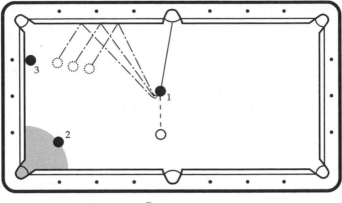

Diagram 10

shoot the cue ball again above center and pocket the 2-ball, the cue ball ends up anywhere within the darkened circle around the 2-ball. Then the 3-ball is an easily pocketed shot.

One of the best ways of improving your game of pool is by repeating shots. Don't repeat long, difficult shots. The ones to repeat are the easy and semi-easy ones that are frequently missed. For the more proficient players, even if you make the object ball and fail to get position, repeat that same shot until you feel comfortable that you can make that ball and get position.

Most people think that if they could make tough shots, they would be better players. The reality is that games are not won by people who make the tough shots; games are lost by players who miss shots that are very easy.

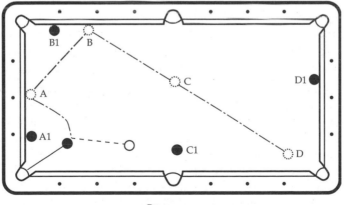

Diagram 11

Diagram 11 shows the many ways the speed of stroke can be used to play position. By using a soft stroke, you can play shape to position A to play A1 for your next shot. A slightly harder stroke will go to position B for B1 as the next shot. Continue working on your speed of stroke until you can play position on shots C1 and D1.

EIGHT-BALL AND NINE-BALL, BALL IN HAND: Another great practice technique for beginners or stronger players is to play Eight-Ball or Nine-Ball with a rule change. When a person breaks and a ball is made on the break, he can take "Ball in Hand" anywhere on the table and shoot until missing. The incoming player also takes "ball in hand" and shoots until missing. The advantage of playing this way is that when you have ball in hand every time you come to the table, you start looking over the table. Even a beginner will start to see patterns of two or maybe three balls. The better player learns very quickly the easiest way to run the balls off. It trains you to see patterns and see the easy way to go for a run out. By playing Ball in Hand pool, whether it is Eight-Ball or Nine-Ball, you learn in one hour the equivalent of what you would learn in about 15 hours of regular practice.

BALL IN HAND EQUAL OFFENSE: Another great practice game is a variation of Equal Offense which is also in this book. In Equal Offense each ball is one point and you can shoot at any ball. No balls count on the break. After the break, the same player who breaks gets ball in hand three times per rack. After each miss, he gets ball in hand again. Then he records how many balls he made that rack. A perfect score is 150 points in 10 racks. By playing this 3-miss way, a person learns to see and play simple patterns. When a person's score approaches 130 or more in ten racks, then he progresses to the 2-miss level. Now he breaks the balls and after the break, he gets ball in hand twice per rack. When his score improves again to 130 or more in ten racks, then he is playing well enough to progress to the 1-miss level. Any player who shoots 130 points or more on the 1-miss level is a very good amateur player. This is a great practice game.

Diagram 12   Diagram 13

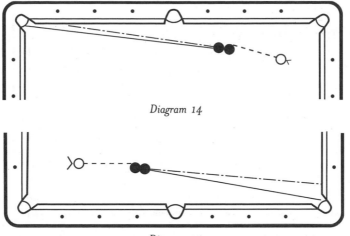

Diagram 14

Diagram 15

Throw Shots: *(Diagrams 12-15)* The object of a "throw" shot is to provide force or english that will move an object ball along an off-center path when two balls are *frozen*.

This situation often arises when the cue ball is touching *(frozen)* to an object ball. If the two are in alignment with a pocket, there is no problem. If not in alignment, it is still possible to pocket the object ball by using a "throw shot," which spins the object ball to the left or right. Diagram 12 shows how, by hitting the cue ball on the left side, the object ball is thrown to the right side. Diagram 13 illustrates that striking the cue ball on the right side moves the object ball to the left.

Another version of the throw shot is when two object balls are frozen together. The cue ball is free, but not in position to pocket either ball easily. In this case, the cue ball *(hit without english)* strikes the closest object ball on either the right side *(Diagram 14)* or the left side *(Diagram 15)* to throw the second object ball in the opposite direction.

Kiss Shots: *(Diagrams 16 & 17)* The object of this exercise is to pocket one of the two balls that are frozen together without the use of english. When two balls are frozen together, an axis or center line is established by their relationship. A cue extended along this imaginary line will readily determine if the closest object ball, when struck on the back half, will follow the line into a pocket. If the cue does not point to a pocket, the object ball will not go into a pocket.

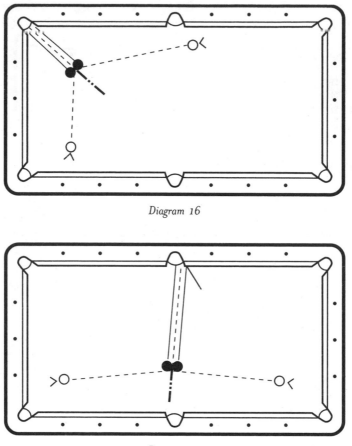

Diagram 16

Diagram 17

Diagram 16 shows how this kiss shot can be made from either side. Diagram 17 demonstrates that one object ball can be pocketed and the other cannot. Arrange two balls in various frozen positions and practice finding the center line. Then, mix throw shots with kiss shots to increase your options under these conditions.

Rules for Tournament Play

The following rules concern the play, scoring, officiating and responsibilities for tournament competition in all pocket billiard games. However, the precepts and principles of these rules are to be considered part of the games' General Rules and should be applied as appropriate to all play, whether or not a formal tournament.

1.1 **PLAYER RESPONSIBILITY**

It is the player's responsibility to be aware of all rules, regulations and schedules applying to competition. While tournament officials will make every reasonable effort to have such information readily available to all players as appropriate, the ultimate responsibility rests with the player. *(For exceptions to this rule, see Rule 2.16.)* The player has no recourse if such information is not volunteered; the responsibility for knowing the situation and/or the rules lies with the player.

1.2 **ACCEPTANCE OF EQUIPMENT**

Tournament players should assure themselves, prior to beginning play, that the balls and other equipment arc standard and legal. Once they begin play of a match, they may no longer question the legality of the equipment in use *(unless the opponent and tournament officials both agree with the objection and any available remedy proposed by the tournament officials)*.

1.3 **USE OF EQUIPMENT**

Players may not use equipment or accessory items for purposes or in a manner other than those for which the items were intended. For example, powder containers, chalk cubes, etc., may not be used to prop up a *mechanical bridge (or natural hand bridge)*; no more than two mechanical bridges may be used at one time, nor may they be used to support anything other than the *cue shaft*. Extra or out-of-play balls may not be used by players to check clearances or for any other reason *(except to lag for break)*; the triangle may be employed by players to ascertain whether a ball is in the rack when a match is unofficiated and the table has not been pencil-marked around the triangle area. *(Also see Rule 2.15.)*

1.4 **EQUIPMENT RESTRICTIONS**

Players may use chalk, powder, mechanical bridge(s) and cue(s) of their choice or design. However, tournament officials may restrict a player if he attempts action that is disruptive of either the house equipment or normal competitive conditions. As examples, a player may: be restrained from using red chalk on green cloth; be advised not to use powder in such an excessive fashion as to unduly affect the balls or table cloth; and be barred from using a cue with a noisemaking device that is clearly disruptive to other competitors. *(Also see Rule 2.15.)*

1.5 MARKING OF TABLES

When racking the balls, a triangle must be used. Prior to competition, each table and the triangle to be used on it shall be marked so as to ensure that the same triangle will be used throughout the tournament on the same table.

An accurate and clearly visible pencil line must also be marked on the cloth: (1) around the outer edge of the triangle to ensure accurate and consistent placement to enable accurate judgement as to ball positions; (2) on the long string to enable accurate spotting of balls; and (3) on the head string to facilitate determinations of whether balls are behind the head string.

The *head spot, center spot* and *foot spot* must also be determined to be accurately marked, whether with discreet penciled "plus" marks, or with standard spots if being employed. In games which do not require them, the center and head spots do not need to be marked.

1.6 ADMINISTRATIVE DISCRETION

The management of each tournament shall reserve the right to set forth rules and procedures appropriate and reasonable for the particular tournament involved, such as may regard players' dress requirements, method of receiving entry fees, refund policy of entry fees, scheduling flexibility, pairing procedures, etc. However, for tournaments to receive a BCA, WPA, WPBA, PCA, or PBT sanction, certain requirements must be met, primarily with regard to safeguarding and ensuring proper distribution of the prize fund.

1.7 LATE START

A player must be ready to begin a match within 15 minutes of the start of the match, or the opponent wins by forfeit. The starting time is considered to be the scheduled time or the time the match is announced, whichever is later.

1.8 NO PRACTICE DURING MATCH

While a match is in progress, practice is not allowed. Taking a shot that is not part of that match is a foul.

1.9   ASSISTANCE NOT ALLOWED

While a match is in progress, players are not allowed to ask spectators for assistance in planning or executing shots. If a player asks for and receives such assistance, he loses the game. Any spectator who spontaneously offers any significant help to a player will be removed from the area.

1.10   FAILURE TO LEAVE THE TABLE

When a player's inning comes to an end, the player must discontinue shooting. Failure to do so is loss of game *(exception in 14.1 - ruled as "deliberate foul")*.

1.11   SLOW PLAY

If in the opinion of the referee a player is impeding the progress of the tournament or game with consistently slow play, the referee can warn the player and then at his discretion impose a maximum 45-second time limit that applies to both players between shots *(that is, both players are put on a shot-clock)*. If the referee does impose a 45-second time limit and that limit is exceeded by a player, a foul will be called and the incoming player is rewarded according to the rules applicable to the game being played.

During a player's inning, the shot-clock starts when the previous shot ends, and runs until tip-to-ball contact begins the next shot. The time while a shot is in progress is not counted. If a player begins with cue ball in hand, the shot-clock starts when he has possession of the cue ball, and any spotting or racking is finished. A warning with the announcement of "time" should be made 10 seconds prior to the time limit being reached. If a player exceeds the time limit specified for the tournament, a foul will be called and the incoming player is rewarded according to the rules applicable to the game being played. If the shot-clock is started late on a shot due to neglect or oversight of the timekeeper, the player receives the benefit of the late start.

1.12   SUSPENDED PLAY

If a player shoots while play is suspended by the referee, he loses the game. Announcement of the suspension is considered sufficient warning. *(Also see Rule 2.27.)*

1.13   TIME OUT

A player is only allowed to take a time out during his/her turn at the table or between sets *(if a format with sets is used)*. During a time out, a sign should be placed on the table by the referee, and no practice will be allowed on that table. In general, each player will be allowed one time out per match, and a maximum of five minutes per time out. When a format with sets is used, each player will be allowed one time out in the final set *(in the third set if playing best-of-3, or in the fifth set if playing the best-of-5 sets)*. This final-set rule applies regardless of whether a player has taken a time out in an earlier set.

1.14   **CONCESSION**

If a player concedes, he loses the game. If a player attempts to unscrew his jointed cue stick while the opponent is at the table, it will be considered a concession of the game. No warning from the referee is required in the case of a concession.

1.15   **SCORING OF FORFEITS**

Matches forfeited for any reason under these rules shall not result in any scores being included in the statistics of a tournament, regardless of whether any score had been reached prior to the declaration of forfeiture. For official records, no point scores should be recorded, but rather the notations "W(F)" and "L(F)" as appropriate should be employed. *(Matches lost through disqualification are considered forfeits for purposes of this rule.)*

If, however, the player awarded a match through the opponent's forfeiture has posted a high run *(or similar accomplishment for which an award is granted)* during play of the match prior to declaration of forfeiture, that high run or other mark shall be eligible for the tournament award or prize.

1.16   **PLAYING WITHOUT A REFEREE**

When a referee is not available, the player who is not shooting will assume the duties of the referee to the extent of play on the table.

1.16.1 **CUE BALL FOULS ONLY**

When a referee is presiding over a match, it is a foul for a player to touch any ball *(cue ball or object ball)* with the cue, clothing, body, mechanical bridge or chalk, before, during or after a shot. However, when a referee is not presiding over a game, it is not a foul to accidentally touch stationary balls located between the cue ball and the shooter while in the act of shooting. If such an accident occurs, the player should allow the Tournament Director to restore the object balls to their correct positions. If the player does not allow such a restoration, and a ball set in motion as a normal part of the shot touches such an unrestored ball, or passes partly into a region originally occupied by a disturbed ball, the shot is a foul. In short, if the accident has any effect on the outcome of the shot, it is a foul. In any case, the Tournament Director must be called upon to restore the positions of the disturbed balls as soon as possible, but not during the shot. It is a foul to play another shot before the Tournament Director has restored any accidentally moved balls.

At the non-shooting player's option, the disturbed balls will be left in their new positions. In this case, the balls are considered restored, and subsequent contact on them is not a foul.

It is still a foul to make any contact with the cue ball whatsoever while it is in play, except for the normal tip-to-ball contact during a shot.

1.16.2 JUMP AND MASSÉ SHOT FOUL

If a match is not refereed, it will be considered a cue ball foul if during an attempt to jump, curve or massé the cue ball over or around an impeding numbered ball that is not a legal object ball, the impeding ball moves *(regardless of whether it was moved by a hand, cue stick follow-through or bridge)*.

1.16.3 THIRD OPINION

When a shot comes up that seems likely to lead to controversy, the player not shooting should temporarily enlist a tournament official or a third party to judge the legality of the execution.

1.16.4 RESOLVING DISPUTES

Any dispute between the two players will be resolved by the Tournament Director or an appointed substitute.

1.16.5 SPLIT HITS

If the cue ball strikes a legal object ball and a non-legal object ball at approximately the same instant, and it cannot be determined which ball was hit first, the judgement will go in favor of the shooter.

1.16.6 RACKING

The balls must be racked as tightly as possible, which means each ball should be touching its neighbor. Refrain from tapping object balls more than absolutely necessary; it is preferable to thoroughly brush the area of the rack to even out the cloth.

(Further instructions for Tournament Play are Included in the Next Section, "Instructions For Referees.")

INSTRUCTIONS FOR REFEREES

2.1 TOURNAMENT OFFICIALS/REFEREES

Where these rules refer to a "referee," it should be noted that the referees' prerogatives and discretion also pertain to other tournament officials as appropriate.

2.2 REFEREE'S AUTHORITY

The referee will maintain order and enforce the rules of the game. The referee is the final judge in all matters of fact, and is in complete charge of the match. The referee may consult other tournament officials for rule interpretations, ball positions, etc. However, all matters of judgement are his and his alone; they cannot be appealed to higher tournament authority by players; only if the referee is in error on a rule or its application may higher tournament authority overrule him.

2.3 REFEREE'S RESPONSIVENESS

The referee shall be totally responsive to players' inquiries regarding objective data, such as whether a ball will be in the rack, if a ball is in the kitchen, what the count is, how many points are needed for a victory, if a player is playing from safety, if a player or his opponent is on a foul, what rule would apply if a certain shot is made, etc. When asked for a clarification of a rule, the referee will explain the applicable rule to the best of his ability, but any misstatement by the referee will not protect a player from enforcement of the actual rules. The referee must not offer or provide any subjective opinion that would affect play, such as whether a good hit can be made on a prospective shot, whether a combination is makeable, or how the table seems to be playing, etc.

2.4 FINAL TOURNAMENT AUTHORITY

Though these rules attempt to cover the vast majority of situations that arise in competition, there still may be the occasional need for interpretation of the rules and their proper application under unusual circumstances. The Tournament Director or other official who assumes final responsibility for a tournament will make any such required decision *(other than referee's judgement calls)* at his discretion, and they shall be final.

2.5 WAGERING BY REFEREES

Referees are strictly prohibited from any wagering of any kind involving the games, players or tournament in any way. Any such wagering by a referee *(or other tournament official)* shall result in his immediate dismissal and the forfeiture of his entire financial compensation for the tournament.

2.6   BEFORE THE MATCH

Before the match, the referee will clean or have the table and balls cleaned as necessary. He will ensure that chalk, powder and mechanical bridges are available. He will mark or have the spots, the head string, the long string and the outer edge of the triangle marked with a pencil when required.

2.7   RACKING

The referee will rack the balls as tightly as possible, which means each ball should be touching its neighbors. Refrain from tapping balls more than necessary; it is preferable to thoroughly brush the area of the rack to even out the cloth. When a referee is racking the balls for a game, neither player is allowed to examine the rack close up at any time during or after the process.

2.8   CALLING SHOTS

For games of call-shot a player may shoot any ball he chooses, but before he shoots, must designate the called ball and called pocket. He need not indicate any detail such as kisses, caroms, combinations, or cushions *(all of which are legal)*. Any additionally pocketed ball(s) on a legal stroke is counted in the shooter's favor. If a referee incorrectly calls a shot, a player should correct him before completing the shot. If a mis-call does occur for any reason, the shot shall be credited if, in the referee's judgement, the player did legally execute the shot as intended.

2.9   CALLING FOULS

Referee will call fouls as soon as they occur and inform the incoming player that he has ball in hand in games where the rule applies.

2.10   SPLIT HITS

When the referee observes that the cue ball strikes a legal object ball and a non-legal object ball at approximately the same instant, and it cannot be determined which ball was hit first, the judgement will go in favor of the shooter.

2.11   CLEARING POCKETS

On tables which do not have ball return systems, the referee will remove pocketed object balls from full or nearly full pockets. It is the player's responsibility to see that this duty is performed; he has no recourse if a ball rebounds from a full pocket.

2.12 CLEANING BALLS

During a game a player may ask the referee to clean one or more balls. The referee will clean any visibly soiled ball.

2.13 SPOTTING BALLS

To avoid any unnecessary guidance to a player when spotting balls, the referee should position each ball so that the number is facing upward.

2.14 SOLICITING INFORMATION

If the referee does not have a clear view of a possible foul, he may form his decision by any means by which he feels comfortable.

2.15 INAPPROPRIATE USE OF EQUIPMENT

The referee should be alert for a player using equipment or accessory items for purposes or in a manner other than those for which the items were intended. Tournament officials should prevent these actions from occurring. Generally, no penalty is applied, because the referee or other tournament official intercedes prior to that point. However, should a player persist in any activity counter to this *(or any other)* general rule after having been advised that the activity is not permissible, tournament officials may take action against him as appropriate under the provisions of "Unsportsmanlike Conduct." *(Also see Rules 1.3 and 1.4.)*

2.16 WARNINGS WHICH ARE MANDATORY. The referee must warn a player who is about to commit a serious foul *(such as three consecutive fouls, requesting coaching assistance, or failure to stop shooting after a foul has been called)* whenever the referee has been given enough time to do so; otherwise, any foul is considered to be a standard foul *(except as specially noted)*. In games where the rule applies the referee must inform a player who has had two consecutive fouls; otherwise, the player is considered to have had only one foul prior to the shot. The referee must inform a player when an object ball is touching a rail; otherwise, any contact on that ball is considered to have driven it to that rail. The referee should notify the player as soon as the corresponding situation arises and whenever enough time to warn was given by the shooter. A caution given just as a shot starts is not considered sufficient; the player as well must be given enough time to react.

2.17 RESTORING A POSITION

When necessary, the referee will restore disturbed balls to their original positions to the best of his ability. The referee may ask for information for this purpose if he is not sure of the original position.

2.18   OUTSIDE INTERFERENCE

When outside interference occurs during a shot that has an effect on the outcome of that shot, the referee will restore the balls to the positions they had before the shot, and the shot will be replayed. If the interference had no effect on the shot, the referee will restore the disturbed balls and play will continue. If the balls cannot be restored to their original positions, the game should be replayed with the original player breaking.

2.19   ILLEGALLY CAUSING BALL TO MOVE

Any player who, in the referee's judgement, intentionally causes a ball to move by any illegal means *(pushing on bed cloth, bumping or slapping table, etc.)* will lose the game and/or match by forfeit. No preliminary warning from the referee is required. *(Referee's judgement and discretion under "Unsportsmanlike Conduct.")*

2.20   JUDGING DOUBLE HITS

When the distance between the cue ball and the object ball is less than the width of a chalk cube, special attention from the referee is required. In such a situation, unless the referee can positively determine a legal shot has been performed, the following guidance may apply: if the cue ball follows through the object ball more than ½ ball, it is a foul.

Center line through object ball

Diagram 18

2.21   OUT OF HEAD STRING WARNING

When player has the cue ball in hand behind the head string, the referee shall warn him before he shoots if he has not placed it within the head string. If the player shoots on or outside the string after having been warned of the legal placement, the stroke is a foul. See specific game rules for penalty. *(Also see Rule 3.9.)*

2.22   REMAINING IN PLAYER'S CHAIR

Players are to remain in the chair designated for their use while opponent is at the table. Should a player need to leave the playing area during matches, he must request and receive permission from the referee. The referee shall apply his good judgement to ensure that undue time is not being used or that a player is not abusing the privilege as a means of unsettling an opponent.

2.23   OUTSIDE ASSISTANCE PROHIBITED

Unless specifically permitted by the rules of a given tournament, players may not knowingly accept any form of playing advice during a match. A player may not engage in communication, either verbal or nonverbal, with persons other than the tournament officials or his opponent during play.

Should a player desire to so communicate, for example to obtain a beverage, get a piece of equipment, or other permissible reason, he should either communicate through a tournament official or with the approval and observance of the referee.

If the referee has reason to believe that a player knowingly solicited or accepted outside assistance in any manner regarding the play of a match, he shall take steps appropriate under the provisions of "Unsportsmanlike Conduct."

2.24 NON-PLAYER INTERFERENCE OR HARASSMENT

If a non-player either verbally or visually interferes with the players, the referee may request that he leave the playing area.

2.25 SLOW PLAY

(See Rule 1.11.)

2.26 PROTESTS

A player may request a rule interpretation or protest a failure to call a foul to the referee or appropriate tournament authority, but the request or protest must be made immediately, prior to any subsequent shot being taken, or it cannot be considered or honored. If the player fails to do so, and the foul goes unpenalized, the foul is considered not to have occurred. The referee is the final judge on matters of fact. If either player thinks that the referee is applying the rules incorrectly, and the dispute cannot be resolved by reference to the rules, the referee must take the protest to the tournament director or an appointed substitute. The tournament director's decision on interpretation of the rules is final. A player may also protest if he thinks that the referee has called a foul incorrectly. In any case play is suspended until the protest is resolved.

All players must honor an opponent's request that play be halted if an official is to be summoned or if a referee is to check or verify a rule question with other officials. Failure to honor such requests may result in disqualification or forfeiture under the provisions of "Unsportsmanlike Conduct."

2.27 SUSPENDING PLAY

The referee has the authority to suspend play during protests by players and whenever he feels that conditions are unsuitable for play to continue. If a spectator is interfering with the game, play may be suspended until that spectator is removed from area. *(Also see Rule 1.12.)*

2.28 UNSPORTSMANLIKE CONDUCT

The referee has the right and obligation to ensure that no player engages in any activity which, in his judgement, is unsportsmanlike in nature, embarrassing, disruptive or detrimental to other players, tournament officials or hosts, or the sport in general. The referee or other officials shall have the right to penalize or disqualify, with or without warning, any player who acts in an unsportsmanlike manner.

GENERAL RULES
OF POCKET BILLIARDS

These general rules apply to all pocket billiard games, UNLESS specifically noted to the contrary in the individual game rules. To facilitate the use and understanding of these general rules, terms that may require definition are set in italics so that the reader may refer to the Glossary of Billiard Terms section for the exact meaning of the term.

3.1 TABLES, BALLS, EQUIPMENT

All games described in these rules are designed for tables, balls and equipment meeting the standards prescribed in the BCA Equipment Specifications.

3.2 RACKING THE BALLS

When racking the balls a triangle must be used, and the apex ball is to be spotted on the foot spot. All the balls must be lined up behind the apex ball and pressed together so that they all have contact with each other.

3.3 STRIKING CUE BALL

Legal shots require that the cue ball be struck only with the cue tip. Failure to meet this requirement is a foul.

3.4 FAILURE TO POCKET A BALL

If a player fails to pocket a ball on a legal shot, then the player's inning is over, and it is the opponent's turn at the table.

3.5 LAG FOR BREAK

The following procedure is used for the lag for the opening break. Each player should use balls of equal size and weight *(preferably cue balls but, when not available, non-striped object balls)*. With the balls in hand behind the head string, one player to the left and one to the right of the head spot, the balls are shot simultaneously to the foot cushion and back to the head end of the table. The player whose ball is the closest to the innermost edge of the head cushion wins the lag. The lagged ball must contact the foot cushion at least once. Other cushion contacts are immaterial, except as prohibited below. It is an automatic loss of the lag if:

(a) The ball crosses into the opponent's half of the table;

(b) The ball fails to contact the foot cushion;

(c) The ball drops into a pocket;

(d) The ball jumps the table;

(e) The ball touches the long cushion;

(f) The ball rests within the corner pocket and past the nose of the head cushion, or;

(g) The ball contacts the foot rail more than once. If both players violate automatic-loss lag rules, or if the referee is unable to determine which ball is closer, the lag is a tie and is replayed.

3.6 OPENING BREAK SHOT

The opening break shot is determined by either lag or lot. (*The lag for break procedure is required for tournament and other formal competition.*) The player winning the lag or lot has the choice of performing the opening break shot or assigning it to the opponent.

3.7 CUE BALL ON OPENING BREAK

The opening break shot is taken with cue ball in hand behind the head string. The object balls are positioned according to specific game rules. On the opening break, the game is considered to have commenced once the cue ball has been struck by the cue tip and crosses the head string.

3.8 DEFLECTING THE CUE BALL ON THE GAME'S OPENING BREAK

On the break shot, stopping or deflecting the cue ball after it has crossed the head string and prior to hitting the racked balls is considered a foul and loss of turn. The opponent has the option of receiving cue ball in hand behind the head string or passing the cue ball in hand behind the head string back to the offending player. (*Exception: 9-Ball, see rule 5.3: "cue ball in hand anywhere on the table"*). A warning must be given that a second violation during the match will result in the loss of the match by forfeiture. (*See Rule 3.28.*)

3.9 CUE BALL IN HAND BEHIND THE HEAD STRING

This situation applies in specific games whereby the opening break is administered or a player's scratching is penalized by the incoming player having cue ball in hand behind the head string. The incoming player may place the cue ball anywhere behind the head string. The shooting player may shoot at any object ball as long as the base of the object ball is on or below the head string. He may not shoot at any ball, the base of which is above the head string, unless he first shoots the cue ball below the head string and then by hitting a rail causes the cue ball to come back above the head string and hit the object ball. The base of the ball *(the point of the ball touching the table)* determines whether it is above or below the head string. If the incoming player inadvertently places the cue ball on or below the head string, the referee or the opposing player must inform the shooting player of improper positioning of the cue ball before the shot is made. If the opposing player does not so inform the shooting player before the shot is made, the shot is considered legal. If the shooting player is informed of improper positioning, he must then reposition the cue ball. If a player positions the cue ball completely and obviously outside the kitchen and shoots the cue ball, it is a foul. When the cue ball is in hand behind the head string, it remains in hand *(not in play)* until the player drives the cue ball past the head string by striking it with his cue tip. The cue ball may be **adjusted** by the player's hand, cue, etc., so long as it remains in hand. Once the cue ball is in play per the above, it may not be impeded in any way by the player; to do so is to commit a foul.

3.10   POCKETED BALLS. A ball is considered pocketed if as a result of an otherwise legal shot, it drops off the bed of the table into the pocket and remains there. *(A ball that drops out of a ball return system onto the floor is not to be construed as a ball that has not remained pocketed.)* A ball that rebounds from a pocket back onto the table bed is not a pocketed ball.

3.11   POSITION OF BALLS
The position of a ball is judged by where its base *(or center)* rests.

3.12   FOOT ON FLOOR
Player must have at least one foot in contact with the floor at the moment the cue tip contacts the cue ball, or the shot is a foul. Foot attire must be normal in regard to size, shape and manner in which it is worn.

3.13   SHOOTING WITH BALLS IN MOTION
It is a foul if a player shoots while the cue ball or any object ball is in motion *(a spinning ball is in motion)*.

3.14   COMPLETION OF STROKE
A stroke is not complete *(and therefore is not counted)* until all balls on the table have become motionless after the stroke *(a spinning ball is in motion)*.

3.15   HEAD STRING DEFINED
The area behind the head string does not include the head string. Thus an object ball that is dead center on the head string is playable when specific game rules require that a player must shoot at a ball past

the head string. Likewise, the cue ball when being put in play behind the head string (*cue ball in hand behind the head string*), may not be placed directly on the head string; it must be behind it.

3.16 GENERAL RULE, ALL FOULS

Though the penalties for fouls differ from game to game, the following apply to all fouls:

(a) Player's inning ends;

(b) If on a stroke, the stroke is invalid and any pocketed balls are not counted to the shooter's credit, and;

(c) Any ball(s) is respotted only if the rules of the specific game require it.

3.17 FAILURE TO CONTACT OBJECT BALL

It is a foul if on a stroke the cue ball fails to make contact with any legal object ball first. Playing away from a touching ball does not constitute having hit that ball.

3.18 LEGAL SHOT

Unless otherwise stated in a specific game rule, a player must cause the cue ball to contact a legal object ball and then:

(a) Pocket a numbered ball, or;

(b) Cause the cue ball or any numbered ball to contact a cushion. Failure to meet these requirements is a foul.

3.19 CUE BALL SCRATCH

It is a foul (*scratch*) if on a stroke, the cue ball is pocketed. If the cue ball touches an object ball that was already pocketed (*for example, in a pocket full of object balls*), the shot is a foul.

3.20 FOULS BY TOUCHING BALLS

It is a foul to strike, touch or in any way make contact with the cue ball in play or any object balls in play with anything (*the body, clothing, chalk, mechanical bridge, cue shaft, etc.*) **except** the cue tip (*while attached to the cue shaft*), which may contact the cue ball in the execution of a legal shot. Whenever a referee is presiding over a match, any object ball moved during a standard foul must be returned as closely as possible to its original position as judged by the referee, and the incoming player does not have the option of restoration. (*Also see Rule 1.16.*)

3.21 FOUL BY PLACEMENT

Touching any object ball with the cue ball while it is in hand is a foul.

3.22 FOULS BY DOUBLE HITS

If the cue ball is touching the required object ball prior to the shot, the player may shoot toward it, providing that any normal stroke is employed. If the cue stick strikes the cue ball more than once on a shot, or if the cue stick is in contact with the cue ball when or after the cue ball contacts an object ball, the shot is foul. *(See Rule 2.20. for judging this kind of shot.)* If a third ball is close by, care should be taken not to foul that ball under the first part of this rule.

3.23 PUSH SHOT FOULS

It is a foul if the cue ball is pushed by the cue tip, with contact being maintained for more than the momentary time commensurate with a stroked shot. *(Such shots are usually referred to as push shots.)*

3.24 PLAYER RESPONSIBILITY FOULS

The player is responsible for chalk, bridges, files and any other items or equipment he brings to, uses at, or causes to approximate the table. If he drops a piece of chalk, or knocks off a mechanical bridge head, as examples, he is guilty of a foul should such an object make contact with any ball in play *(or the cue ball only if no referee is presiding over the match)*.

3.25 ILLEGAL JUMPING OF BALL

It is a foul if a player strikes the cue ball below center *("digs under" it)* and intentionally causes it to rise off the bed of the table in an effort to clear an obstructing ball. Such jumping action may occasionally occur accidentally, and such "jumps" are not to be considered fouls on their face; they may still be ruled foul strokes, if for example, the ferrule or cue shaft makes contact with the cue ball in the course of the shot.

3.26 JUMP SHOTS

Unless otherwise stated in rules for a specific game it is legal to cause the cue ball to rise off the bed of the table by elevating the cue stick on the shot, and forcing the cue ball to rebound from the bed of the table. Any miscue when executing a jump shot is a foul.

3.27 BALLS JUMPED OFF TABLE

Balls coming to rest other than on the bed of the table after a stroke *(on the cushion top, rail surface, floor, etc.)* are considered jumped balls. Balls may bounce on the cushion tops and rails of the table in play without being jumped balls if they return to the bed of the table under their own power and without touching anything not a part of the table. The table shall consist of the permanent part of the table proper.

(Balls that strike or touch anything not a part of the table, such as the light fixture, chalk on the rails and cushion tops, etc., shall be considered jumped balls even though they might return to the bed of the table after contacting items which are not parts of the table proper). In all pocket billiard games, when a stroke results in the cue ball or any object ball being a jumped ball off the table, the stroke is a foul. All jumped object balls are spotted *(except in Nine-Ball)* when all balls have stopped moving. See specific game rules for putting the cue ball in play after a jumped cue ball foul.

3.28 SPECIAL INTENTIONAL FOUL PENALTY. The cue ball in play shall not be intentionally struck with anything other than a cue's attached tip *(such as the ferrule, shaft, etc.)*. While such contact is automatically a foul under the provisions of Rule 3.19., if the referee deems the contact to be intentional, he shall warn the player once during a match that a second violation during that match will result in the loss of the match by forfeiture. If a second violation does occur, the match must be forfeited.

3.29 ONE FOUL LIMIT. Unless specific game rules dictate otherwise, only one foul is assessed on a player in each inning; if different penalties can apply, the most severe penalty is the factor determining which foul is assessed.

3.30 BALLS MOVING SPONTANEOUSLY. If a ball shifts, settles, turns or otherwise moves "by itself," the ball shall remain in the position it assumed and play continues. A hanging ball that falls into a pocket "by itself" after being motionless for 5 seconds or longer shall be replaced as closely as possible to its position prior to falling, and play shall continue. If an object ball drops into a pocket "by itself" as a player shoots at it, so that the cue ball passes over the spot the ball had been on, unable to hit it, the cue ball and object ball are to be replaced to their positions prior to the stroke, and the player may shoot again. Any other object balls disturbed on the stroke are also to be replaced to their original positions before the shooter replays.

Spotting Balls

3.31 SPOTTING BALLS. When specific game rules call for spotting balls, they shall be replaced on the table on the long string after the stroke is complete. A single ball is placed on the foot spot; if more than one ball is to be spotted, they are placed on the long string in ascending numerical order, beginning on the foot spot and advancing

Diagram 19

toward the foot rail. When balls on or near the foot spot or long string interfere with the spotting of balls, the balls to be spotted are placed on the long string as close as possible to the foot spot without moving the interfering balls. Spotted balls are to be placed as close as possible or frozen *(at the referee's discretion)* to such interfering balls, except when the cue ball is interfering; balls to be spotted against the cue ball are placed as close as possible without being frozen. If there is insufficient room on the long string between the foot spot and the foot rail cushion for balls that must be spotted, such balls are then placed on the extension of the long string "in front" of the foot spot *(between the foot spot and the center spot)*, as near as possible to the foot spot and in the same numerical order as if they were spotted "behind" the foot spot *(lowest numbered ball closest to the foot spot)*.

3.32 JAWED BALLS. If two or more balls are locked between the jaws or sides of the pocket, with one or more suspended in air, the referee shall inspect the balls in position and follow this procedure: he shall visually *(or physically if he desires)* project each ball directly downward from its locked position; any ball that in his judgement would fall in the pocket if so moved directly downward is a pocketed ball, while any ball that would come to rest on the bed of the table is not pocketed. The balls are then placed according to the referee's assessment, and play continues according to specific game rules as if no locking or jawing of balls had occurred.

3.33. ADDITIONAL POCKETED BALLS

If extra balls are pocketed on a legal scoring stroke, they are counted in accord with the scoring rules for the particular game.

3.34. NON-PLAYER INTERFERENCE

If the balls are moved *(or a player bumped such that play is directly affected)* by a non-player during the match, the balls shall be replaced as near as possible to their original positions immediately prior to the incident, and play shall resume with no penalty on the player affected. If the match is officiated, the referee shall replace the balls. This rule shall also apply to "act of God" interference, such as earthquake, hurricane, light fixture falling, power failure, etc. If the balls cannot be restored to their original positions, replay the game with the original player breaking. This rule is not applicable to 14.1 Continuous where the game consists of successive racks: the rack in progress will be discontinued and a completely new rack will be started with the requirements of the normal opening break *(players lag for break)*. Scoring of points is to be resumed at the score as it stood at the moment of game disruption.

3.35. BREAKING SUBSEQUENT RACKS. In a match that consists of short rack games, the winner of each game breaks in the next. The following are common options that may be designated by tournament officials in advance:

(a) Players alternate break.

(b) Loser breaks.

(c) Player trailing in game count breaks the next game.

3.36 PLAY BY INNINGS

During the course of play, players alternate turns *(innings)* at the table, with a player's inning ending when he either fails to legally pocket a ball, or fouls. When an inning ends free of a foul, the incoming player accepts the table in position.

3.37 OBJECT BALL FROZEN TO CUSHION OR CUE BALL

This rule applies to any shot where the cue ball's first contact with a ball is with one that is frozen to a cushion or to the cue ball itself. After the cue ball makes contact with the frozen object ball, the shot must result in either:

(a) A ball being pocketed, or;

(b) The cue ball contacting a cushion, or;

(c) The frozen ball being caused to contact a cushion attached to a separate rail, or;

(d) Another object ball being caused to contact a cushion with which it was not already in contact. Failure to satisfy one of those four requirements is a foul. *(Note: 14.1 and other games specify additional requirements and applications of this rule; see specific game rules.)* A ball which is touching a cushion at the start of a shot and then is forced into a cushion attached to the same rail is not considered to have been driven to that cushion unless it leaves the cushion, contacts another ball, and then contacts the cushion again. An object ball is not considered frozen to a cushion unless it is examined and announced as such by either the referee or one of the players prior to that object ball being involved in a shot.

3.38 PLAYING FROM BEHIND THE STRING

When a player has the cue ball in hand behind the string *(in the kitchen)*, he must drive the cue ball to a point outside the kitchen before it contacts either a cushion or an object ball. Failure to do so is a foul if a referee is presiding over a match. If no referee, the opponent has the option to call it either a foul or to require the offending player to replay the shot again with the balls restored to their positions prior to the shot *(and with no foul penalty imposed)*. Exception: if an object ball lies on or outside the head string *(and is thus playable)* but so close that the cue ball contacts it before the cue ball is out of the kitchen, the ball can be legally played. If, with cue ball in hand behind the headstring and while the shooter is attempting a legitimate shot, the cue ball accidentally hits a ball behind the head string, and the cue ball crosses the line, it is a foul. If with cue ball in hand behind the head string, the shooter causes the cue ball to hit an object ball accidentally, and the cue ball does not cross the headstring, the following applies: the incoming player has the option of calling a foul and having cue ball in hand, or having the balls returned to their original position, and having the offending player replay the shot. If a player under the same conditions intentionally causes the cue ball to contact an object ball behind the headstring, it is unsportsmanlike conduct.

3.39 CUE BALL IN HAND FOUL

During cue ball in hand placement, the player may use his hand or any part of his cue *(including the tip)* to position the cue ball. When placing the cue ball in position, any forward stroke motion contacting the cue ball will be a foul, if not a legal shot.

3.40 INTERFERENCE

If the non-shooting player distracts his opponent or interferes with his play, he has fouled. If a player shoots out of turn, or moves any ball except during his inning, it is considered to be interference.

3.41 DEVICES

Players are not allowed to use a ball, the triangle or any other width - measuring device to see if the cue ball or an object ball would travel through a gap, etc. Only the cue stick may be used as an aid to judge gaps, etc., so long as the cue is held by the hand. To do so otherwise is a foul and unsportsmanlike conduct. *(Also see Rules 1.3., 1.4. and 2.15.)*

3.42 ILLEGAL MARKING

If a player intentionally marks the table in any way to assist in executing the shot, whether by wetting the cloth, by placing a cube of chalk on the rail, or by any other means, it is a foul. If the player removes the mark prior to the shot, no penalty is imposed.

RULES FOR
WHEELCHAIR COMPETITION

The International Stoke Mandeville Wheelchair Sports Federation (ISMWSF) is recognized by the World Pool–Billiard Association (WPA), the world governing body of pocket billiards, as governing all international competitions concerning wheelchair pocket billiards. The ISMWSF has adopted the rules of play within these pages except for the amendments, exceptions and alterations stipulated below.

CUE SPORTS CLASSIFICATION

There are Three (3) Classes for those competing in wheelchairs.

1. Those players with hand or arm disabilities who cannot make or sustain a functional bridge while playing a shot.

2. Those players who can make and sustain a functional bridge but who have no stability and balance due to a lack of functional trunk muscles. These players support themselves at the table with their bridge hand.

3. All other players with a good to normal balance meeting the criteria for minimal disability.

MINIMAL DISABILITY

A minimal disability is a significant disability that prevents a player from playing standing up.

GENERAL RULES

1. Players must remain seated on the cushion or seat of the wheelchair when playing a shot.

2. Feet must be kept clear of the floor, should the feet or footplates touch the floor it will be deemed a foul.

3. Players in Class 1 may request the referee for assistance with rest and equipment, etc.

4. Below the knee strapping is allowed to keep the feet on the footplates. However, strapping above the waist is not allowed except for medical reasons when it will be taken into account for classification purposes.

TOURNAMENT
POCKET BILLIARD GAMES

EIGHT-BALL
World Standardized Rules
Except when clearly contradicted by these additional rules, the General Rules of Pocket Billiards apply.

4.1 **OBJECT OF THE GAME**
Eight-Ball is a call shot game played with a cue ball and 15 object balls, numbered 1 through 15. One player must pocket balls of the group numbered 1 through 7 (*solid colors*), while the other player has 9 through 15 (*stripes*). **The player pocketing either group first, and then legally pocketing the 8-ball wins the game.**

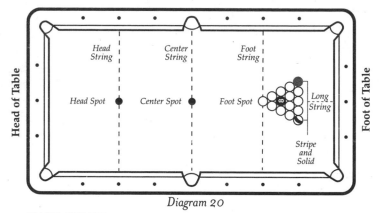

Diagram 20

4.2 **CALL SHOT**
In Call Shot, obvious balls and pockets do not have to be indicated. It is the opponent's right to ask which ball and pocket if he is unsure of the shot. Bank shots and combination shots are not considered obvious, and care should be taken in calling both the object ball and the intended pocket. When calling the shot, it is never necessary to indicate details such as the number of cushions, banks, kisses, caroms, etc. Any balls pocketed on a foul remain pocketed, regardless of whether they belong to the shooter or the opponent.

The opening break is not a "called shot." Any player performing a break shot in 8-Ball may continue to shoot so long as any object ball is legally pocketed on the break.

4.3 RACKING THE BALLS

The balls are racked in a triangle at the foot of the table with the 8-ball in the center of the triangle, the first ball of the rack on the foot spot, a stripe ball in one corner of the rack and a solid ball in the other corner.

4.4 ALTERNATING BREAK

Winner of the lag has the option to break. During individual competition, players will alternate breaking on each subsequent game.

4.5 JUMP AND MASSÉ SHOT FOUL

While "cue ball fouls only" is the rule of play when a match is not presided over by a referee, a player should be aware that it will be considered a cue ball foul if during an attempt to jump, curve or Massé the cue ball over or around an impeding numbered ball that is not a legal object ball, the impeding ball moves *(regardless of whether it was moved by a hand, cue stick follow-through or bridge)*.

4.6 LEGAL BREAK SHOT

(Defined) To execute a legal break, the breaker *(with the cue ball behind the head string)* must either (1) pocket a ball, or (2) drive at least four numbered balls to the rail. When the breaker fails to make a legal break, it is a foul, and the incoming player has the option of (1) accepting the table in position and shooting, or (2) having the balls reracked and having the option of shooting the opening break or allowing the offending player to rebreak.

4.7 SCRATCH ON A LEGAL BREAK

If a player scratches on a legal break shot, (1) all balls pocketed remain pocketed *(exception, the 8-ball: see rule 4.9)*, (2) it is a foul, (3) the table is open. **Please Note**: The incoming player has cue ball in hand behind the head string and may not shoot an object ball that is behind the head string, unless he first shoots the cue ball past the head string and causes the cue ball to come back behind the head string and hit the object ball.

4.8 OBJECT BALLS JUMPED OFF TABLE ON THE BREAK

If a player jumps an object ball off the table on the break shot, it is a foul and the incoming player has the option of (1) accepting the table in position and shooting, or (2) taking cue ball in hand behind the head string and shooting.

4.9   8-BALL POCKETED ON THE BREAK

If the 8-ball is pocketed on the break, breaker may ask for a rerack or have the 8-ball spotted and continue shooting. If the breaker scratches while pocketing the 8-ball on the break, the incoming player has the option of a rerack or having the 8-ball spotted and begin shooting with ball in hand behind the head string.

4.10   OPEN TABLE

(Defined) The table is "open" when the choice of groups *(stripes or solids)* has not yet been determined. When the table is open, it is legal to hit a solid first to make a stripe or vice-versa. **Note: The table is always open immediately after the break shot.** When the table is open it is legal to hit any solid or stripe or the 8-ball first in the process of pocketing the called stripe or solid. However, when the table is open and the 8-ball is the first ball contacted, no stripe or solid may be scored in favor of the shooter. The shooter loses his turn; any balls pocketed remain pocketed; and the incoming player addresses the balls with the table still open. On an open table, all illegally pocketed balls remain pocketed.

4.11   CHOICE OF GROUP

The choice of stripes or solids is not determined on the break even if balls are made from only one or both groups, because the table is always open immediately after the break shot. The choice of group is determined only when a player legally pockets a called object ball after the break shot.

4.12   LEGAL SHOT

(Defined) On all shots *(except on the break and when the table is open)*, the shooter must hit one of his group of balls first and (1) pocket a numbered ball, or (2) cause the cue ball or any numbered ball to contact a rail. **Please Note**: It is permissible for the shooter to bank the cue ball off a rail before contacting the object ball; however, after contact with the object ball, an object ball must be pocketed, **or** the cue ball or any numbered ball must contact a rail. Failure to meet these requirements is a foul.

4.13   "SAFTEY" SHOT

For tactical reasons, a player may choose to pocket an obvious object ball and also discontinue a turn at the table by declaring "safety" in advance. A safety shot is defined as a legal shot. If the shooting player intends to play safe by pocketing an obvious object ball, then prior to the shot, the shooter must declare a "safety" to the opponent. If this is **not** done, and one of the shooter's object

88

balls is pocketed, the shooter will be required to shoot again. Any ball pocketed on a safety shot remains pocketed.

4.14 SCORING

A player is entitled to continue shooting until failing to legally pocket a ball of his group. After a player has legally pocketed all of his group of balls, he shoots to pocket the 8-ball.

4.15 FOUL PENALTY

Opposing player gets cue ball in hand. This means that the player can place the cue ball anywhere on the table *(does not have to be behind the headstring except on opening break)*. This rule prevents a player from making intentional fouls which would put an opponent at a disadvantage. With "cue ball in hand," the player may use a hand or any part of a cue *(including the tip)* to position the cue ball. When placing the cue ball in position, any forward stroke motion contacting the cue ball will be a foul, if not a legal shot. *(Also see Rule 3.39.)*

4.16 COMBINATION SHOTS

Combination shots are allowed; however, the 8-ball can't be used as a first ball in the combination except when the table is open.

4.17 ILLEGALLY POCKETED BALLS

An object ball is considered to be illegally pocketed when (1) that object ball is pocketed on the same shot a foul is committed, or (2) the called ball did not go in the designated pocket, or (3) a safety is called prior to the shot. Illegally pocketed balls remain pocketed.

4.18 OBJECT BALLS JUMPED OFF THE TABLE

If any object ball is jumped off the table, it is a foul and loss of turn, unless it is the 8-ball, which is a loss of game. Any jumped object balls are spotted in numerical order according to General Rules for spotting balls.

4.19 PLAYING THE 8-BALL

When shooting at the 8-ball, a scratch or foul is not loss of game if the 8-ball is not pocketed or jumped from the table. Incoming player has cue ball in hand. **Note:** A combination shot can never be used to legally pocket the 8-ball.

4.20 LOSS OF GAME

A player loses the game by committing any of the following infractions:

1. Fouls when pocketing the 8-ball *(exception: see 8-Ball Pocketed On The Break)*.

2. Pockets the 8-ball on the same stroke as the last of his group of balls.

3. Jumps the 8-ball off the table at any time.

4. Pockets the 8-ball in a pocket other than the one designated.

5. Pockets the 8-ball when it is not the legal object ball.

Note: All infractions must be called before another shot is taken, or else it will be deemed that no infraction occurred.

4.21   STALEMATED GAME

If, after 3 consecutive turns at the table by each player (*6 turns total*), the referee judges (*or if no referee, both players agree*) that attempting to pocket or move an object ball will result in loss of game, the balls will be reracked with the original breaker of the stalemated game breaking again. The stalemate rule may only be used when there are only two object balls and the 8-ball remaining on the table. **Please Note**: Three consecutive fouls by one player is not a loss of game.

NINE-BALL

World Standardized Rules

Except when clearly contradicted by these additional rules, the General Rules of Pocket Billiards apply.

5.1   OBJECT OF THE GAME

Nine-Ball is played with nine object balls numbered one through nine and a cue ball. On each shot, the first ball the cue ball contacts must be the lowest numbered ball on the table, but the balls need not be pocketed in order. If a player pockets any ball on a legal shot, he remains at the table for another shot, and continues until missing, comitting a foul, or wining the game by pocketing the 9-ball. After a miss, the incoming player must shoot from the position left by the previous player, but after any foul the incoming player may start with the cue ball anywhere on the table. Players are not required to call any shot. A match ends when one of the players has won the required number of games.

5.2   RACKING THE BALLS

The object balls are racked in a diamond shape, with the 1-ball at the top of the diamond and on the foot spot, the 9-ball in the center of the diamond, and the other balls in random order, racked as tightly as possible. The game begins with cue ball in hand behind the head string.

5.3 **LEGAL BREAK SHOT**

The rules governing the break shot are the same as for other shots except:

Diamond Shaped Rack

1-ball must be on the foot spot.
9-ball must be in the center of the rack.

Diagram 21

1. The breaker must strike the 1-ball first and either pocket a ball or drive at least four numbered balls to the rail.

2. If the cue ball is pocketed or driven off the table, or the requirements of the opening break are not met, it is a foul, and the incoming player has cue ball in hand anywhere on the table.

3. If on the break shot, the breaker causes an object ball to jump off the table, it is a foul and the incoming player has cue ball in hand anywhere on the table. The object ball is not respotted *(exception: if the object ball is the 9-ball, it is respotted)*.

5.4 **CONTINUING PLAY**

On the shot immediately following a legal break, the shooter may play a "push out." *(See Rule 5.5)*. If the breaker pockets one or more balls on a legal break, he continues to shoot until he misses, fouls, or wins the game. If the player misses or fouls, the other player begins an inning and shoots until missing, comitting a foul, or winning. The game ends when the 9-ball is pocketed on a legal shot, or the game is forfeited for a serious infraction of the rules.

5.5 **PUSH OUT**

The player who shoots the shot immediately after a legal break may play a push out in an attempt to move the cue ball into a better position for the option that follows. On a push out, the cue ball is not required to contact any object ball nor any rail, but all other foul rules still apply. The player must announce the intention of playing a push out before the shot, or the shot is considered to be a normal shot. Any ball pocketed on a push out does not count and remains pocketed except the 9-ball. Following a legal push out, the incoming player is permitted to shoot from that position or to pass the shot back to the player who pushed out. A push out is not considered to be a foul as long as no rule *(except rules 5.7 and 5.8)* is violated. An illegal push out is penalized according to the type of foul committed. After a player scratches on the break shot, the incoming player cannot play a push out.

5.6 FOULS

When a player commits a foul, he must relinquish his run at the table and no balls pocketed on the foul shot are respotted *(exception: if a pocketed ball is the 9-ball, it is respotted)*. The incoming player is awarded ball in hand; prior to his first shot he may place the cue ball anywhere on the table. If a player commits several fouls on one shot, they are counted as only one foul.

5.7 BAD HIT

If the first object ball contacted by the cue ball is not the lowest numbered ball on the table, the shot is foul.

5.8 NO RAIL

If no object ball is pocketed, failure to drive the cue ball or any numbered ball to a rail after the cue ball contacts the object ball on is a foul.

5.9 IN HAND

When the cue ball is in hand, the player may place the cue ball anywhere on the bed of the table, except in contact with an object ball. The player may continue to adjust the position of the cue ball until shooting.

5.10 OBJECT BALLS JUMPED OFF THE TABLE

An unpocketed ball is considered to be driven off the table if it comes to rest other than on the bed of the table. It is a foul to drive an object ball off the table. The jumped object ball(s) is not respotted *(exception: if the object ball is the 9-ball, it is respotted)* and play continues.

5.11 JUMP AND MASSÉ SHOT FOUL

If a match is not refereed, it will be considered a cue ball foul if during an attempt to jump, curve or massé the cue ball over or around an impeding numbered ball, the impeding ball moves *(regardless of whether it was moved by a hand, cue stick follow-through or bridge)*.

5.12 THREE CONSECUTIVE FOULS

If a player fouls three consecutive times on three successive shots without making an intervening legal shot, the game is lost. The three fouls must occur in one game. The warning must be given between the second and third fouls. A player's inning begins when it is legal to take a shot and ends at the end of a shot on which he misses, fouls or wins, or when he fouls between shots.

5.13   END OF GAME
A game starts as soon as the cue ball crosses over the head string on the opening break. The 1-ball must be legally contacted on the break shot. The game ends at the end of a legal shot which pockets the 9-ball, or when a player forfeits the game as the result of a foul.

14.1 CONTINUOUS
World Standardized Rules
Except when clearly contradicted by these additional rules, the General Rules of Pocket Billiards apply.

6.1   OBJECT OF THE GAME
14.1 is a nomination game. The player must nominate a ball and a pocket. The player is awarded one point for every correctly nominated and pocketed ball on a legal stroke, and is allowed to continue a turn until failure to pocket a nominated ball or commits a foul. The player can pocket the first 14 balls, but before continuing a turn by shooting at the 15th *(and last remaining)* ball on the table, the 14 pocketed balls are racked as before, except with the apex space vacant. The player then attempts to pocket the 15th ball in a manner so that the racked balls are disturbed and he can continue the run. The player who scores the predetermined point total for a game *(usually 150 in major tournament play or any agreed upon total in casual play)* prior to the opponent, wins the game.

6.2   PLAYERS
2, or 2 teams.

6.3   BALLS USED
Standard set of object balls numbered 1-15, plus the cue ball.

6.4   THE RACK
Standard triangle rack with the apex ball on the foot spot, 1-ball on the racker's right corner, 5-ball on left corner. Other balls are placed at random and must touch their neighbors.

6.5   SCORING
Any ball legally pocketed counts one point for the shooter.

6.6   OPENING BREAK

Starting player must either (1) designate a ball and a pocket into which that ball will be pocketed and accomplish the shot, or (2) cause the cue ball to contact a ball and then a cushion, plus cause two object balls to contact a cushion. Failure to meet at least one of the above requirements is a breaking violation. Offender's score is assessed a 2-point penalty for each breaking violation. In addition, the opponent has the choice of (1) accepting the table in position, or (2) having the balls reracked and requiring the offending player to repeat the opening break. That choice continues until the opening break is not a breaking violation, or until the opponent accepts the table in position. The three successive fouls rule does not apply to breaking violations. If the starting player scratches on a legal opening break, he is charged with a foul and assessed a one point penalty, which applies toward the "Successive Fouls Penalties." The incoming player is awarded cue ball in hand behind the head string, with object balls in position.

6.7 RULES OF PLAY

1. A legally pocketed ball entitles a shooter to continue at the table until he fails to legally pocket a called ball on a shot. A player may shoot any ball, but before the shot, must designate the called ball and called pocket. Details such as kisses, caroms, combinations, or cushions (all of which are legal) need not be indicated. Any additionally pocketed ball(s) on a legal stroke is scored as one point for the shooter.

2. On all shots, a player must cause the cue ball to contact an object ball and then (1) pocket a numbered ball, or (2) cause the cue ball or any numbered ball to contact a cushion. Failure to meet these requirements is a foul. When an object ball is not frozen to a cushion, but is within a ball's width of a cushion (referee to determine by measurement if necessary), a player is permitted only two consecutive legal safeties on that ball using only the near rail. If such safety play is employed, that object ball is then considered frozen to the rail on the player's next inning. The General Rules of Pocket Billiards "Frozen Balls" requirements apply if the player chooses to make the first cue ball contact with that object ball on the third shot. (**Note**: If a player has committed a foul on the shot immediately before or the shot immediately after playing this ball, then he must immediately meet the requirements of the "Frozen Ball" rule when playing this object ball. Also, if he has committed two consecutive fouls, he must immediately meet the requirements of the Frozen Ball rule when playing this object ball. If such player fails to meet the requirements of the Frozen Ball rule, he is considered to have committed a third successive foul and the appropriate

point penalty is assessed as well as one point for each of the previous fouls. All 15 balls are then reracked and the player committing the infraction is required to break, as at the beginning of the game.)

3. When the 14th ball of a rack is pocketed, play stops momentarily with the 15th ball remaining in position on the table; the 14 pocketed balls are then racked *(with the space at the foot spot vacant in the triangle)*. Player then continues, normally pocketing the 15th *(or "break" ball)* in such manner as to have the cue ball carom into the rack and spread the balls to facilitate the continuance of his run. However, player is not compelled to shoot the 15th ball; he may shoot any ball he desires. See Diagram 22 if the 15th ball is pocketed on the same stroke as the 14th ball.

4. A player may call a safety rather than an object ball *(for defensive purposes)*. Safety play is legal, but must comply with all applicable rules. The player's inning ends when a safety is played, and pocketed balls are not scored. Any object ball pocketed on a called safety is spotted.

5. A player may not catch, touch, or in any way interfere with a ball as it travels toward a pocket or the rack area on a shot *(to include catching a ball as it enters a pocket by having a hand in the pocket)*. Doing so is a special "deliberate foul" and is penalized one point for the foul and an additional 15 point penalty, for a total of 16 points. The incoming player then has choice of (1) accepting the table in position with the cue ball in hand behind the head string, or (2) having all 15 balls reracked and requiring the offending player to shoot under the requirements of the opening break.

Cue Ball Lies / 15th Ball Lies	IN THE RACK	NOT IN THE RACK & NOT ON HEAD SPOT*	ON HEAD SPOT*
IN THE RACK	15th Ball: foot spot. Cue Ball: in kitchen.	15th Ball: head spot. Cue Ball: in position.	15th Ball: center spot. Cue Ball: in position.
POCKETED	15th Ball: foot spot. Cue Ball: in kitchen.	15th Ball: foot spot. Cue Ball: in position.	15th Ball: foot spot. Cue Ball: in position.
IN KITCHEN BUT NOT ON HEAD SPOT*	15th Ball: in position. Cue Ball: head spot.		
NOT IN KITCHEN & NOT IN THE RACK	15th Ball: in position. Cue Ball: in kitchen.		
ON HEAD SPOT*	15th Ball: in position. Cue Ball: center spot.		*On head spot means to interfere with spotting a ball on the head spot.

Diagram 22

6. If the 15th *(unpocketed)* ball of a rack and/or the cue ball interferes with the triangle being lowered straight down into position for racking, refer to the diagram, which indicates the proper manner of relocating balls. *(The gray boxes are those situations in which there is no interference, both balls remain in position.)*

7. When a player has the cue ball in hand behind the head string *(as after a scratch)* and all object balls are behind the head string, the object ball nearest the head string may be spotted upon request. If two or more balls are an equal distance from the head string, the player may designate which of the equidistant balls is to be spotted.

6.8 ILLEGALLY POCKETED BALLS
All spotted. No penalty.

6.9 OBJECT BALLS JUMPED OFF THE TABLE
The stroke is a foul. Any jumped ball(s) is spotted after the balls come to rest.

6.10 CUE BALL AFTER JUMPING OFF TABLE/SCRATCH
Incoming player has cue ball in hand behind the head string, unless the provision of Rule of Play 6.7.2, 6.7.5 or 6.12 *(below)* apply to the offender's foul and dictate alternate choices or procedures.

6.11 PENALTIES FOR FOULS
One point deducted for each foul. **Note**: penalties are more severe for deliberate fouls *(Rule of Play 6.7.5)* and third "Successive Fouls" *(6.12 below)*. Incoming player accepts cue ball in position unless foul was a jumped cue ball, pocket scratch, deliberate foul *(Rule of Play 6.7.5)* or third successive foul.

6.12 SUCCESSIVE FOUL PENALTIES
When a player commits a foul, penalization is one point *(or more as appropriate)* and a notation is made and posted by the scorer that the player is "on a foul." The player remains "on a foul" until the next shot attempt, at which time the foul may be removed by successfully pocketing a called ball, or completing a legal safety. If failing to meet these requirements on the next turn at the table, the player is penalized one point. The notation is changed to "on two fouls." If he fails to meet the requirements of successfully pocketing a called ball or completing a legal safety on the third consecutive turn at the table, penalization is one point and an additional penalty of 15 points is assessed *(a total of 18 points for three consecutive fouls equals −18 points)*. The commission of a third successive foul automatically clears the offender's record of fouls.

All balls are then reracked and the player committing the infraction is required to break as at the beginning of the game. Rules for the opening break apply.

It should be emphasized that successive fouls must be committed in successive turns *(or playing attempts)*, not merely in successive innings. For example, if a player ends inning six with a foul, steps to the table for inning seven and fouls *(he is "on two fouls")*, and then starts inning eight with a legally pocketed ball before scratching on his second shot attempt of the inning, he has not committed three successive fouls, even though there were fouls in three successive innings. As soon as he legally pocketed the ball to start inning eight, he cleared the two fouls. He is, of course, "on one foul" when he plays the first stroke attempt of inning nine.

6.13   SCORING NOTE

The deduction of penalty points can result in negative scores. A running score can read "minus one," "minus two," "minus 15," etc. *(A player can win a game with a score of 150 while the opponent has scored but two fouls. The final score would read 150 to -2.)*

If a player fouls on a shot that has not pocketed a ball, the point penalty is deducted from his score at the end of the previous inning. If a player fouls and pockets a ball on the same shot, that ball is spotted *(not scored)* and the point penalty is deducted from his score at the end of the previous inning.

SEVEN-BALL

World Standardized Rules

Except when clearly contradicted by these additional rules, the General Rules of Pocket Billiards apply.

TYPE OF GAME

Seven-Ball is at least three years old. Speedy rotational game designed to meet the time requirements of television. Averaging only about three minutes per game, contestants shoot at the same seven object balls, permiting players to show skills in making combination and carom shots, defensive shots and placement. At the same time, it is attractive to players of moderate skills, and readily adapts to handicapping by limiting the number of pockets in which the better contestant can legally pocket the game-winning 7-ball. Any nationwide commercial use of this game *(patent pending)* should be cleared in advance with Big Fights, Inc., 9 East 40th St., New York, NY 10016.

Seven Ball Rack

Diagram 23

PLAYERS

2, or 2 teams.

BALLS USED

Object balls numbered 1-7, plus cue ball.

THE RACK

A special circular rack has been designed for this game. A standard diamond rack *(as used in Nine-Ball)* may also be used by turning it sideways.

The balls are racked in a circle on the foot spot, with the 1-ball at the apex *(12 o'clock)* and the balls increasing numerically 1-6 *(clockwise in a circle)* with the 7-ball in the middle of the circle. *(See Diagram 23.)*

OBJECT OF THE GAME

To legally pocket the 7-ball.

SCORING

The balls have no point value. The player legally pocketing the 7-ball is credited with a game won.

OPENING BREAK

The starting player must (1) make an open break, or (2) legally pocket an object ball. If not, the incoming player has choice of foul Penalty 1, or having the balls reracked and shooting the opening break shot. In subsequent games, players alternate the break shot.

RULES OF PLAY:

1. A legal shot requires that the cue ball's first contact be with the lowest numbered ball on the table. A player must then (1) pocket a numbered ball, or (2) cause the cue ball or any object ball to contact a cushion. Failure to meet these requirements is a foul and Penalty for Fouls 2 applies.

2. A legally pocketed ball entitles a shooter to remain at the table until failing to pocket a ball on a legal shot.

3. After a legal opening break, the opponent chooses which side of the table *(any of the three pockets on one side)* into which he will pocket the 7-ball. Balls 1-6 may be pocketed on either side of the table.

4. Pocketing the 7-ball on a fair opening break wins the game.

5. Any violation of General Rules results in Penalty for Fouls 2.

LOSS OF GAME

A player loses the game by committing any of the following infractions: (a) pockets the 7-ball in a non-assigned pocket after the break, (b) scratches when the 7-ball is the legal object ball, (c) pockets the 7-ball on an illegal shot; (d) misses when the 7-ball is the object ball *(optional—an alternative is to assess Foul Penalty 2)*; (e) commits three successive fouls.

ILLEGALLY POCKETED OBJECT BALLS
All spotted; Penalty for Fouls 2 applies. *(Optional for coin-operated tables: all balls remain pocketed; Penalty for Fouls 2 applies.)*

OBJECT BALLS JUMPED OFF THE TABLE
All spotted. The stroke is a foul, and Penalty for Fouls 2 applies.

CUE BALL AFTER JUMP OR SCRATCH
Incoming player has cue ball in hand.

PENALTY FOR FOULS
No point penalty. (1) Incoming player has cue ball in hand behind the head string and object balls in position, but if the lowest numbered object ball is also behind head string it must be spotted. (2) Cue ball in hand anywhere on the table.

VARIATION
Players of unequal ability may be handicapped by assigning them more or less pockets in which they can play the 7-ball. It is suggested that more skilled players shoot the 7-ball into the side pocket on their side of the table. Players may also agree that the 7-ball can be pocketed anywhere on table.

TEN-BALL
World Standardized Rules
Except when clearly contradicted by these additional rules, the General Rules of Pocket Billiards apply.

TYPE OF GAME
Ten-Ball is a variation of Rotation in which a rack of just 10 object balls is employed. As you will discern from the following rules, it is virtually the same game as Nine-Ball, but with the extra ball adding both additional difficulty and generally fewer balls being pocketed on the opening break *(particularly the 10-, or game-ball)*. Still, accomplished players turn it into a fast, action packed game!

PLAYERS
2 or more, though 2, 3, or 4 is generally preferred.

BALLS USED
Object balls 1-10, plus cue ball.

THE RACK
Triangle rack truncated by removal of the rear row of balls *(rows 1-2-3-4)* with the 1-ball on the foot spot, and the 10-ball in the center of the row-of-

3; other balls may be placed entirely at random.

OBJECT OF THE GAME
To legally pocket the 10-ball.

SCORING
The balls have no point value. The player legally pocketing the 10-ball is credited with a game won.

OPENING BREAK
The starting player must either (1) make an open break, or (2) legally pocket an object ball. If failing to do so, the incoming player has choice of (1)cue ball in hand behind the head string and object balls in position, or (2) having the balls reracked and shooting the opening break shot.

RULES OF PLAY

1. A legal shot requires that the cue ball's first contact with a ball is with the lowest numbered ball on the table, **and then** either (1) pocket a numbered ball, or (2) cause the cue ball or any object ball to contact a cushion. Failure to meet this requirement is a foul.

2. A legally pocketed ball entitles the shooter to remain at the table until failing to pocket a ball on a legal shot.

3. When a player legally pockets a ball, he must shoot again. The player may not call a safety and spot a legally pocketed ball.

4. It is a loss of the game if a player commits three successive fouls.

ILLEGALLY POCKETED BALLS
All spotted, no penalty. *(Common option, coin-op play: None spotted except the game-ball, no penalty.)*

OBJECT BALLS JUMPED OFF THE TABLE
All spotted. The stroke is a foul, and the incoming player has cue ball in hand, except after the break shot.

CUE BALL AFTER JUMPING OFF THE TABLE OR SCRATCH
Incoming player has cue ball in hand, except after the break shot.

PENALTY FOR FOULS
Incoming player is awarded cue ball in hand. *(**Note**: Rule of Play 4 calls for loss of game if the foul is a 3rd successive one.)*

ROTATION
World Standardized Rules
Except when clearly contradicted by these additional rules, the General Rules of Pocket Billiards apply.

Rotation requires that the cue ball contact the lowest numbered object ball first on each shot; any ball pocketed on a legal shot counts. It is not necessary to call balls or pockets. It is a formidable test of a player's imagination, shot-making ability and repertoire. Few games require more exacting position play.

PLAYERS
2 or more.

BALLS USED
Standard set of object balls 1-15, plus cue ball.

THE RACK
Standard triangle rack with the 1-ball on the foot spot, 2-ball on the right rear corner, 3-ball on the left rear corner, and 15-ball in the center. All other balls placed entirely at random.

OBJECT OF THE GAME
To score balls of greater total point value than the opponent(s).

SCORING
Each legally pocketed object ball has a point value equal to its number. When a player's point total mathematically eliminates an opponent(s) from outscoring him *(61 points in a two-player game)*, the game is ended. If two or more players tie for highest point total after all 15 object balls have been pocketed, the tied player who legally pocketed the last object ball is credited with an extra tie-breaking point and wins the game.

OPENING BREAK
The starting player must (1) make an open break, or (2) legally pocket an object ball. If failing to do so, the incoming player has the choice of (1) shooting with cue ball in hand behind the head string and object balls in position, or (2) having the balls reracked and shooting the opening break shot.

RULES OF PLAY

1. A legal shot requires that the cue ball's first contact be with the lowest numbered ball on the table. A player must then (1) pocket a numbered ball, or (2) cause the cue ball or any numbered ball to contact a cushion. Failure to do so is a foul.

2. A legally pocketed ball entitles a shooter to remain at the table until failing to pocket a ball on a legal shot. If necessary, a player is permitted only two legal safeties played by merely hitting that object ball *(only)* to the near cushion.

3. When a player legally pockets a ball, he must shoot again. The shooter can't call a safety and spot a legally pocketed object ball.

4. When a player has the cue ball in hand behind the head string *(as after a scratch)* and the legal object ball is also behind the head string, the object ball may be spotted on the foot spot upon request.

5. It is a loss of the game if a player commits three successive fouls. In more than a two player game, balls pocketed by disqualified players remain off the table.

ILLEGALLY POCKETED BALLS
All spotted.

OBJECT BALLS JUMPED OFF THE TABLE
All spotted. The stroke is a foul, and the penalty for fouls is followed.

CUE BALL AFTER JUMPING OFF THE TABLE OR SCRATCH
Incoming player has cue ball in hand behind the head string.

PENALTY FOR FOULS
No point penalty. Incoming player has the option of (1) accepting the balls in position, or (2) requiring offending player to shoot again with the table in position *(if cue ball is in hand behind the head string it is so for either player)*. Rule of Play 5 takes precedence in the case of a third consecutive foul.

BANK POOL
World Standardized Rules
Except when clearly contradicted by these additional rules, the General Rules of Pocket Billiards apply.

TYPE OF GAME
In Bank Pool, each shot must be a bank of an object ball into at least one cushion before the ball is pocketed. "Straight-in" shots are not legal. It is by definition a demanding game, and fascinating to observe, particularly when the players are accomplished at the art of banking.

PLAYERS
2, 3, 4 or 5 players, though 2 players are generally preferred.

BALLS USED
Standard set of object balls 1–15, plus *cue ball* for long rack; or any nine balls racked in the shaped of a diamond, plus the *cue ball* for a short rack (*a popular form of competition*).

THE RACK
Standard triangle rack; balls placed entirely at random.

OBJECT OF THE GAME
To score a greater number of balls than the opponent(s).

SCORING
Each legally pocketed object ball is scored as one ball. In two-player games, the first player to score eight balls wins (*long rack*). In short rack the first player to score five balls wins. When 3, 5 or 5 players compete, long rack is generally played. In those contest, the first player to score five balls, four balls, and three balls respectively are considered winners.

OPENING BREAK
Starting player must make an open break. If failing to do so, the incoming player has choice of (1) accepting the table in position and shooting, or (2) having the balls reracked and shooting the opening break shot.

If any balls are pocketed on a legal opening break shot, the breaker continues shooting. Any balls pocketed on a legal break shot are spotted after the breaker completes his turn at the table.

RULES OF PLAY

1. A legal shot requires that the cue ball contact any numbered ball and then (1) pocket a numbered ball, or (2) cause the cue ball or any numbered ball to contact a cushion. Failure to do so is a foul.

2. A legally pocketed ball entitles shooter to remain at the table until failing to legally pocket a ball. Player may shoot any object ball, but must designate which ball, pocket and the cushion(s) that ball will contact. A legally pocketed ball must be driven into at least one cushion and rebounded into the called pocket.

3. A legally pocketed ball must be "cleanly" banked (*i.e., no kisses, no combinations, or caroms involving the object ball are permitted*). The cue ball may contact the object ball only once on a stroke.

4. On a legal scoring stroke, only the object ball is credited to the shooter. Any other balls pocketed on the same stroke do not count for the shooter, and may be subject to special spotting provisions regarding "Illegally Pocketed Balls."

5. When a player has the cue ball in hand behind the head string *(as after a scratch)* and all object balls are also behind the head string, the object ball nearest the head string may be spotted on the foot spot upon request. If two or more balls are an equal distance from the head string, the player may also designate which balls are to be spotted.

6. Cushion impact shall mean clear and distinct contact with a cushion by the object ball. Incidental contact with a cushion as the object ball approaches the called pocket shall not be considered an "extra" cushion(s) that would otherwise disqualify a legal shot. Rebounding of the object ball in the jaws of the pocket before dropping shall not be considered "extra" cushions unless otherwise designated by the player.

ILLEGALLY POCKETED BALLS

All spotted; no penalty. **Special spotting rule:** When in the course of a legal scoring stroke, an additional ball(s) is pocketed, spotting of the ball(s) is delayed until the shooter's inning ends. Should a player score the last ball on the table while any illegally pocketed balls are being held for delayed spotting, those balls are then spotted so the player may continue the inning.

OBJECT BALLS JUMPED OFF THE TABLE

All spotted. The stroke is a foul, and the penalty for fouls is followed. The incoming player accepts the cue ball in position.

CUE BALL AFTER JUMPING THE TABLE OR SCRATCH

Incoming player has cue ball in hand behind the head string.

PENALTY FOR FOULS

The player committing the foul must spot one of the previously scored object balls for each foul committed. If a player fouls when there are no previously pocketed balls to spot up, the shooter "owes" for such fouls, and must spot balls after each scoring inning until all "owed" fouls are eliminated. After fouls other than jumped cue ball or cue ball scratch, the incoming player accepts the cue ball in position.

ONE POCKET
World Standardized Rules
Except when clearly contradicted by these additional rules, the General Rules of Pocket Billiards apply.

TYPE OF GAME
One Pocket is a unique game in which only two of the six pockets are employed for legal scoring. Any ball may be played and need not be called. What is required is that an object ball falls in the player's "target" pocket. It requires a wide variety of strokes, cue ball control, shot-making ability, patience and defensive strategy.

PLAYERS
2, or 2 teams.

BALLS USED
Standard set of object balls 1-15, plus cue ball.

THE RACK
Standard triangle rack; balls placed entirely at random.

OBJECT OF THE GAME
Score a total of eight object balls in a player's target pocket before opponent.

SELECTION OF POCKETS
Prior to the opening break shot, the starting player chooses one of the corner pockets on the foot end of the table as a target pocket; the opponent then has the other foot end corner as a target pocket.

SCORING
A legally pocketed ball is scored as one ball for shooter. Any ball pocketed in opponent's target pocket counts, unless the cue ball should scratch on the same shot. If the shot constitutes a foul other than a scratch, the opponent is allowed to keep the ball. A shooter's inning ends on a scratch or foul and any balls pocketed in shooter's pocket don't count on a foul or scratch. In addition, the shooter is penalized one ball for a foul or scratch.

OPENING BREAK
Starting player must (1) legally pocket an object ball into his targeted pocket, or (2) cause the cue ball to contact an object ball and after contact, at least one object ball must contact a cushion. Failure to do so is a foul. **Note**: The cue ball does not have to strike a rail on the opening break.

RULES OF PLAY:
1. A legal shot requires that the cue ball contact an object ball and then (1) pocket a numbered ball, or (2) cause the cue ball or any

numbered ball to contact a cushion. Failure to do so is a foul.

2. A legally pocketed ball in a target pocket entitles shooter to remain at the table until failing to pocket a ball in the target pocket on a legal shot. Player may choose to shoot any object ball, any ball pocketed in the target pocket on an otherwise legal stroke is a scored ball.

3. Balls pocketed in the four non-target pockets are "Illegally Pocketed Balls."

4. Balls pocketed by a shooter in an opponent's target pocket are scored for the opponent, even if the stroke was a foul, but would not count if the cue ball should scratch or jump the table. However, if the stroke is not a foul and the shooter pockets a ball(s) in both target pockets, the shooter's inning continues, with all legally pocketed balls scored to the appropriate player. If a shooter pockets a ball that brings the opponent's score to the number opponent needed to win the game, the shooter has lost unless the cue ball scratches or jumps off the table.

5. When a player has the cue ball in hand behind the head string *(as after a scratch)* and all object balls are also behind the head string, the object ball nearest the head string may be spotted upon request. If two or more balls are an equal distance from the head string, the highest numbered ball is spotted.

6. Three successive fouls by the same player is loss of game.

ILLEGALLY POCKETED BALLS

All spotted. **Special spotting rules:** When a ball(s) is pocketed in a non-target pocket, spotting is delayed until the shooter's inning ends. Should a player legally score the last ball(s) on the table while any illegally pocketed balls are being held for delayed spotting, those balls are then spotted so the player may continue the inning.

OBJECT BALLS JUMPED OFF THE TABLE

All spotted. The stroke is a foul, and penalty for fouls is followed. The incoming player accepts the cue ball in position.

CUE BALL AFTER JUMPING OFF THE TABLE OR SCRATCH

Incoming player has cue ball in hand behind the head string.

PENALTY FOR FOULS

The player committing the foul must spot one of the previously scored object balls for each foul committed. If a player who fouls has no previously pocketed balls to spot up, the shooter "owes" for such fouls, and must spot balls after each scoring inning until all "owed" fouls are eliminated. After fouls other than jumped cue ball or cue ball scratch, incoming player accepts the cue ball in position.

THREE FOUL PENALTY

If a player fouls three consecutive times on three successive shots without making an intervening legal shot, he loses the game. The three fouls must occur in one game. The warning must be given between the second and third fouls. A player's inning begins when it is legal to take a shot and ends at the end of a shot on which he misses, fouls or wins, or when he fouls between shots.

BREAKING SUBSEQUENT RACKS

If a "race" or set of games is being played as a match, player's alternate the break shot in subsequent games.

OTHER POPULAR POCKET
BILLIARD GAMES

BASEBALL POCKET BILLIARDS

Except when clearly contradicted by these additional rules, the General Rules of Pocket Billiards apply.

TYPE OF GAME
The game is played with 21 object balls, numbered from 1-21, and a white cue ball. The object balls are racked at the foot spot *(in a 21-ball triangle)*. The 1-ball is placed on the foot spot, which is called "home plate." The 2- and 3-balls, respectively, are placed at the left and right corners of the triangle. The 9-ball, called the "pitcher," is placed near the center of the rack. *(See Diagram 24.)* Starting player has cue ball in hand.

SCORING
Players are credited with all balls legally pocketed. Each player has nine shots or innings at the table, which are played in succession. In other words, each player continues at the table until completing nine innings. An inning continues until a player misses or commits a foul, which results in a loss of turn.

The number of runs scored correspond to the number on the balls pocketed by the player. If a player scores the 12- and 13-balls in one inning, the player gets credit for 25 runs in that inning. Scores are posted by innings on a score sheet. The game ends when all players have completed nine innings of play.

The winner is the player with the most runs after all have played.

START OF PLAY
Rotation of play may be determined by lag or lot. The starting player has the cue ball in hand within the string. The starting player is credited with all balls scored on the break shot. After the break, the player continues, but must "call shots"— ball and pocket.

SUBSEQUENT PLAY
Incoming players have balls racked and proceed as above, playing nine innings.

SPOTTING BALLS
If a player pockets a ball and makes a scratch, the object ball must be spotted on the "home plate" *(foot spot)*. If home plate is occupied, balls are spotted

according to general rules for spotting balls in pocket billiards.

SCRATCHES

If the player scratches, it completes the inning and an "O" is placed in that inning on the score sheet. He then plays the next inning. If the shooter scratches and no object ball is pocketed, it is still regarded as a scoreless inning. Scratches are penalized by forfeit of all balls pocketed on the foul stroke, plus the last called ball legally pocketed. If the player has no balls to his credit, he spots next called ball scored.

CALL SHOTS

If a player makes a called ball as designated, all other balls pocketed on the same stroke accrue to his credit. If failing to pocket the called ball, however, and other balls drop in the pockets, the pocketed balls are spotted, it counts as a scoreless inning and player continues, unless miss occurred in ninth inning.

NINE INNINGS

Any number of players may play baseball pocket billiards, but before the game is complete, all players must have nine innings at the table. If a player runs all the balls before completing nine innings of play, the balls are reracked and player continues until completing nine innings, and then the total score is posted.

GENERAL RULES

Unless conflicting with provisions for this game, the General Rules of Pocket Billiards apply to Baseball Pocket Billiards.

Baseball Pocket Billiards

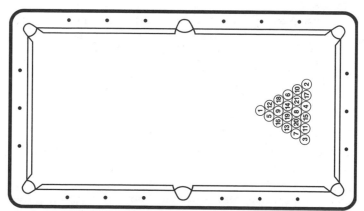

Diagram 24

BASIC POCKET BILLIARDS

Except when clearly contradicted by these additional rules, the General Rules of Pocket Billiards apply.

TYPE OF GAME
The game of Basic Pocket Billiards is a combination of the call shot aspects of 14.1 Continuous and the "anything goes" character of Fifteen Ball. It's a game well-suited for "mixed" *(beginners and accomplished players)* play, particularly in a team mode.

PLAYERS
2, or 2 teams.

BALLS USED
Standard set of object balls 1-15, plus *cue ball*.

THE RACK
Standard *triangle* rack; balls placed entirely at random.

OBJECT OF THE GAME
To score eight balls before the opponent.

SCORING
Any legally pocketed ball is scored as one ball.

OPENING BREAK
Starting player must:

1. legally pocket any numbered ball into a target pocket, or

2. cause the cue ball to contact any numbered ball and after contact, at least one numbered ball must contact a cushion. Failure to do so is a foul. **Note**: The cue ball does not have to strike a rail on the opening break. Failure is a breaking violation; the opponent can accept the table in position and shoot, or require that the balls be reracked and offending player repeat the opening break until the requirements are satisfied.

   If a starting player pockets a ball on the opening break, it is a legally pocketed ball if no foul or other violation is committed, and continues at the table. On all subsequent shots, however, the shooter must comply with all the "Rules of Play" below.

RULES OF PLAY

1. A legally pocketed ball entitles the shooter to continue at the table until failing to pocket a ball on a legal shot. The player may choose

and shoot any ball, but before shooting, must designate a single ball that will be pocketed; the shooter need not indicate *kisses, caroms, combinations* or *cushions (all of which are legal)*.

2. On all shots subsequent to the opening break, the player must cause the cue ball to contact an object ball, and then:

    (a) pocket an object ball, or;

    (b) cause an object ball or the cue ball to contact a cushion. Failure to do so is a foul.

3. When a player has the cue ball in hand behind the head string and all remaining object balls are behind the head string as well, the object ball nearest the head string may be spotted on the foot spot upon request. If two or more balls are an equal distance from the head string, the player may designate which of the equidistant balls should be spotted.

ILLEGALLY POCKETED BALLS
All *spotted*, no penalty.

OBJECT BALLS JUMPED OFF THE TABLE
All spotted. The stroke is a foul, and the penalty for fouls is followed.

CUE BALL AFTER JUMPING OFF THE TABLE OR SCRATCH
All spotted. The stroke is a foul, and the penalty for fouls is followed.

PENALTY FOR FOULS
One scored ball is returned to the table (*spotted*) by fouling player for each foul committed. If player who fouls has no previously pocketed balls to spot up, he "owes" for such fouls, and must spot balls after each scoring inning until his "owed" fouls are eliminated. After fouls other than cue ball jump or cue ball *scratch*, the incoming player accepts cue ball in position.

BOTTLE POOL

Except when clearly contradicted by these additional rules, the General Rules of Pocket Billiards apply.

TYPE OF GAME
A unique pocket billiard game, Bottle Pool requires the use of an inexpensive but specially shaped and balanced leather or plastic container (*"bottle"* or *"shaker bottle"*), shaped much like some disposable beverage bottles. The play of Bottle Pool combines the ball pocketing abilities of pocket billiards with the carom-making requirements of *carom* games.

PLAYERS

2 or more.

BALLS USED

Object balls 1 and 2, plus *cue ball*.

THE RACK

No triangle needed; at the start of the game, the 1-ball is frozen to the *foot cushion*, centered on the first diamond in from the racker's right corner pocket; the 2-ball is *frozen* to the *foot cushion*, centered on the first diamond in from the racker's left corner pocket; the bottle is placed open end down on the *center spot*. *(See Diagram 25.)*

Bottle Pool

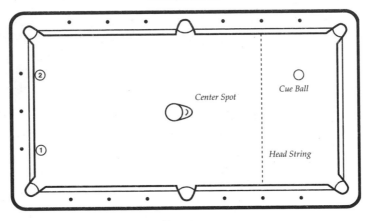

Diagram 25

OBJECT OF THE GAME

To score exactly 31 points prior to opponent(s).

SCORING

There are five scoring possibilities. Executing a legal stroke scores as follows:

1. Pocketing the 1-ball: one point.

2. Pocketing the 2-ball: two points.

3. Carom of the cue ball on the two object balls: one point.

4. Carom of the cue ball from an object ball(s) to the bottle which knocks the bottle onto its side: five points.

5. Carom of the cue ball from an object ball(s) to the bottle which stands the bottle onto its base: automatic win of the game.

Should a player accomplish more than one scoring possibility on a shot, he scores for each; a single shot can result in a total of nine points scored. Since exactly 31 points must be scored for victory *(unless #5 above applies)*, a player must not exceed 31; if he does, his inning ends and his score becomes only the total by which he exceeded 31.

OPENING BREAK

No "break shot" as such. Beginning with *cue ball in hand behind the head string*, starting player must cause the cue ball to contact either the 1-ball or the 2-ball. If failing to do so, the incoming player can require that offending player repeat the opening shot until that requirement is satisfied.

RULES OF PLAY

1. A legally executed scoring stroke entitles shooter to continue at the table until failing to legally score on a shot, exceeds 31 points on a shot, causes an object ball to contact the bottle before the cue ball contacts the bottle *(the entire shot is invalid and inning ends)*, or causes the bottle to be forced off the table or into a pocket *(the entire shot is invalid and inning ends)*.

2. On all shots, player must cause the cue ball to contact an object ball. Failure to do so is a foul.

3. Cue ball must contact an object ball before it contacts the bottle. Failure to do so is a foul.

4. If player causes the bottle to be upset, or upended by an object ball, the shot is a foul.

5. Player loses the game if he fouls in each of three consecutive innings at the table.

REPLACING UPSET BOTTLE

Whenever the bottle is upset, it is replaced on the table, open end down, with the open end as close as possible to its position when the bottle came to rest. It is, of course, replaced prior to the next shot.

When the bottle is forced off the table or into a pocket *(or into such position that the open end is over the pocket opening, making replacement as in the preceding paragraph impossible)*, then bottle is replaced on the center spot. If occupied, then replace on the head spot; if occupied, use the foot spot; if occupied, hold out until center spot is vacant.

ILLEGALLY POCKETED BALLS

All spotted. The stroke is a foul, and the penalty for fouls is followed.

OBJECT BALLS JUMPED OFF THE TABLE
All spotted. The stroke is a foul, and the penalty for fouls is followed.

SPECIAL SPOTTING RULES
After each shot is completed, any pocketed object balls are spotted prior to the next shot. They are spotted in the positions as at the start of the game. If a ball or the bottle prevents the free placement of an object ball to be spotted, the object ball is spotted on the center spot; if that is also occupied, the object ball is then spotted on the head spot. If both object balls are being spotted, follow the above, first spotting the 1-ball, then the 2-ball.

CUE BALL AFTER JUMP OR SCRATCH
Incoming player has cue ball in hand behind the head string.

PENALTY FOR FOULS
One point is deducted from offender's score for each foul. Fouls other than cue ball jumped/scratched, incoming player accepts the cue ball in position.

BOWLLIARDS

Except when clearly contradicted by these additional rules, the General Rules of Pocket Billiards apply.

TYPE OF GAME
Bowlliards applies the scoring concepts of bowling to pocket billiards. It's one of the few games that can be quite interesting as a solitary exercise since, like bowling, there is a perfect game score to strive for, and a player can measure improvement quite easily over the course of time playing Bowlliards.

PLAYERS
Any number.

BALLS USED
Any ten objects balls, plus *cue ball*.

THE RACK
Standard triangle position *(front apex ball on foot spot)*, using a 1-2-3-4 rack configuration.

OBJECT OF THE GAME
To score a perfect score of 300 points in 10 frames *(innings)* in solitary play. In competition, to score a higher point total in 10 innings than opponent(s).

SCORING
Each legally pocketed ball is scored as one point, regardless of ball number. The points scored per the "Rules of Play" below are treated exactly as is the pinfall in bowling.

OPENING BREAK

At the start of player's inning *(frame)*, he has a *free break (no special balls-to-cushion or other requirements once break stroke commences, and a jumped or scratched cue ball is without penalty)*. Any balls pocketed on the break are spotted, and player follows break by beginning scoring play with object balls in position and *cue ball in hand behind the head string. (The opening break takes place at the start of every inning.)*

RULES OF PLAY

1. A legally pocketed ball entitles the shooter to continue at the table until failing to pocket a *called ball* on a shot, or until scoring (10), the maximum total per inning possible. The player may choose and shoot any ball, but before shooting, must designate a single ball that will be pocketed and the pocket into which the ball will score; the shooter need not indicate *kisses, caroms, combinations* or *cushions (none of which are illegal)*.

2. Player has two chances to pocket the 10 possible balls of each frame. If player legally pockets 10 consecutive balls on the first chance of a frame, that frame is completed and player scores the frame exactly as a strike in bowling. If player fails to pocket 10 consecutive balls on the first chance, the player takes a second chance immediately. If the shooter succeeds in legally pocketing the remaining balls of the 10 on the second chance, the frame is completed and player scores it exactly as a spare in bowling. If player fails to legally pocket all 10 balls in two chances, the frame is then completed and is scored just as in bowling; a "strike" in the 10th inning earns two extra shots, a spare one extra shot.

3. If players tie for high game total in competition, additional innings are played alternately by the tied players, with the first player posting a superior score to that of the opponent(s) being the winner *("sudden death")*.

ILLEGALLY POCKETED BALLS

On the break, illegally pocketed balls are spotted prior to player beginning scoring play *(first chance of the frame)*. During scoring play, illegally pocketed balls are spotted.

OBJECT BALLS JUMPED OFF THE TABLE

All spotted. The stroke is a foul, and the penalty for fouls is followed.

CUE BALL AFTER JUMP OR SCRATCH

Only applies if occurring as player's first foul of a frame, player has cue ball in hand behind the head string to begin a second chance of the frame.

PENALTY FOR FOULS

One point is deducted from offender's score for each *foul*. If a foul ends the player's first chance of a frame, he has cue ball in hand behind the head string to begin his second chance of the frame.

BUMPER POOL

Rules and Regulations (Reprinted with permission of The Valley Company, Bay City, Michigan).

PLAYERS

Bumper Pool® is played by two players or by four as partners

BALLS USED

Each side has five red balls or five white balls, one of each color being a marked cue ball.

THE RACK

To set up Bumper Pool, place two red balls on each side of the white cup (*pocket*) on markers, placing marked red ball directly in front of white cup. Place white balls in same position around the red cup (*pocket*).

Bumper Pool

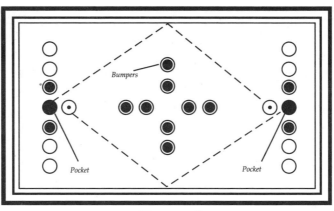

Diagram 26

OBJECT OF THE GAME

The first player or team to sink all five balls is the winner, except that player forfeits game if he shoots his last ball into his opponent's cup.

OPENING BREAK

Both players shoot the marked ball at the same time, hitting first the side-cushion, banking the ball into or near his color cup. The player who plays his ball into or nearest his cup shoots again.

RULES OF PLAY

1. Marked cue balls must be pocketed first. If a player sinks another ball before his marked ball is pocketed, his opponent may remove two of his own balls and drop them into his cup. In the event that both marked balls are pocketed on first shots, each player takes one of the remaining balls and spots it in front of cup and both shoot at same time, just as they did with marked balls. From there on they take turns, beginning with the player who pockets his ball or is nearest to his cup.

2. A player receives another shot upon sinking his own color ball in his own color cup.

3. In the event that a player causes a ball to leave the table, his opponent may place this ball anywhere he wishes, and in addition can remove two of his own balls and drop them into his cup as an additional bonus.

4. No player is allowed to jump his ball over balls or bumpers in making shots. Penalty for this will be the same as in Rule 7.

5. The length of time that the winners may continue playing is governed by House Rule.

PENALTY FOR FOULS

If a player sinks one of an opponent's balls there is no penalty, but if sinking one of his own into an opponent's cup, or shooting one of the opponent's, the opponent may then drop two of his own balls into his cup.

COWBOY

Except when clearly contradicted by these additional rules, the General Rules of Pocket Billiards apply.

TYPE OF GAME
Cowboy is another game that combines carom and pocket billiards skills, and employs a very unusual set of rules. It's certainly a change of pace game: how many games have you played in which the cue ball must be pocketed on a carom of the 1-ball on the last shot?

Cowboy Pocket Billiards

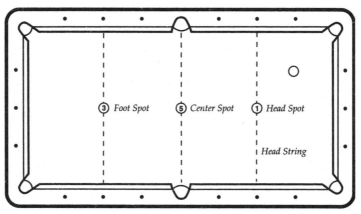

Diagram 27

PLAYERS
Any number.

BALLS USED
Object balls 1, 3 and 5, plus the *cue ball*.

THE RACK
No *triangle* needed; the 1-ball is placed on the *head spot*, the 3-ball on the *foot spot*, and the 5-ball on the *center spot*.

OBJECT OF THE GAME
To score 101 points prior to opponent(s).

SCORING
The first ninety points exactly may be scored by any of these means on legal scoring strokes:

    1. Pocketing any of the objects balls: points equal to the balls' numbers.

2. *Carom* of the cue ball off two of the object balls: one point.

3. *Carom* of the cue ball off the three object balls: two points.

Points 91 through 100 *(exactly)* must, and may only, be scored by execution of carom shots 2 and 3 above.

Point 101 *(winning point)* must be scored by caroming the cue ball off the 1-ball into a *called pocket* without the cue ball contacting any other object ball.

Should a player accomplish more than one scoring possibility permitted by these rules, he scores for each; thus a single shot can result in a total of 11 points scored.

OPENING BREAK

No "break shot" as such. Beginning with *cue ball in hand behind the head string*, starting player must cause the cue ball to contact the 3-ball first. If starting player fails to do so, incoming player has choice of

1. requiring starting player to repeat the opening shot, or

2. executing the opening shot.

RULES OF PLAY

1. A legally executed shot, conforming to the requirements of "Scoring," entitles the shooter to continue at the table until failing to legally execute and score on a shot.

2. On all shots, a player must cause the cue ball to contact an object ball, and then the cue ball or object ball must contact a *cushion*. Failure to do so is a *foul*.

3. At the completion of each shot, any pocketed object balls are *spotted* on their same positions as at the start of the game. If the appropriate position is occupied, the ball(s) in question remain off the table until the correct position is vacant after a shot. If, however, the 1-ball would be held out as a player with exactly 100 points is to shoot, the balls are all placed as at the start of the game, and the player shoots with cue ball in hand behind the head string.

4. When a player scores the 90th point, the shot must score the number of points exactly needed to reach 90; if the shot producing the 90th point also scores a point(s) in excess of 90 for the player, the shot is a *foul*.

5. When a player is playing for points 91 through 100 *(which must all be scored on caroms solely)*, it is a foul to pocket an object ball on a shot.

6. When a player is playing for the 101st point, it is a foul if the cue ball is pocketed in a pocket other than the one called, or if the cue ball fails to contact the 1-ball, or if the cue ball contacts any other object ball.

7. When a player pockets the cue ball on an otherwise legal shot, and according to the special requirements given in "Scoring" for counting the 101st point, pocketing the cue ball on such a shot on the 101st point is not a foul.

8. The player loses the game when fouling in each of three consecutive plays at the table.

ILLEGALLY POCKETED BALLS
All spotted per the provision of Rule of Play 3 *(above)*, with no penalty, except in the special cases covered by the Rules of Play 4 and 5.

OBJECT BALLS JUMPED OFF THE TABLE
All spotted. The stroke is a foul, and the penalty for fouls is followed.

CUE BALL AFTER JUMP OR SCRATCH
Incoming player has cue ball in hand behind the head string.

PENALTY FOR FOULS
No point deduction, but any points scored on previous shots of the inning are not scored, and player's inning ends. After fouls other than cue ball jump or cue ball *scratch*, incoming player accepts the cue ball in position.

CRIBBAGE

Except when clearly contradicted by these additional rules, the General Rules of Pocket Billiards apply.

TYPE OF GAME
Cribbage Pocket Billiards derives its name from the fact that a score can be made *(with two exceptions)* only by pocketing two consecutive balls which add up to fifteen; a similarity exists with the popular card game of Cribbage. In a sense, it represents a combination of a call-shot game and a set-order game, and is a bit different and quite interesting to play.

PLAYERS
2 players.

BALLS USED
Standard set of object balls 1-15 plus *cue ball*.

THE RACK

Standard *triangle* rack, with the 15-ball in the center; with the exception that no two of the three corner balls shall add up to a total of 15 points, all other balls may be placed entirely at random.

OBJECT OF THE GAME

To *score* five points *(cribbages)* out of a possible total of eight.

DEFINITION OF A CRIBBAGE

A cribbage is a pair of object balls, legally pocketed, numerically totaling 15. There are just these seven regular cribbages: 1-14, 2-13, 3-12, 4-11, 5-10, 6-9 and 7-8. No other ball combinations can be cribbages except that when all seven regular cribbages have been legally pocketed, the 15 ball becomes a legal cribbage by itself.

SCORING

Each legally pocketed cribbage counts one point for scoring player.

OPENING BREAK

Starting player must attempt an *open break*. Failure to do so is a *breaking violation*; opponent has the choice of:

1. requiring offending player to repeat the opening break *(until requirements are satisfied)*, or;

2. playing the opening break shot.

Starting player is not required to call the shot; if any balls are pocketed on the break shot, they accrue to him and he may continue at the table.

RULES OF PLAY

1. To legally pocket a cribbage, the two balls must be pocketed in the same inning. When a player has legally pocketed a single ball on a shot, he must legally pocket the appropriate companion ball on his next shot, or it is a *foul*.

2. If a player scores a legal cribbage, he can continue his inning and attempt to score more cribbages in the same inning.

3. When not "on a cribbage," if a player pockets two or more balls on a shot that do not constitute a cribbage, he may next pocket any of the proper companion balls as he chooses, but must successively pocket each of those companion balls if he is to continue at the table. If he fails, it is a foul. If, while satisfying the requirements of scoring companion balls, other ball(s) are incidentally pocketed, they likewise accrue to him; he must continue to complete one of

the cribbages he is "on" on each successive stroke *(though in no special order)*. Failure to do so is a foul; all balls of uncompleted cribbages are spotted.

4. When a ball is pocketed legally, but player fails to complete the cribbage legally during the same inning, the ball is spotted.

5. On all shots, the player must cause the cue ball to contact an object ball and then either :

    (a) pocket a numbered ball, or;

    (b) cause ay numbered ball or the cue ball to contact a cushion. Failure to do so is a foul.

6. A player loses the game if committing three *successive fouls*.

7. If the 15-ball is pocketed before all the other cribbages have been legally pocketed, it is an illegally pocketed ball and is *spotted* immediately following the stroke *(not inning)* on which it was pocketed. No penalty.

8. When a player has the *cue ball in hand behind the head string (as after a scratch)* and all the object balls are also behind the head string, the object ball nearest the head string may be spotted on the foot spot at his request. If two or more balls are an equal distance from the head string, the player may also designate which of the equidistant balls should be spotted.

ILLEGALLY POCKETED BALLS
All spotted; no penalty.

OBJECT BALLS JUMPED OFF THE TABLE
All spotted. The stroke is a foul, and the penalty for fouls is followed.

CUE BALL AFTER JUMPING OFF THE TABLE OR SCRATCH
Incoming player has cue ball in hand behind the head string.

PENALTY FOR FOULS
Inning ends; no point or ball penalty *(except per Rule of Play 6 above)*. Incoming player has the option of:

1. accepting the table in position and shooting, or;

2. shooting with cue ball in hand behind the head string.

CUT-THROAT

Except when clearly contradicted by these additional rules, the General Rules of Pocket Billiards apply.

TYPE OF GAME

Cut-Throat *(also known as Elimination)* is a very popular game in social situations, rather than for serious competitive play. It is very enjoyable to play—fast and with simple rules. A perfect game when an odd number of participants are available.

PLAYERS

3 or 5.

BALLS USED

Standard set of object balls 1-15 plus *cue ball*.

THE RACK

Standard *triangle* rack with the 1 ball on the foot spot, and the 6 and 11 balls on the two corners; all other balls placed at random.

DETERMINATION OF GROUPS

In three-player games, starting player has the group of balls 1-5; second 6-10; third player has balls 11-15. In five-player games, starting player 1-3; second player 4-6; third 7-9; fourth 10-12; and fifth 13-15.

OBJECT OF THE GAME

To legally pocket your opponents' balls before the opponents legally pocket your group of balls.

SCORING

Group balls have no point value. The player with a ball(s) still on the table, when all the other groups' balls are legally pocketed, wins the game.

OPENING BREAK

Starting player must make an *open break*. If failing to do so, incoming player may:

1. accept the *table in position* and shoot, or;

2. require that the balls be reracked and shoot the opening break himself. All balls pocketed on a legal break remain pocketed.

RULES OF PLAY

1. Players must decide prior to the game whether they are playing call shot or not.

2. A legal shot requires that the cue ball's first contact be with an

opponents' object ball. On all shots, player must cause the cue ball to contact an object ball and then either

(a) pocket a numbered ball, or

(b) cause any numbered ball or the cue ball to contact a cushion. Failure to meet these requirements is a foul. Any legally pocketed ball entitles shooter to continue at the table until failing to pocket an object ball on a shot. (*Also see exception: Rule of Play 4.*)

3. If player pockets any opponents' balls on an illegal shot, they are spotted; but if he pockets his own group balls on an illegal shot, they remain pocketed. If player pockets the last ball of his own group, whether or not a legal shot, it remains pocketed and his inning ends.

4. When a player's last group ball is legally pocketed, he is eliminated from the shooting rotation. He remains eliminated for the duration of the game unless a foul is committed by a player still in the game; when a player is reinstated due to a foul, he resumes his normal position in the original order of play.

5. When a player has the *cue ball in hand behind the head string (as after a scratch)*, and all balls of all opponents' groups are behind the head string, the object ball nearest the head string may, at the shooter's request, be spotted on the foot spot. If two or more balls are an equal distance from the head string, the player may designate which of the equidistant balls he desires to be spotted.

6. When successive games are played, the order of play for the next game is the same as the order of final elimination in the preceding game. (*First player eliminated breaks; winner shoots last; others in order of elimination.*)

ILLEGALLY POCKETED BALLS
Opponents' group balls are *spotted*; no penalty. Shooter's group balls remain pocketed, no penalty.

OBJECT BALLS JUMPED OFF THE TABLE
All spotted. The stroke is a foul, and the penalty for fouls is followed. The incoming player accepts the cue ball in position.

CUE BALL AFTER JUMPING OFF THE TABLE OR SCRATCH
Incoming player has cue ball in hand behind the head string.

PENALTY FOR FOULS
Shooter's inning ends. In addition, one ball from each of the opponents'

groups that is off the table is brought back into play. Players who had been eliminated can be reinstated at any time until the game is over. If a player's group has no pocketed balls at the time of a foul by one of his opponents, then the penalty has no effect on that group or player; the penalty is not carried forward.

EQUAL OFFENSE

Except when clearly contradicted by these additional rules, the General Rules of Pocket Billiards apply.

TYPE OF GAME
Equal Offense is a game in which each player shoots until he misses a shot, fouls or pockets the maximum amount of balls allowed for the inning. The winner is determined by the total inning score *(similar to bowling)*. Based on 14.1 Continuous, the game is ideal for leagues, tournaments, handicapping and averaging; fair, fun and interesting for beginners as well as the advanced player. Although copyrighted by BCA Master Instructor Jerry Briesath, he has placed no restrictions on its use.

PLAYERS
Any number.

BALLS USED
Standard set of object balls 1-15, plus *cue ball*.

THE RACK
Standard *triangle* rack; balls placed entirely at random. The balls are racked at the beginning of each inning for each player.

OBJECT OF THE GAME
To score more total points than opponent(s) in a predetermined number of innings *(200 points in 10 innings maximum)*.

SCORING
Any legally pocketed ball counts one point for shooter.

OPENING BREAK
At the start of each player's inning, he has a *free break (no special balls to cushion or other requirements once break stroke commences, and a jumped or scratched cue ball is without penalty)*. Any balls pocketed on the break are spotted, and player then begins shooting with object balls in position and *cue ball in hand behind the head string*. The *opening break* takes place at the start of every inning of each player *(10 times per match in championship play for each player)*.

RULES OF PLAY

1. Player may shoot any ball, but before shooting must designate an object ball and call a pocket. He need not indicate *kisses, caroms, combinations* or *cushions (none of which are illegal)*. A legally pocketed ball entitles the shooter to continue at the table until he fails to pocket a *called ball*, or until he has scored the maximum total per inning permissible *(20 points in championship play)*.

2. Player is entitled to any additional balls pocketed on a shot, as long as he pockets his called ball.

3. Shooting order for subsequent innings is determined by the scoring results of preceding innings — player with the highest score shooting first. In the event of a tie inning, the order does not change.

4. If players are tied for high match total *(10 inning)* score, additional innings are played by each tied player with the first player posting a superior score to his opponent(s) in an equal number of innings being the winner *("sudden death")*.

OBJECT BALLS JUMPED OFF THE TABLE
The stroke is a foul, and the penalty for fouls is followed.

CUE BALL AFTER JUMP OFF THE TABLE OR SCRATCH
This does not apply to Equal Offense, since a jumped or scratched cue ball ends player's inning, and all players' innings begin with the opening break.

PENALTY FOR FOULS: No point penalty; player's inning ends.

SOME VARIATIONS
For purposes of scheduling, handicapping, etc., variations can be made as follows:

1. A given number of misses or *fouls* may be allowed per inning *(use 14.1 Continuous rules for "Cue Ball After Jump or Scratch")*.

2. Maximum number of balls per inning permissible may be increased or decreased.

3. Number of innings constituting a *match* may be increased or decreased.

4. Each player's inning may be restricted by a time limit.

5. Combinations of any of the variations above may be utilized, and may be applied in a non-uniform manner as a means of handicapping players.

6. As an exercise for beginners to progress in finding patterns of play, three chances should be allowed *(two misses, cue ball in hand)* to reach a score of 15. An intermediate player should be allowed two chances. The 10-inning perfect score would thus be 150.

7. Third miss ends the player's inning.

INTERNET EQUAL OFFENSE

Except when clearly contradicted by these additional rules, the Rules of Equal Offense and the General Rules of Pocket Billiards apply.

TYPE OF GAME
Internet Equal Offense is the game of Equal Offense played using the Internet. Instead of players being on opposite sides of the table during the game, they can be, and are, on opposite sides of the world linked together via computer. Players' scores are typed into the computer and shared with participants via the Internet. Sven Davies of the USA and Jari Kokko of Finland pioneered this form of competition and direct regularly scheduled International Internet Equal Offense Tournaments each year.

PLAYERS
Two or more teams of five players each.

EQUIPMENT
In order to participate in scheduled Internet Equal Offense tournaments, you must have a computer dial-up or direct line connection to the Internet, or be a member of an online service that allows you to e-mail and telnet on the Internet. Your computer will need to be placed near one or more pocket billiard tables for play. All other equipment used is the same as in the game of Equal Offense.

COST
This form of international competition is very inexpensive; depending on your area and connection to the Internet, you will pay as little as a local phone call.

  Because of the international appeal of the game and the fact that it's affordable, Internet Equal Offense is popular with colleges and universities around the world.

FOR MORE INFORMATION
If you want more information about Internet Equal Offense, please call the BCA offices at (319) 351-2112.

FIFTEEN-BALL

Except when clearly contradicted by these additional rules, the General Rules of Pocket Billiards apply.

TYPE OF GAME
Fifteen-Ball is a basic game variation that does not require calling balls or pockets, and yet rewards good shot selection because scoring is based on the numerical values of the balls *(numbers)* as in Rotation. It is a game well-suited for developing skills at beginning and intermediate player levels.

PLAYERS
2 or more, though 2 players are generally preferred.

BALLS USED
Standard set of object balls 1-15, plus *cue ball*.

THE RACK
Standard *triangle* rack with the 15-ball on the *foot spot*; other balls have no exact positions, but the higher numbered balls are placed at the front of the rack near the 15-ball, with the lower numbered balls near the back of the rack.

OBJECT OF THE GAME
To *score* balls of greater total point value than the opponent(s).

SCORING
Each legally pocketed object ball has a point value equal to its number. The game ends when a player's point total mathematically eliminates opponent(s) *(61 in a two player game)*. If two or more players tie for highest point total, the tied player legally pocketing the last object ball is credited with the game.

OPENING BREAK
Starting player must either:

1. pocket a ball *(does not have to call either ball or pocket)*, or

2. cause the cue ball to contact an object ball, and then the cue ball and two object balls must contact a *cushion*. If failing to do so, the incoming player has the choice of:

    (a) accepting the *table in position* and shooting, or;

    (b) having the balls reracked and shooting the opening break , or;

    (c) requiring offending player to repeat the opening break.

RULES OF PLAY

1. Any ball pocketed on a legal shot entitles shooter to continue at the table until failing to do so.

2. On all shots subsequent to the opening break, player must cause the cue ball to contact an object ball, and then either:

   (a) pocket an object ball, or;

   (b) cause an object ball or the cue ball to contact a cushion. Failure to do so is a foul.

3. When a player has the *cue ball in hand behind the head string* (*as after a scratch*) and all object balls are also behind the head string, the object ball nearest the head string may be spotted on the foot spot at his request. If two or more balls are an equal distance from the head string, the player may designate which of the equidistant balls should be spotted.

ILLEGALLY POCKETED BALLS
All spotted; no penalty.

OBJECT BALLS JUMPED OFF THE TABLE
All spotted. The stroke is a foul, and the penalty for fouls is followed.

CUE BALL AFTER JUMPING OFF TABLE OR SCRATCH
Incoming player has cue ball in hand behind the head string.

PENALTY FOR FOULS
Three points are deducted from the offender's score for each foul committed. After fouls other than jumped cue ball or cue ball *scratch*, incoming player accepts the table in position.

FORTY-ONE

Except when clearly contradicted by these additional rules, the General Rules of Pocket Billiards apply.

TYPE OF GAME
Forty-One Pocket Billiards is another game that is well-suited for social play at parties or other gatherings where players of mixed abilities will take part. Since no one knows what number "pea" is held by the opponent(s), it is difficult to play defensively. In addition, the rules are designed to greatly equalize all the players' chances. An unusual and interesting game.

PLAYERS
2 to 15 *(though 3, 4, or 5 are generally preferred)*.

BALLS USED
Standard set of object balls 1-15 plus cue ball. A set of 15 numbered peas *(or "pills")* and a *shake bottle* are also used.

THE RACK
Standard *triangle* rack with balls placed entirely at random.

DETERMINING PRIVATE NUMBERS
After the balls are racked but before play begins, each player is given a pea from the shake bottle containing the peas numbered from 1-15. The number of the pea is the player's private number and is kept secret.

OBJECT OF THE GAME
To score points which, when added to the player's private number, total exactly 41.

SCORING
Each legally pocketed ball has a point value equal to its number.

OPENING BREAK
Starting player must make an *open break*. He is not obligated to pocket a ball on the break shot; but if he fails to make a legal *open break*, it is a foul.

RULES OF PLAY

1. Any ball(s) scored on a legal stroke count for the shooter. Players may shoot any ball and need not call ball, pocket or mode of shot.

2. A player is permitted only one shot or turn per inning, regardless of whether or not he scores.

3. An illegally pocketed ball is a foul, and does not score for the shooter.

4. On all shots, player must cause the cue ball to contact an object ball and then either

    (a) pocket an object ball, or

    (b) cause an object ball or the cue ball to contact a cushion. Failure to do so is a foul.

5. When a player has the *cue ball in hand behind the head string (as after a scratch)* and all object balls are also behind the head string, the object ball nearest the head string may be spotted on the foot spot at his

request. If two or more balls are an equal distance from the head string, the player may designate which of the equidistant balls he desires to be spotted.

6. When player has a total count of 41, he must announce his victory and present his pea for confirmation before the next player shoots. If he fails to declare his 41 total until the next player has shot, he must wait until his next turn to so declare. If, in the meantime, another player succeeds in attaining a legal total count of 41 and properly declares, the latter player wins the game.

7. If a player totals more than 41 points, he has "burst" and must so declare immediately *(before the next player shoots)*. All balls the burst player had pocketed are spotted, and the burst player may request a new pea prior to his next turn if he so desires. Any player who bursts and does not declare it prior to the following player's shot is disqualified from further play in the game; if a two-player game, the opponent is automatically the winner.

8. If all balls are pocketed prior to any player attaining a total count of 41, the player whose count is closest to 41 wins the game. If two or more players are tied for nearest to 41 in this situation, the game is a tie.

ILLEGALLY POCKETED BALLS
All spotted; no penalty.

OBJECT BALLS JUMPED OFF THE TABLE
All spotted. The stroke is a foul, and the penalty for fouls is followed.

CUE BALL AFTER JUMPING OFF THE TABLE OR SCRATCH
Incoming player has cue ball in hand behind the head string.

PENALTY FOR FOULS
The player committing a foul must spot one of his previously scored object balls for each foul committed. If a player has no previously pocketed balls to his credit when he commits a foul, he is exempt from a penalty for that particular foul.

HONOLULU

Except when clearly contradicted by these additional rules, the General Rules of Pocket Billiards apply.

TYPE OF GAME
Honolulu is a unique and fascinating pocket billiard game that confronts the player with an unending kaleidoscope of strategic and shot-making challenges.

Essentially, Honolulu is just a game of one-rack call shot. Call any ball in any pocket; score one point per legally pocketed ball; the first player to make eight points wins. *(Said score, incidentally, being kept the same as in One Pocket: Put your balls in your bin (just pick a side) and respot out of your bin any time you scratch or foul.)*

The major critical difference being — absolutely no "straight-in" shots are allowed. Each and every legally pocketed ball must be made by means of either (1) a bank, (2) a combination, (3) a carom, (4) a "kick" shot, or (5) some combination thereof.

PLAYERS
2, or 2 teams.

BALLS USED
Standard set of 15 object balls, plus cue ball.

THE RACK
Standard triangle; balls racked at random.

OBJECT OF THE GAME
Winner of game must score eight (8) points before opponent. *(Each legally pocketed ball scores one (1) point.)*

SCORING
Player must call ball and pocket. If called ball is made in designated pocket by means of either a bank, combination, carom, or kick shot *(or any combination thereof)*, it is considered a legally pocketed ball and scores one (1) point.

It is not necessary to call or specify kisses, caroms, rails, etc. Only called balls legally score. Any balls accidentally *(or illegally)* pocketed are re-spotted at end of inning. **Note**: 1985 Vaso Amendment may be implemented at player's option. To wit: Shooter may call any number of balls *(two or more)* on any one shot — as long as all balls called are pocketed as called — or none are scored. In other words, call all you want, but make all you call — or none qualify. Shooter calling two balls but pocketing only one (a) loses inning and (b) must respot pocketed ball.

KICK SHOTS
No short-rail kicks. Kick shots are legal only when cue ball is first banked

off rail not connected with designated pocket *(or if cue ball is banked off any two, or more, rails before striking object ball). (See Diagram 28.)*

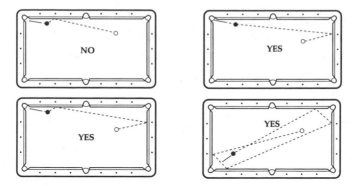

Diagram 28

OPENING BREAK

On the opening break the shooter must either:

1. call and pocket a ball out of the rack, or;

2. cause two numbered balls plus the cue ball to hit the cushion after striking rack with cue ball.

   Failure to do either is a foul. Penalty: One (1) point. Incoming player accepts cue ball where it lies. Breaker owes one (1) ball *(i.e., must respot first ball he legally pockets)*.

   All subsequent play is subject to standard BCA Pocket Billiard Regulations. *(Legal safety: Contact between cue ball and object ball, after which either cue ball — or object ball — or both — hit a cushion.)*

FOULS AND PENALTIES

One (1) point penalty *(one ball either re-spotted or owed)* per scratch or foul. Following scratch, incoming player has cue ball in hand in kitchen; following foul, incoming shooter accepts cue ball where it lies. The accidental touching or moving of any ball on the table is considered a foul. In Honolulu there is no three consecutive foul penalty.

ILLEGALLY POCKETED BALLS

Are all respotted at end of inning.

LINE-UP

Except when clearly contradicted by these additional rules, the General Rules of Pocket Billiards apply.

TYPE OF GAME
Line-Up is a forerunner of 14.1 Continuous.

PLAYERS
2.

BALLS USED
Standard set of object balls numbered 1-15, plus *cue ball*.

THE RACK
Standard *triangle* rack with the front apex ball on the *foot spot*, 1- ball on the rack's right corner, 5-ball on left corner; other balls placed at random.

OBJECT OF THE GAME
To score the predetermined point total *(usually 150 in tournaments, or any agreed upon total)* for game prior to opponent.

SCORING
Any ball legally pocketed counts one point for shooter.

OPENING BREAK
Starting player must pocket a *called ball* or drive two object balls to a *cushion*. If he fails to do so, he is assessed a two point penalty. Incoming player may accept the *table in position* and shoot, or require that offender repeat the opening break until the requirements are satisfied. Each successive failure is a two point penalty for offending player.

RULES OF PLAY

1. A legally pocketed ball entitles shooter to continue at the table until failing to pocket a called ball on a shot. Player may shoot any ball he chooses, but before he shoots, must designate the ball he will pocket and the pocket into which the ball will score; he need indicate no other detail.

2. On all shots, player must cause the cue ball to contact an object ball and then either

   (a) pocket a numbered ball, or

   (b) cause the cue ball or any numbered ball to contact a cushion. Failure to do so is a *foul*.

3. A player may call a *safety* rather than an object ball if he so desires

(for defensive purposes). Safety play is legal, but must comply with all applicable rules. Player's inning ends when safety is played, and pocketed balls are not scored. Any object ball pocketed on a called safety is *spotted*.

4. When the 15th ball of the rack has been pocketed, shooter records his scored balls from the rack. The balls are then spotted, and player continues shooting, playing the cue ball from where it came to rest after preceding shot, before the balls were spotted. *(If player misses or fouls during the rack, he records his score and incoming player shoots, accepting the table in position.)*

ILLEGALLY POCKETED BALLS
All spotted; no penalty.

OBJECT BALLS JUMPED OFF THE TABLE
All spotted. The stroke is a foul, and the penalty for fouls is followed.

CUE BALL AFTER JUMPING OFF THE TABLE OR SCRATCH
Incoming player has *cue ball in hand behind the head string* (*unless the foul was a third successive foul; see "Successive Fouls Penalty"*).

PENALTY FOR FOULS
One point is deducted from offender's score for each foul committed, unless the foul is a third *successive foul* (*see "Successive Fouls Penalty"*). After fouls other than cue ball jump, cue ball *scratch*, or third *successive foul*, incoming player accepts the table in position.

SUCCESSIVE FOULS PENALTY
If a player commits three successive fouls, he is penalized one point for each foul, and an additional deduction of 15 points. The balls are reracked and offending player is required to break the balls under the requirements of the opening break.

MR. AND MRS.

Except when clearly contradicted by these additional rules, the General Rules of Pocket Billiards apply.

TYPE OF GAME
Mr. and Mrs. (*also called Boy Meets Girl*) is a game that combines the general forms of Rotation and Basic Pocket Billiards. The rules are different for players of widely differing skill levels.

PLAYERS
Any number from two to six.

BALLS USED
Standard set of object balls numbered 1-15, plus *cue ball*.

THE RACK
Standard *triangle* rack with the 1-ball on the *foot spot*, 2-ball on racker's right corner, 3-ball on left corner, 15-ball in the center. All other balls are placed at random.

OBJECT OF THE GAME
To score balls of greater total point value than opponent(s).

SCORING
Each legally pocketed object ball has a point value equal to its number. Game ends when a player's point total mathematically eliminates opponent(s) — 61 points in a two-player game. If two or more players tie for highest point total, the tied player that legally pocketed the last object ball is credited with a game won.

OPENING BREAK
Starting player must cause the cue ball's first contact to be with the 1-ball. If starting player fails to meet this requirement, incoming player has the choice of (1) accepting the *table in position* and shooting, or (2) requiring that the balls be reracked and offending player repeat the *opening break*.

RULES OF PLAY

1. A legally pocketed ball entitles shooter to continue at the table until failing to legally pocket a ball.

2. On all shots, the more skilled player must cause the cue ball's first contact with a ball to be with the lowest numbered object ball on the table and then either

   (a) pocket a ball, or

   (b) cause the cue ball or any object ball to contact a *cushion*. Failure to do so is a foul.

3. The less skilled player may shoot any ball, regardless of number. He need not call ball, pocket or mode of shot. Any ball pocketed on a legal shot is a scored ball.

4. Player loses game if he commits three *successive fouls*. If more than a two-player game, balls previously pocketed by disqualified player remain off the table.

5. When a skilled player has the *cue ball in hand behind the head string (as after a*

scratch) and the legal object ball is also behind the head string, the object ball may be spotted on the foot spot at his request.

6. When a less skilled player has the cue ball in hand behind the head string *(as after a scratch)* and all of the object balls are also behind the head string, the object ball nearest the head string may be spotted at his request. If two or more object balls are an equal distance from the head string, he may also designate which of the equidistant object balls should be spotted.

ILLEGALLY POCKETED BALLS
All spotted; no penalty.

OBJECT BALLS JUMPED OFF THE TABLE
All spotted. The stroke is a foul, and the player's inning ends. The penalty for fouls is followed.

CUE BALL AFTER JUMPING OFF THE TABLE OR SCRATCH
Incoming player has cue ball in hand behind the head string.

PENALTY FOR FOULS
No point penalty. If foul is other than jumped cue ball or cue ball scratch, incoming player accepts the cue ball in position. A third consecutive foul by the same player is loss of game.

PEA (KELLY) POOL

Except when clearly contradicted by these additional rules, the General Rules of Pocket Billiards apply.

TYPE OF GAME
Pea *(or Kelly)* Pool is an old favorite among pocket billiard players who enjoy a group game in which the competitors play individually, and which entails a bit of luck *(not so much in the actual play but rather in the pea or pill each player receives during each game)*. The game is very popular since it can accommodate players of widely differing levels of ability.

PLAYERS
2 or more, with the best game being from four to six.

BALLS USED
Standard set of object balls numbered 1-15, plus cue ball. A set of 15 number peas *(or "pills")* and a *shake bottle* are also used.

THE RACK

Standard *triangle* rack with 1-ball on the *foot spot*, 2-ball on racker's right corner, 3-ball on left corner. All other balls placed at random.

DETERMINING PRIVATE NUMBERS

After the balls are racked, but before play begins, each player is given a pea from the shake bottle *(containing the peas numbered 1-15)*. The number of the pea is the player's private number and is kept secret.

OBJECT OF THE GAME

To legally pocket the object ball with the numerical value equivalent to the player's private number.

SCORING

No point value for object balls except the ball equivalent to pocketing player's private number; when a player legally pockets that object ball, he wins the game. Option: Game is played until a player legally pockets "his own" ball and wins, as above; he receives two points from each player for winning the game. In addition, when any player's "private number ball" is legally pocketed by any player other than himself, the pocketing player receives one point and the player whose ball was pocketed loses one point. Players whose private number balls have been pocketed by other players continue to shoot in the regular rotation, but if a player fails to announce that his object ball was pocketed by another player prior to a subsequent shot is being taken, the offending player is disqualified from further play during the game, and the forfeiture of points to the pocketing player is increased from one to two. If no player succeeds in pocketing his private number ball, the game ends when the last private number ball is pocketed, and another game is played with all point values doubled and player who pocketed the last private number ball being the starting player.

OPENING BREAK

Starting player must make an *open break*. If he fails to do so, incoming player has choice of either:

1. *cue ball in hand behind the head string* and *table in position*, or;

2. having the balls reracked and shooting the opening break shot.

RULES OF PLAY

1. A legally pocketed ball entitles shooter to continue at the table until he fails to legally pocket a ball.

2. On all shots, the cue ball's first contact must be with the lowest numbered object ball on the table and then must either

(a) pocket a numbered ball, or

(b) cause the cue ball or any object ball to contact a *cushion*. Failure to do so is a *foul*.

3. A player legally pocketing a ball must shoot again. He may not call a *safety* and *spot* a pocketed ball.

4. When a player has the cue ball in hand behind the head string *(as after a scratch)* and the legal object ball is also behind the head string, the object ball may be spotted on the foot spot at his request.

ILLEGALLY POCKETED BALLS
All spotted; no penalty.

OBJECT BALLS JUMPED OFF THE TABLE
All spotted. The stroke is a foul, and the penalty for fouls is followed.

CUE BALL AFTER JUMP OR SCRATCH
Incoming player has cue ball in hand behind the head string.

PENALTY FOR FOULS

No point penalty. Incoming player has choice of either:

1. accepting the table in position and shooting, or

2. requiring offending player to shoot again *(if cue ball is in hand behind the string, it is so for either player)*.

POKER POCKET BILLIARDS

Except when clearly contradicted by these additional rules, the General Rules of Pocket Billiards apply.

THE GAME
Poker Pocket Billiards is played with a white cue ball and a special set of 16 object balls.

15 of the object balls are numbered from 1 to 15, while the 16th ball has a "J" marked on two sides. Three of the numbered balls are also marked with a "J", which represents a "Jack," as in poker played with cards.

Four of the numbered balls are marked with an "A" for ace; four are marked with a "K" for king, and the remaining four marked with a "Q" for queen.

START OF THE GAME
Rotation of play may be determined by lag or lot. The object balls are racked in any order on the foot spot in a 16-ball rectangle. *(See Diagram 29.)* Starting

player has cue ball in hand.

SCORING

The object of the game is to get a better poker hand than your opponents. The best hand is four of a kind — four aces, for example. The next best hand is a full house; then three of a kind; then two pairs; then a straight *(ace, king, queen, jack)* and finally a pair *(two of a kind)*.

No player is allowed to score more than five balls in a single inning. Balls pocketed legally remain off the table.

THE BREAK

Starting player is credited with all balls scored on the break shot, providing he doesn't foul. If he counts, he continues shooting until he misses or pockets the limit of five balls allowed in one inning.

Poker Pocket Billiards

Diagram 29

INCOMING PLAYER

Incoming player accepts balls in position and is limited to five scores in a single inning.

NUMBER OF PLAYERS

Two or more players can play.

GAME ENDS

Game ends when all the balls have been legally pocketed. For example, one player may have five balls to his credit. Another may have three scores. A third player may have four balls in his "hand." A fourth player may have two counts. In this event, two object balls remain on the table. The player with five balls to his credit can continue to shoot in turn, spotting a ball from his hand each time he pockets a ball. He continues to pocket and spot balls in an attempt to better his hand, until he misses or scores the limit of five balls in an inning. The player with four counts to his credit, shooting in turn, can pocket a fifth ball and continue to shoot for the lone ball on the table in an effort to better his hand, spotting a ball each time he pockets one. He continues until he misses.

A player with three balls to his credit, however, with only two object balls on the table, ends the game if he pockets the two balls. In other words, he doesn't spot a ball after scoring, since he has only five counts to his credit.

ORDER OF FINISH

When all the balls are pocketed to end the game, players make the best poker hand out of the balls to their credit. A player with only three balls — if, for example, they are three kings — would win over a player who has five scores, but can get only two pairs out of this hand. A player with one ball to his credit defeats a player with no counts. A player with no balls to his credit finishes ahead of a player with no counts, who owes a ball as the result of a foul.

DELIBERATE MISS

It is obvious that if a player who has five balls to his credit can't better his hand by pocketing the balls on the table, he will miss deliberately rather than pocket a ball that will not better his hand. In making a deliberate miss, player must drive an object ball to a cushion or cause the cue ball to hit a cushion after striking an object ball. Failure is a foul.

PENALTIES

Players are penalized one ball for each foul. If a player fouls with no balls to his credit, he owes one to the table. If a player is forced to spot a ball from his hand as the result of a foul, he can choose the ball to be spotted.

FOULS

A player has fouled in Poker Pocket Billiards when:

1. Failing to hit an object ball.

2. Driving the cue ball or any object ball off the table.

3. Failing to have one foot on the floor when stroking.

4. Touches the cue ball except with the tip of the cue on a legitimate stroke or touches any object ball on the table, except on legal contact by the cue ball.

5. Fails to comply with rule on "deliberate miss." *(Above.)*

GENERAL RULES

When not in conflict with specific game provisions, the rules of 14.1 Continuous Pocket Billiards apply.

WILD GAMES

1. By agreement, players can make the "J" ball "wild," players pocketing the "J's" designating them as any "card" they wish when the "hands are laid down" at the conclusion of the game. For example, a player with three "A" balls *(aces)* and a "J" ball *(jack, which is wild)* can call his hand "four aces."

2. Players may draw a ball from the shake bottle, the number of which is kept secret from all the players until the game is over. At the conclusion of the game, the secret number is revealed. If, for example, the number corresponds to a "K" ball, all the kings are wild, players holding kings thus having the advantage of a wild card in finally calling their hands.

3. Each player can draw a number from the shake bottle, which makes all balls he scores of that number wild.

SIX-BALL

Except when clearly contradicted by these additional rules, the General Rules of Pocket Billiards apply.

TYPE OF GAME

Six Ball is a variation of Rotation in which the lowest numbered ball on the table must always be the player's first cue ball contact. If a player complies, any pocketed ball counts. For example, if a player strikes the 1-ball legally, which then caroms into the 6-ball and causes it to be pocketed, that player wins the game. It's fast, and with only six object balls on the table, single inning racks are very common!

PLAYERS

2 or more, though 2 players are generally preferred.

BALLS USED

Object balls 1-6, plus *cue ball*.

THE RACK

Triangle rack *(rows of 1-2-3)* with the 1-ball on the *foot spot*, and the 6-ball in the center of the rear row. all other balls placed entirely at random.

OBJECT OF THE GAME
To legally pocket the 6-ball.

SCORING
The balls have no point value. The player legally pocketing the 6-ball is credited with a game won.

OPENING BREAK

The starting player must:

1. make an *open break*, or;

2. legally pocket an object ball. If failing to do so, the incoming player has choice of:

    (a) *cue ball in hand behind the head string* and object balls in position, or;

    (b) having balls reracked and shooting the opening break shot.

RULES OF PLAY

1. A legal shot requires that the cue ball's first contact be with the lowest numbered ball on the table. A player must then:

    (a) pocket a numbered ball, or;

    (b) cause the cue ball or any numbered ball to contact a cushion. Failure to do so is a foul.

2. A legally pocketed ball entitles a shooter to remain at the table until he fails to pocket a ball on a legal shot.

3. When a player legally pockets a ball, he must shoot again. He may not call a safety and spot a legally pocketed object ball.

4. It is a loss of game if a player commits three *successive fouls*.

ILLEGALLY POCKETED BALLS
All spotted; no penalty, *(Common Option, coin-operated play: None spotted except game ball.)*

OBJECT BALLS JUMPED OFF THE TABLE
All spotted. The stroke is a foul, and the penalty for fouls is followed.

CUE BALL AFTER JUMPING OFF THE TABLE OR SCRATCH
Incoming player has *cue ball in hand*.

PENALTY FOR FOULS
Incoming player is awarded *cue ball in hand*. However, if a 3rd consecutive foul, Rule of Play 4 provides for a penalty of loss of game. The player's inning ends and no count can be scored.

GAMES OF YESTERYEAR

Editor's Note: In keeping with celebrating its 50th anniversary in 1998, the BCA is happy to provide the following rules for once-popular billiard games. Sources of the rules of these games are noted at the end of each game. For a change of pace, try these great billiard games of yesteryear! In most cases, the exact text of the rules is reprinted to catch the flavor of the language then or any unusual game circumstance.

BBC CO. POCKET BILLIARDS

A forerunner of Eight-Ball, the game is played with seven yellow, seven red, one black and one cue ball. The object is to pocket the black after having pocketed all seven balls of one color. The black is racked behind the apex ball. Balls pocketed on the break count. BBC refers to the Brunswick-Balke-Collender Co., now known as Brunswick Billiards. As now, Brunswick was a major manufacturer of billiard tables and equipment in the late nineteenth century. BBC pool was introduced by Brunswick and was still referred to by its original name as late as 1925. The sets are no longer sold *(although they can usually be found at billiards supply houses)*, the public having realized that a regular set of pocket balls, including seven solids, seven stripes and an 8-ball serves just as well. BBC pool is also called casino pool. There are, however, slight variations in the rules.

1. The players can either shake or bank for the break. All balls count on the break.

2. In racking the balls at the commencement of the game they are placed on the table in the form of a triangle or pyramid, as customary, the black ball being placed immediately behind the head ball of the triangle, and the other balls placed indiscriminately in the triangle.

3. If on the break a player pockets either a red or a yellow ball the aim is to secure the remaining balls of that color, and the player proceeds accordingly. Should both red and yellow balls be pocketed during the break, the breaker must choose between the two colors, and continue to play for the balls of the color chosen. After pocketing the seven balls of the color chosen, the black ball must be pocketed next. Successful pocketing of the black ball wins the game.

4. When balls of both colors are pocketed on the opening stroke, or simultaneously at any time thereafter, they must count for both players. Thus, if A, on the break, pockets a red and a yellow ball, and he selects the red, the yellow is placed back in the rack to the credit of his opponent.

5. If the black ball is pocketed out of turn, that is, before either player or side has secured the seven red or seven yellow balls, the game terminates, and the player who pocketed the black ball loses the game.

6. A player pocketing a ball of his opponent's color, and, failing simultaneously to pocket a ball of his own color, forfeits his shot, and his opponent is entitled to the ball pocketed.

7. In event of a scratch by reason of the cue ball being pocketed, or jumped off the table, the player loses his inning, but any balls pocketed on the stroke count for the player or his opponent, according to color. The cue ball being in hand, the next player must play from inside the string, or balk, but should there be no ball outside the string, of the color he is playing, the ball of that color nearest the string line is to be spotted on the spot at the foot of the table. Should the player with cue ball in hand already have spotted the seven balls of his color, then the black ball shall be spotted as above.

8. At the commencement of the game, should the player fail to break the balls - that is, fail to pocket a ball, or drive at least two of the object balls to a cushion - the next player has the option of selecting his color before playing, or he can break the balls and select his color afterward, whether he pockets a ball or not.

9. The rules of American Pyramid, and the General Rules of Billiards when not conflicting with the above rules, govern this game also.

Source: The Illustrated Encyclopedia of Billiards; 1925 Brunswick rulebook.

ONE AND 15 IN THE SIDE

Editor's Note: The following rules were the rules for 8-Ball in 1963 and prior.

THE GAME

The game is played with a cue ball and 15 object balls; numbered from 1 to 15. Balls are racked at the foot spot, with 8-ball in the center of the triangle. One player or side must pocket balls numbered from 1 to 7 or from 9 to 15. Opponent pockets group of balls not selected by player with original choice. For example, if the player with the first choice chooses to score balls from 1 to 7, the opponent must pocket balls from 9 to 15. Player or side pocketing numerical group first and then legally pocketing 8-ball wins the game.

OPENING BREAK

Order of play can be determined by lagging or lot. Starting player is not compelled to make a choice on opening shot, nor must he call his shot on the break. If opening player pockets one or more balls on the break, he has his choice of the high or low group. If the breaker fails to pocket a ball on the break, the incoming player accepts balls in position and has his choice of the high or low balls.

SCORING

The striker is entitled to all balls legally pocketed, unless he pockets a ball belonging to his opponent, in which case, the opponent is credited with that ball. If player pockets only an opponent's ball and none of his own group, it is a miss. Combination shots are allowed at all times, except in an attempt to pocket the 8-ball. Player may play combination off opponent's ball. The rules of Eight Ball specify that the player pocketing the high numerical group of balls must pocket the 15-ball in the left side pocket, that is, in the side pocket to his left as he stands at the head of the table facing the foot of the table. The player scoring the low numbered balls must pocket the 1-ball in the right side pocket. If the 1- and 15-balls are not placed in these pockets as required by the rules, they are spotted and respotted until the player is successful in accomplishing this purpose. After a player has pocketed all the balls in his numerical group, he shoots to pocket the 8-ball, calling his shot. If shooting directly at the 8-ball (*not banking*), the player must pocket that ball or case the 8-ball or the cue ball to contact a cushion. Loss of Game: If the player, shooting directly at the 8-ball, fails to cause the cue ball to go to a cushion after hitting 8-ball, or the 8-ball to contact a cushion, he loses the game. If banking 8-ball, players must hit the 8-ball. If a player accidentally pockets the 8-ball before he pockets all the balls of his numerical group, he loses the game. When playing for the 8-ball, player must hit that ball first. If he pockets the 8-ball on a bank, he loses game. Since a player is required to call his shot when playing for the 8-ball, he loses the game if the 8-ball drops into a pocket not designated on the call. When player is shooting to make the 8-ball, he loses the game if cue ball scratches in pocket.

Source: 1963 BCA Rules and Records Book.

AMERICAN PYRAMID FIFTEEN-BALL POCKET BILLIARDS

TYPE OF GAME

The game of American Pyramid Fifteen-ball Pocket Billiards is played with 15 balls, numbered from 1 to 15 respectively, and a white cue ball. The player opening the game plays from any point inside the string, and after the opening shot plays with the cue ball as he finds it. Each ball counts one point, and in match or two-hand games, the player first scoring eight balls wins game.

1. In the opening stroke the cue ball, aimed directly or as the result of a bank shot, must strike the pyramid with force sufficient to cause at least two object balls to touch a cushion, or at least one object ball to go into a pocket. Failure to do either forfeits the stroke and one ball to the table. In case of a forfeit by a player having no ball to his credit, the first ball scored by him shall be placed on the deep-red spot, or as near therto as possible. All balls pocketed on the opening stroke count and need not be called. In match or tournament games, when the player on the opening stroke fails to drive at least two balls to a cushion or one ball to a pocket, the balls are set up again, and the player forfeits on ball from his score, and must continue to play until he shall have made a legal leading stroke.

2. After the opening stroke the player must call the number of the ball he intends to pocket, but need not call the pocket. Should the called ball not be pocketed no ball pocketed on that stroke is counted, but must be placed on the deep-red spot, or as near as possible on a line below it; the player's hand is out, but he incurs no penalty. Should more than one ball be called, and one or more thus called should not be pocketed, none can be counted. Failure to hit a called ball involves no penalty, provided any other ball be hit.

3. One ball is forfeited if, after the opening stroke, the player fails to pocket a ball, or fails to make at least one object ball, or the cue ball, after hitting an object ball, strike a cushion. Should the player also pocket the cue ball after failure as above described he forfeits but one ball on the stroke.

4. When one or more balls, in addition to the ball called, are pocketed, the player is entitled to all pocketed.

5. When more than two players are engaged, the game is ended when the balls remaining on the table are not sufficient to tie the next lowest score; and all that may be depending upon the game shall be decided in accordance with the standing of each player when game is called.

6. A player forfeits one ball for making a miss, pocketing the cue ball,

forcing the cue ball off the table, for failing as described in Rule 3, and for striking the cue ball twice.

7. It is a stroke, and one ball is forfeited, if the striker touches the cue ball with his cue and make a miss, or touch it with his clothing, or any other object.

8. A stroke is made when any ball is in motion is foul, one ball is forfeited, and the incoming striker may either have the balls replaced or play as he finds them.

9. When the cue ball is struck twice, the balls disturbed in consequence of the second stroke shall be replaced, or the incoming striker, if he choose, may play as he finds them; the striker forfeits one ball.

10. The rules of Pocket Billiards for the Championship, and the General Rules of Billiards, except as above specified, govern this game also.

Source: 1925 Brunswick rulebook.

18.2 BALKLINE

18.2 Balkline is a style of Balkline in which the lines are drawn 18 inches from the rails and if both balls are in balk or in anchor the player must drive one of them out on or before his second shot. The 14-inch line was widened to 18 inches because of a popular feeling that 14.2 Balkline was too easy a game for professional competition. The first 18.2 tournament was played in New York in March 1896.

Source: The Illustrated Encyclopedia of Billiards

SNOOKER GAMES

Pocket billiard games in America in the 1800s generally evolved from English Billiards *(with two cue balls and one red ball)*, which was played on a 6 x 12' table with rails that sloped into the pocket openings. By 1860, New York table manufacturer, author and noted player Michael Phelan replaced the sloping sides of the pockets with straight corners, thus changing the direction of American pocket billiards from the English game from that time to the present.

English Billiards could only be played with two players, so eventually multi-player variations such as Life Pool and Pyramid Pool became popular in America, England, and territories in which English soldiers were stationed. Life Pool featured different colored balls used as both cue balls and/or object balls, depending on the situation and the number of players. Pyramid Pool featured 15 red balls racked on the Pyramid *(foot)* Spot, and each player received one point for each red ball legally potted. Black Pool was a form of Pyramid Pool which used the black ball from a Life Pool set so that a player could alternately pot a red and then attempt the black for extra points. Legend has it that in 1875, Sir Neville Chamberlain, an English regiment soldier stationed in Jubbulpore, India, was playing Black Pool with his fellow officers when he got the idea to add other colored balls to the game so that the variation eventually featured 15 red balls, a yellow, green, pink and black ball *(a blue and brown ball were added some years later)*. In the course of play, one day a visiting military cadet remarked that first-year cadets at his particular academy were known as "snookers." When the cadet missed a particularly easy pot, Chamberlain exclaimed to him, "Why, you're a regular snooker!" After explaining the meaning of the word to his fellow peers, Chamberlian added that perhaps they were all snookers at the game. The term was adopted for this particular variation, and the game has been called snooker ever since.

Snooker spread to other posts, and soldiers returning to England introduced the game there. Champion player John Roberts, Jr. learned the rules of the game on one of his exhibition tours of India, and he may have had some influence in further popularizing the game in the UK. When English Billiards started losing spectator interest at professional matches in England in the 1930s, champion billiardist Joe Davis recognized snooker as a more appealing alternative, and his cue prowess at the game eventually led to snooker being embraced as the more popular championship discipline in that country.

Snooker has never gained as much popularity in the U.S., but its appeal to many American players, its rank as the #1 televised sport on English television, and the skillful variations it has bred around the world warrants the inclusion of three pertinent sets of rules in this section.

English Snooker – 6x12 Table

Diagram 30

INTERNATIONAL SNOOKER
World Standardized Rules

The rules of Snooker as printed below are recognized by the International Billiards and Snooker Federation and the World Professional Billiards & Snooker Association as of September, 1995. The BCA is authorized to print these rules through the kind permission of the United States Snooker Association, the IBSF-recognized body governing the game and the rules in the United States.

EQUIPMENT (Section 1)
Measurements parentheses state the metric equivalent to the nearest millimeter.

THE STANDARD TABLE

DIMENSIONS
The playing area within the cushion faces shall measure 11' 8 ½" x 5'10" *(3569mm x 1778mm)* with a tolerance on both dimensions of ±½" *(±13mm)*.

HEIGHT
The height of the table from the floor to the top of the cushion rail shall be from 2'9½" to 2' 10½" *(851mm to 876mm)*.

POCKET OPENINGS

1. There shall be pockets at the corners *(two at the Spot end known as the top pockets and two at the Baulk end known as the bottom pockets)* and one each at the middle of the longer sides *(known as the center pockets)*.

2. The pocket openings shall conform to the templates authorized by the World Professional Billiards and Snooker Association *(WPBSA)*.

BAULK-LINE AND BAULK

A straight line drawn 29" *(737mm)* from the face of the bottom cushion and parallel to it is called the Baulk-line, and that line and the intervening space is termed the Baulk.

THE "D"

The "D" is a semi-circle described in Baulk with its center at the middle of the Baulk-line and with a radius of 11 ½" *(292mm)*.

SPOTS

Four spots are marked on the center longitudinal line of the table:

1. The Spot *(known as the Black Spot)*, 12 ¾" *(324mm)* from a point perpendicularly below the face of the top cushion.

2. The Center Spot *(known as the Blue Spot)*, located midway between the faces of the top and bottom cushions.

3. The Pyramid Spot *(known as the Pink Spot)*, located midway between the Center Spot and the face of the top cushion.

4. The Middle of the Baulk-line *(known as the Brown Spot)*. Two other spots used are located at the corners of the "D." Viewed from the baulk end, the one on the right is known as the Yellow Spot and the one on the left as the Green Spot.

BALLS

The Balls shall be of an approved composition and shall each have a diameter of 52.5mm with a tolerance of ± 0.05mm and:

1. They shall be of equal weight within a tolerance of 3g per set

2. A ball or set of balls may be changed by agreement between the players or on a decision by the referee.

CUE

A cue shall be not less than 3' *(914mm)* in length and shall show no sub-stantial departure from the traditional and generally accepted shape and form.

ANCILLARY

Various cue rests, long cues (*called butts and half-butts according to length*), extensions and adaptors may be used by players faced with difficult positions for cueing. These may form part of the equipment normally found at the table but also include equipment introduced by either player or the referee (*see also Section 3 Use of Ancillary Equipment*). All extensions, adaptors and other devices to aid cueing must be of a design approved by the WPBSA.

DEFINITIONS (Section 2)

Standard definitions used throughout these Rules are hereinafter italicized.

FRAME

A *frame* of snooker is the period of play from the first *stroke*, with all the balls set as described in Section 3 *Position of Balls*, until the frame is completed by:

1. Concession by any player during his turn,

2. Claim by the striker when only the Black remains and there is more than seven points difference between the scores in his favor.

3. The final pot or foul when only the Black remains, or

4. Being awarded by the referee under Section 3 *Foul And A Miss(3)* or Section 4 *Unfair Conduct*.

GAME

A *game* is an agreed or stipulated number of *frames*.

MATCH

A *match* is an agreed or stipulated number of *games*.

BALLS

1. The White ball is the cue ball.

2. The 15 Reds and the 6 colors are the object balls.

STRIKER

The person about to play or in play is the striker and remains so until the referee has decided he has left the table at the end of his turn.

STROKE

1. A stroke is made when the striker strikes the cue ball with the tip of the cue.

2. A stroke is fair when no infringement of Rule is made.

3. A stroke is not completed until all balls have come to rest.

4. A stroke may be made directly or indirectly, thus:

    (a) a stroke is direct when the cue ball strikes an object ball without first striking a cushion.

    (b) a stroke is indirect when the cue ball strikes one or more cushions before striking an object ball.

POT

A pot is when an object ball, after contact with another ball and without any infringement of these Rules, enters a pocket. Causing a ball to be potted is known as potting.

BREAK

A break is a number of pots in successive strokes made in any one turn by a player during a frame.

IN HAND

1. The cue ball is in hand

    (a) before the start of each frame,

    (b) when it has entered a pocket, or

    (c) when it has been forced off the table.

2. It remains in hand until

    (a) it is played fairly from in hand, or

    (b) a foul is committed whilst the ball is on the table.

3. Striker is said to be in hand when the cue ball is in hand as above.

BALL IN PLAY

1. The cue ball is in play when it is not in hand.

2. Object balls are in play from the start of the frame until pocketed or forced off the table.

3. Colors become in play again when respotted.

BALL ON

Any ball which may be lawfully struck by the first impact of the cue ball, or any ball which may not be so struck but which may be potted, is said to be on.

NOMINATED BALL

1. A nominated ball is the object ball which the striker declares, or indicates to the satisfaction of the referee, he undertakes to hit with the first impact of the cue ball.

2. If requested by referee, the striker must declare which ball is on.

FREE BALL

A free ball is a ball which the striker nominates as the ball on when snookered after a foul *(see Section 3 Snookered After A Foul)*.

FORCED OFF THE TABLE

A ball is forced off the table if it comes to rest other than on the bed of the table or in a pocket, or if it is picked up by the striker while it is in play except as provided for in Section 3 *Foul And A Miss 14 (8)*.

FOUL

A foul is any infringement of these Rules.

SNOOKERED

The cue ball is said to be snookered when a direct stroke in a straight line to every ball on is wholly or partially obstructed by a ball or balls not on. If one or more balls on can be struck at both extreme edges free of obstruction by any ball not on, the cue ball is not snookered.

1. If in hand, the cue ball is snookered if it is obstructed as described above from all possible positions on or within the lines of the "D."

2. If the cue ball is so obstructed from hitting a ball on by more than one ball not on:

    (a) The ball nearest to the cue ball is considered to be the effective snookering ball, and

    (b) Should more than one obstructing ball be equidistant from the cue ball, all such balls will be considered to be effective snookering balls.

3. When Red is the ball on, if the cue ball is obstructed from hitting different Reds by different balls not on, there is no effective snookering ball.

4. The striker is said to be snookered when the cue ball is snookered as above.

5. The cue ball cannot be snookered by a cushion. If the curved face of a cushion obstructs the cue ball and is closer to the cue ball than any obstructing ball not on, the cue ball is not snookered.

SPOT OCCUPIED

A spot is said to be occupied if a ball cannot be placed on it without that ball touching another ball.

PUSH STROKE

A push stroke is made when the tip of the cue remains in contact with the cue ball:

1. After the cue ball has commenced its forward motion, or

2. As the cue ball makes contact with an object ball except, where the cue ball and an object ball are almost touching, it shall not be deemed a push stroke if the cue ball hits a very fine edge of the object ball.

JUMP SHOT

A jump shot is made when the cue ball passes over any part of an object ball, whether touching it in the process or not, except:

1. when the cue ball first strikes one object ball and then jumps over another ball,

2. when the cue ball jumps and strikes and object ball, but does not land on the far side of that ball,

3. when, after striking an object ball lawfully, the cue ball jumps over that ball after hitting a cushion or another ball.

MISS

A miss is when the cue ball fails to first contact a ball on and the referee considers that the striker has not made a good enough attempt to hit a ball on.

THE GAME (Section 3)

DESCRIPTION

Snooker may be played by two or more players, either independently or as sides. The game can be summarized as follows:

1. Each player uses the same white cue ball and there are 21 object balls — 15 Reds each have a value of 1, and six colors: Yellow valued 2, Green 3, Brown 4, Blue 5, Pink 6 and Black 7.

2. Scoring strokes in a player's turn are made by potting Reds and colors alternately until all the Reds are off the table and the colors in the ascending order of their value.

3. Points awarded for scoring strokes are added to the score of striker.

4. Penalty points from fouls are added to the opponent's score.

5. A tactic employed at any time during a frame is to leave the cue ball behind a ball not on such that it is snookered for the next player. If a player or side is more points behind than are available from the balls left on the table, then the laying of snookers in the hope of gaining points from fouls becomes most important.

6. The winner of a frame is the player or side:

   (a) Making the highest score;

   (b) To whom the frame is conceded;

   (c) To whom it is awarded under Section 3 *Foul And A Miss,* or Section 4 *Unfair Conduct.*

7. The winner of a game is the player or side:

   (a) Winning most, or the required number of frames;

   (b) Making the greatest total where aggregate points are relevant, or

   (c) To whom the game is awarded under Section 4 *Unfair Conduct.*

8. The winner of a match is the player or side winning most games or, where aggregate points are relevant, with the greatest total.

POSITION OF BALLS

At the start of each frame the cue ball is in hand and the object balls are positioned on the table as follows:

1. The Reds in the form of a tightly-packed equilateral triangle, with the Red at the apex standing on the center line of the table, above the Pyramid Spot such that it will be as close to the Pink as possible without touching it, and the base of the triangle nearest to, and parallel with, the top cushion.

2. Yellow on the right-hand corner of the "D,"

3. Green on the left-hand corner of the "D,"

4. Brown on the Middle of the Baulk-line,

5. Blue on the Center Spot,

6. Pink on the Pyramid Spot, and

7. Black on the Spot.

After a frame has started, a ball in play may only be cleaned by the referee upon reasonable request by the striker and:

8. The position of the ball, if not spotted, shall be marked by a suitable device prior to the ball being lifted for cleaning.

9. The device used to mark the position of a ball being cleaned shall be regarded as and acquire the value of the ball until such time as the ball has been cleaned and replaced. If any player other than the striker should touch or disturb the device, he shall be penalized as if he were the striker, without affecting the order of play. The referee shall return the device or ball being cleaned to its position, if necessary, to his satisfaction even if it was picked up.

MODE OF PLAY

The players shall determine the order of play by lot or in any mutually agreed manner.

1. The order of play thus determined must remain unaltered throughout the frame, except that a player may be asked by the next player to play again after any foul.

2. The player or side to strike first must alternate for each frame during a game.

3. The first player plays from in hand, the frame commencing when the cue ball has been placed on the table and contacted by the tip of the cue, either:

   (a) As a stroke is made, or

   (b) While addressing the cue ball.

4. For a stroke to be fair, none of the infringements described below in *Penalties*, must occur.

5. For the first stroke of each turn, until all Reds are off the table, Red or a free ball nominated as a Red is the ball on, and the value of each Red and any free ball nominated as a Red potted in the same stroke, is scored.

   (a) If a Red, or free ball nominated as a Red, is potted, the same player plays the next stroke and the next ball on is a color of the striker's choice which, if potted, is scored and the color is then spotted.

   (b) The break is continued by potting Reds and colors alternately until all Reds are off the table and, where applicable, a color has been played at following the potting of the last Red.

(c) the colors then become on in the ascending order of their value as per Section 3 *Description*(1) and when next potted remain off the table, except as provided for in *End Of Frame, Game Or Match* below, and the striker plays the next stroke at the next color on.

6. Reds are not replaced on the table once pocketed or forced off the table regardless of the fact that a player may thus benefit from a foul. Exceptions to this concept are provided for in Section 3 *Ball Of Position*(9), *Ball On Edge Of Pocket, Foul And A Miss*(6 & 8) and *Ball Moved By Other Than Striker*.

7. If the striker fails to score or commits a foul, his turn ends and the next player plays from where the cue ball comes to rest, or from in hand if the cue ball is off the table.

END OF FRAME, GAME OR MATCH

1. When only the Black is left, the first score or foul ends the frame excepting only if the following conditions both apply:

   (a) The scores are then equal, and

   (b) Aggregate scores are not relevant.

2. When both conditions in (1) above apply,

   (a) The Black is spotted;

   (b) The players draw lots for choice of playing;

   (c) The next player plays from in hand, and;

   (d) The next score or foul ends the frame.

3. When aggregate scores determine the winner of a game or match, and the aggregate scores are equal at the end of the last frame, the players in that frame shall follow the procedure for a respotted Black set out in (2) above.

PLAYING FROM IN HAND

To play from in hand, the cue ball must be struck from a position on or within the lines of the "D," but it may be played in any direction.

1. The referee will state, if asked, whether the cue ball is properly placed *(that is, not outside the lines of the "D")*.

2. If the tip of the cue should touch the cue ball while positioning it, and the referee is satisfied that the striker was not attempting to play a stroke, then the cue ball is not in play.

HITTING TWO BALLS SIMULTANEOUSLY

Two balls, other than two Reds or a free ball and a ball on, must not be struck simultaneously by the first impact of the cue ball.

SPOTTING COLORS

Any color pocketed or forced off the table shall be spotted before the next stroke is made, until finally potted under Section 3 *Mode Of Play (a and b)*.

1. A player shall not be held responsible for any mistake by the referee in failing to spot any ball correctly.

2. If a color is spotted in error after being potted in ascending order as per Section 3 *Mode Of Play (5c)*, it shall be removed from the table without penalty when the error is discovered and play shall continue.

3. If a stroke is made with a ball or balls not correctly spotted, they will be considered to be correctly spotted for subsequent strokes. Any color incorrectly missing from the table will be spotted:

   (a) without penalty when discovered if missing due to previous oversight

   (b) subject to penalty if the striker played before the referee was able to effect the spotting.

4. If a color has to be spotted and its own spot is occupied, it shall be placed on the highest value spot available.

5. If there is more than one color to be spotted and their own spots are occupied, the highest value ball shall take precedence in order of spotting.

6. If all spots are occupied, the color shall be placed as near its own spot as possible, between that spot and the nearest part of the top cushion.

7. In the case of Pink and Black, if all spots are occupied and there is no available space between the relevant spot and the nearest part of the top cushion, the color shall be placed as near to its own spot as possible on the center line of the table below the spot.

8. In all cases, the color when spotted must not be touching another ball.

9. A color, to be properly spotted, must be placed by hand on the spot designated in these Rules.

TOUCHING BALL

1. If the cue ball comes to rest touching another ball or balls that are, or could be, on, the referee shall state TOUCHING BALL and indicate which ball or balls on the cue ball is touching.

2. When a touching ball has been called, the striker must play the cue ball away from that ball without moving it or it is a push stroke.

3. Providing the striker does not cause the object ball to move, there shall be no penalty if:

   (a) The ball is on:

   (b) The ball could be on and the striker declares he is on it, or

   (c) The ball could be on and the striker declares, and first hits, another ball that could be on.

4. If the cue ball comes to rest touching or nearly touching a ball that is not on, the referee, if asked whether it is touching, will answer YES or NO. The striker must play away without disturbing it as above but must first hit a ball that is on.

5. When the cue ball is touching both a ball on and a ball not on, the referee shall only indicate the ball on as touching. If the striker should ask the referee whether the cue ball is also touching the ball not on, he is entitled to be told.

6. If the referee is satisfied that any movement of a touching ball at the moment of striking was not caused by the striker, he will not call a foul.

7. If a stationary object ball, not touching the cue ball when examined by the referee, is later seen to be in contact with the cue ball before a stroke has been made, the balls shall be repositioned by the referee to his satisfaction.

BALL ON EDGE OF POCKET

1. If a ball falls into a pocket without being hit by another ball, and being no part of any stroke in progress, it shall be replaced and any points scored shall count.

2. If it would have been hit by any ball involved in a stroke:

   (a) with no infringement of these Rules, all balls will be replaced and the same stroke played again or a different stroke maybe played at his discretion, by the same striker.

(b) if a foul is committed, the striker incurs the penalty prescribed, all balls will be replaced and the next player has the
usual options after a foul.

3. If a ball balances momentarily on the edge of a pocket and then falls
in, it shall count as in the pocket and not be replaced.

SNOOKERED AFTER A FOUL

After a foul, if the cue ball is snookered, the referee shall state FREE BALL
(*see Section 2, Snookered*).

1. If the player next in turn elects to play the next stroke,

(a) he may nominate any ball as the ball on, and

(b) any nominated ball shall be regarded as, and acquire the value
of, the ball on except that, if potted, it shall then be spotted.

2. It is a foul if the cue ball should

(a) fail to hit the nominated ball first, or first simultaneously with
the ball on, or

(b) be snookered on all Reds, or the ball on, by the free ball thus
nominated, except when Pink and Black are the only object
balls remaining on the table.

3. If the free ball is potted, it is spotted and the value of the ball on is
scored.

4. If a ball on is potted, after the cue ball struck the nominated ball
first, or first simultaneously with a ball on, the ball on is scored and
remains off the table.

5. If both the nominated ball and a ball on are potted, only the ball
on is scored unless it was a Red, when each ball potted is scored.
The free ball is then spotted and the ball on remains off the table.

6. If the offender is asked to play again, the free ball call becomes
void.

FOULS

If a foul is committed, the referee shall immediately state FOUL.

1. If the striker has not made a stroke, his turn ends immediately and
the referee shall announce the penalty.

2. If a stroke has been made, the referee will wait until completion of
the stroke before announcing the penalty.

3. If a foul is neither awarded by the referee, nor successfully claimed by the non-striker before the next stroke is made, it is condoned.

4. Any color not correctly spotted shall remain where positioned except that if off the table it shall be correctly spotted.

5. All points scored in a break before a foul is awarded are allowed but the striker shall not score any points for any ball pocketed in a stroke called foul.

6. The next stroke is played from where the cue ball comes to rest or, if the cue ball is off the table, from in hand.

7. If more than one foul is committed in the same stroke, the highest value penalty shall be incurred.

8. The player who committed the foul

   (a) incurs the penalty described in *Penalties* below, and

   (b) has to play the next stroke if requested by the next player.

PENALTIES

All fouls will incur a penalty of four points unless a higher one is indicated in paragraphs 1 to 4 below. Penalties are:

1. Value of the ball on by

   (a) Striking the cue ball more than once;

   (b) Striking when both feet are off the floor;

   (c) Playing out of turn;

   (d) Playing improperly from in hand, including at the opening stroke;

   (e) Causing the cue ball to miss all object balls;

   (f) Causing the cue ball to enter a pocket;

   (g) Playing a snooker behind a free ball;

   (h) Playing a jump shot;

   (i) Playing with a non-standard cue, or;

   (j) Conferring with a partner contrary to Section 3 *Four-Handed Snooker(5)*.

2. Value of the ball on or ball concerned, whichever is higher, by:

   (a) Striking when any ball is not at rest;

    (b) Striking before referee has completed the spotting of a color;

    (c) Causing a ball not on to enter a pocket;

    (d) Causing the cue ball to first hit a ball not on;

    (e) Making a push stroke;

    (f) Touching a ball in play, other than the cue ball with the tip of the cue as a stroke is made, or;

    (g) Causing a ball to be forced off the table.

3. Value of the ball on or higher value of the two balls concerned by causing the cue ball to first hit simultaneously two balls, other than two reds or a free ball and a ball on.

4. A penalty of seven points is incurred if the striker

    (a) Uses a ball off the table for any purpose;

    (b) Uses any object to measure gaps or distance;

    (c) Plays at Reds, or a free ball followed by a Red, in successive strokes;

    (d) Uses any ball other than White as the cue ball for any stroke once the frame has started;

    (e) Fails to declare which ball he is on when requested to do so by the referee, or;

    (f) After potting a Red or free ball nominated as a Red, commits a foul before nominating a color.

PLAY AGAIN

Once a player has requested an opponent to play again after a foul, such request cannot be withdrawn. The offender, having been asked to play again, is entitled to:

1. Change his mind as to

    (a) Which stroke he will play, and

    (b) Which ball on he will attempt to hit.

2. Score points for any ball or balls he may pot.

FOUL AND A MISS

The striker shall, to the best of his ability, endeavour to hit the ball on. If the referee considers the Rule infringed, he shall call FOUL AND A MISS unless only the Black remains on the table, or a situation exists where it is impossible to hit the ball on. In the latter case it must be asumed the striker is attempting to hit the ball on provided that he plays, directly or indirectly, in the direction of the ball on with sufficient strength, in the referee's opinion, to have reached the ball on but for the obstructing ball or balls.

1. After a foul and a miss has been called, the next player may request the offender to play again from the position left or, at his discretion, from the original position, in which latter case the ball on shall be the same as it was prior to the last stroke made, namely:

   (a) Any Red, where Red was the ball on,

   (b) The color on, where all Reds were off the table, or

   (c) A color of the striker's choice, where the ball on was a color after a Red had been potted.

2. If the striker, in making a stroke, fails to first hit a ball on when there is a clear path in a straight line from the cue ball to any part of any ball that is or could be on, the referee shall call FOUL AND A MISS unless either player needed snookers before, or as a result of, the stroke played and the referee is satisfied that the miss was not intentional.

3. After a miss has been called under paragraph (2) above when there was a clear path in a straight line from the cue ball to a ball that was on or that could have been on, such that central, full ball, contact was available *(in the case of Reds, this to be taken as a full diameter of any Red that is not obstructed by a color)*, then:

   (a) a further failure to first hit a ball *on* in making a *stroke* from the same position shall be called as a FOUL AND A MISS regardless of the difference in scores, and

   (b) if asked to play again from the original position, the offender shall be warned by the referee that a third failure will result in the *frame* being awarded to his opponent.

4. After the cue ball has been replaced under this Rule, when there is a clear path in a straight line from the cue ball to any part of any ball that is or could be on, and the striker fouls any ball, including the cue ball while preparing to play a stroke a miss will not be called if a stroke has not been played. In this case the appropriate penalty will be imposed and

   (a) the next player may elect to play the stroke himself or ask the offender to play again from the position left, or

(b) the next player may ask the referee to replace all balls moved to their original position and have the offender play again from there, and

(c) If the above situation arises during a sequence of miss calls, any warning concerning the possible awarding of the frame to his opponent shall remain in effect.

5. All other misses will be called at the discretion of the referee.

6. After a miss and a request by the next player to replace the cue ball, any object balls disturbed will remain where they are unless the referee considers the offending player would or could gain an advantage. In the latter case, any or all disturbed balls may be replaced to the referee's satisfaction and in either case, colors incorrectly off the table will be spotted or replaced as appropriate.

7. When any ball is being replaced after a miss, both the offender and the next player will be consulted as to its position, after which the referee's decision shall be final.

8. During such consultation, if either player should touch any ball in play, he shall be penalized as if he were the striker, without affecting the order of play. The ball touched shall be replaced by the referee, to his satisfaction, if necessary, even if it was picked up.

9. The next player may ask if the referee intends to replace balls other than the cue ball in the event that he should ask for the stroke to be played from the original position, and the referee shall state his intentions.

BALL MOVED BY OTHER THAN STRIKER

If a ball, stationary or moving, is disturbed other than by the striker, it shall be repositioned by the referee to the place he judges the ball was, or would have finished, without penalty.

1. This rule shall include cases where another occurence or person, other than the striker's partner, causes the striker to move a ball.

2. No player shall be penalized for any disturbance of balls by the referee.

STALEMATE

If the referee thinks a position of stalemate exists, or is being approached, he shall offer the players the immediate option of restarting the frame. If any player objects, the referee shall allow play to continue with the proviso that the situation must change within a stated period, usually after three more strokes to each side but at the referee's discretion. If the situation remains basically unchanged after the stated period has expired, the referee shall nullify all scores and reset all balls as for the start of a frame and

    (a) The same player shall again make the opening stroke.

    (b) The same order of play shall be maintained.

FOUR-HANDED SNOOKER

1. In a four-handed, game each side shall open alternate frames and the order of play shall be determined at the start of each frame and, when so determined, must be maintained throughout that frame.

2. Players may change the order of play at the start of each new frame.

3. If a foul is committed and a request to play again is made, the player who committed the foul plays again, even if the foul was made out of turn, and the original order of play is maintained, such that the offender's partner may lose a turn.

4. When a frame ends in a tie, Section 3 *End Of Frame, Game Or Match* applies. If a respotted Black is necessary, the pair who play the first stroke have the choice of which player will make that stroke. The order of play must then continue as in the frame.

5. Partners may confer during a frame but not:

    (a) While one is the striker and at the table, nor

    (b) After the first stroke of the striker's turn until the break ends.

USE OF ANCILLARY EQUIPMENT

It is the responsiblity of the striker to both place and remove any equipment to be used at the table.

1. The striker is responsible for all items including, but not limited to, rests and extensions brought to the table, whether owned by him or borrowed *(except from the referee)* and he will be penalized for any fouls made by him when using this equipment.

2. Equipment normally found at the table which has been provided by another party, including the referee, is not the responsibility of the striker. Should this equipment prove to be faulty and thereby cause the striker to touch a ball or balls, no foul will be called. The referee will, if necessary, reposition any balls in accordance with

Ball Moved By Other Than Striker (above) and the striker, if in a break, will be allowed to continue without penalty.

INTERPRETATION

1. Throughout these Rules and Definitions, words implying the male gender shall equally apply to and include the female gender.

2. Circumstances may necessitate adjustment in how Rules are applied for persons with physical handicaps. In particular and for example:

    (a) Section 3 *Penalties(1b)* cannot be applied to players in wheelchairs, and

    (b) a player, upon request to the referee, shall be told the color of a ball if he is unable to differentiate between colors as, for example, red and green.

3. When there is no referee, the opposing player or side will be regarded as such for the purpose of these Rules.

THE PLAYERS (Section 4)

TIME WASTING

If the referee considers that a player is taking an abnormal amount of time over a stroke or the selection of a stroke, he shall warn the player that he is liable to have the frame awarded to his opponent.

UNFAIR CONDUCT

For refusing to continue a frame, or for conduct which, in the opinion of the referee is wilfully or persistently unfair, including continued time wasting after being warned under *Time Wasting (above)* or ungentlemanly conduct, a player shall lose the frame and the referee shall issue a warning that if such conduct continues, he shall lose the game.

PENALTY

1. If a frame is forfeited under this Section, the offender shall

    (a) lose the frame, and

    (b) forfeit all points scored and the non-offender shall receive a number of points equivalent to the value of the balls remaining on the table, with each Red counting as eight points and any color incorrectly off the table being counted as if spotted.

2. If a game is forfeited under this section, the offender shall

    (a) lose the frame in progress as in (1), and

(b) additionally lose the required number of unplayed frames to complete the game where frames are relevant, or

(c) additionally lose the remaining frames, each valued at 147 points, where aggregate points apply.

NON-STRIKER

The non-striker shall, when the striker is playing, avoid standing or moving in the line of sight of the striker. He shall sit or stand at a reasonable distance from the table.

ABSENCE

In the case of his absence from the room, the non-striker may appoint a deputy to watch his interests and claim a foul if necessary. Such appointment must be made known to the referee prior to departure.

CONCEDING

1. A player may only concede when he is the striker. The opponent has the right to accept or refuse the concession, which becomes null and void if the opponent chooses to play on.

2. When aggregate scores apply and a frame is conceded, the value of any balls remaining on the table is added to the score of the other side. In such case, Reds shall count as eight points each and any color incorrectly off the table shall be counted as if spotted.

THE OFFICIALS (Section 5)

THE REFEREE

1. The referee shall:

   (a) Be the sole judge of fair and unfair play;

   (b) Be free to make a decision in the interests of fair play for any situation not covered adequately by Rule;

   (c) Be responsible for the proper conduct of the game under these Rules;

   (d) Intervene if he sees any infringement of these Rules;

   (e) Tell a player the color of a ball if requested, and;

   (f) Clean any ball upon reasonable request by a player.

2. The referee shall not:

(a) Answer any questions not authorized in these Rules;

(b) Give any indication that player is about to make a foul stroke;

(c) Give any advice or opinion on points affecting play, nor;

(d) Answer any questions regarding the difference in scores,

3. If the referee has failed to notice any incident, he may take the evidence of the marker or other officials or spectators best placed for observation to assist his decision.

THE MARKER
The marker shall keep the score on the scoreboard and assist the referee in carrying out his duties. He shall also act as recorder if necessary.

THE RECORDER
The recorder shall maintain a record of each stroke played, showing fouls where appropriate and how many points are scored by each player or side as required. He shall also make note of break totals.

ASSISTANCE BY OFFICIALS
1. At the striker's request, the referee or marker shall move and hold in position any lighting apparatus that interferes with the action of the striker in making a stroke.

2. It is permissible for the referee or marker to give necessary assistance to handicapped players according to their circumstances.

AMERICAN SNOOKER

TYPE OF GAME
American Snooker is a cousin of Snooker as it is played widely around the world, the rules giving it a distinct orientation toward the structure of many American pocket billiard games. It is generally played on either 4 ½ x 9', 5 x 10' or 6 x 12' Snooker tables, with cushions that are more narrow than other pocket billiard tables, and curve smoothly into the pocket openings. The balls used are either 2-¹⁄₁₆" or 2-⅛" diameter. *(See BCA Specifications.)*

PLAYERS
2.

BALLS USED
Set of Snooker balls: 15 object balls that are not numbered and are solid red *(called reds)*, six object balls that may or may not be numbered *(called colors)* and

a cue ball. Point values for object balls: red–1, yellow–2, green–3, brown–4, blue–5, pink–6, black–7.

THE RACK
Play begins with balls placed as in Diagram 31.

OBJECT OF THE GAME
To score a greater number of points than opponent.

SCORING
Points are scored in two ways; players are awarded points for fouls by the opponent (*see "Penalty For Foul" below*), and by legally pocketing reds or colors. Each legally pocketed red ball has a point value of one; each legally pocketed color ball has a point value as indicated (*"Balls Used" above*). Game ends when all balls have been pocketed, following the Rules of Play; if, however, only the black 7-ball is left on the table, the game ends with the first score or foul.

If the players' scores are equal after that scoring, the black ball is spotted on its original position and the players lag for the choice of shooting at, or assigning opponent to shoot at the black ball with the cue ball in hand within the D; the first score or foul then ends the game.

American Snooker-5x10 Table

Diagram 31

OPENING BREAK
Starting player has cue ball in hand within the "D." He must:

1. Cause the cue ball to contact a red ball prior to contacting a color, and

2. Cause a red ball to contact a cushion or drop into a pocket, and

3. Cause the cue ball to contact a cushion after it contacts a red ball. Failure to meet these requirements is a foul and a breaking violation. A foul is scored and incoming player has choice of:

(a) Accepting the table and shooting, or;

(b) Requiring offender to break again.

RULES OF PLAY

1. A legally pocketed ball entitles the shooter to continue at the table until failing to legally pocket a ball.

2. On all shots, player must comply with the appropriate requirements of Rules of Play 5 and 6, plus cause the cue ball or an object ball to contact a cushion or drop in a pocket after the cue ball has contacted a legal object ball *(on ball)*. Failure to do so is a foul.

3. As long as reds are on the table, an incoming player *(player taking his first shot of an inning)* always has a red as his legal object ball *(on ball)*.

4. Any red balls pocketed on a legal shot are legally pocketed balls; player need not call any particular red ball(s), pocket(s) or mode of pocketing.

5. When a player has a red ball as his "on ball" *(required legal object ball)*, he must cause the cue ball's first contact to be with a red ball. Failure to do so is a foul. Rule of Play 2 also applies.

6. After a player has scored a red ball initially, his next legal object is a color, and as long as reds remain on the table he must alternate play between reds and colors *(though within each group he may play ball of his choice)*. When reds remain on the table and a color is his object, the player must (a) designate prior to shooting which color ball is his object *(that specific color is then his "on ball")*, and (b) cause the cue ball's first contact with a ball to be with that color ball. If a player fails to meet these requirements, it is a foul. Rule 2 requirements also apply.

7. If player's on ball is a red and he pockets a color, it is a foul.

8. If player's on ball is a color and he pockets any other ball, it is a foul.

9. It is a foul if a player intentionally causes the cue ball to jump *(rise from the bed of the table)* by any means, if the jump is an effort to clear an obstructing ball.

10. While reds remain on the table, each pocketed color ball is spotted prior to the next stroke. *(See "Spotting Balls" below for spotting rules.)* If a player shooting after a color has been spotted plays while that ball is incorrectly spotted *(and opponent or referee calls it before two such shots have*

been taken), the shot taken is a foul. If such shooting player shoots twice after such error without its being announced by opponent or referee, he is free of penalty and continues shooting and scoring normally as though the spotting error simply had not occurred.

11. If a player fouls and the incoming player is blocked from seeing any part of a ball on, the player may remove the impeding ball *(mark the spot)* and shoot the ball on. The player cannot score by pocketing this ball on that had been blocked, and the next player returns to the table when the stroke is completed.

12. When no reds remain on the table, player's on balls become the colors, in ascending numerical order *(2, 3, 4, 5, 6, 7)*. These legally pocketed colors are not spotted after each is pocketed; they remain off the table *(the seven-ball is an exception in the case of a tie score; see "Scoring.")*

ILLEGALLY POCKETED BALL
Reds illegally pocketed are not spotted; they remain off the table. Colors illegally pocketed are spotted *(See "Spotting Balls.")*

OBJECT BALLS JUMPED OFF THE TABLE
Reds jumped off the table are not spotted. Colors jumped off the table are spotted. The stroke is a foul, and the penalty for fouls is followed.

SPOTTING BALLS
Reds are never spotted. Colors to be spotted are placed as at the start of the game. If a color's spot is occupied *(to mean that to spot it would make it touch a ball)*, it is placed on the spot of the highest value color that is unoccupied. If all spots are occupied, the color is spotted as close as possible to its original spot on a straight line between its spot and the nearest point on the foot cushion.

CUE BALL AFTER JUMPING OFF THE TABLE OR SCRATCH
Incoming player has cue ball in hand within the D. When cue ball is in hand within the D *(except on the opening break)*, there is no restriction *(based on position of reds or colors)* as to what balls may be played; player may play at an on ball regardless of where it is on the table.

PENALTY FOR FOULS
Seven points are added to non-fouling player's score for each foul committed *(no deduction from offender's score)*. Incoming *(non-offending)* player has the choice of either

1. accepting the table in position and shooting, or

2. requiring the offending player to shoot again. If the foul is a cue

ball jumped off the table or a cue ball scratch, the cue ball is in hand within the D for either player. If the foul is other than cue ball jumped off the table or scratch, the cue ball remains in position. If a player pockets a ball and fouls, the player is not credited with any points.

GOLF

TYPE OF GAME
In many sections of the United States the most popular game on a snooker table is Golf. It is usually played on a 4 ½' x 9', 5 x 10' or 6 x 12' snooker table with either 2-⅛ " or 2-¹⁄₁₆ " diameter snooker balls. *(See BCA Specifications.)*

PLAYERS
2 or more, with a game often including 4 players or more.

BALLS USED
The numbered group of snooker balls *(2-Yellow through 7-black)* and a white snooker cue ball.

THE RACK
Starting player's object ball is spotted on the foot *(pyramid)* spot.

OBJECT OF THE GAME
For a player to successfully pocket his object ball in each of the six pockets in numerical pocket order *(Diagram 30)* before his opponent(s) does.

DETERMINING ORDER OF PLAY
Players draw lots *(or numbered peas)* from a shake bottle. Lowest-drawn number goes first with the remainder of the order corresponding to the ascending draw of peas for each player. Starting player's object ball throughout the game is the 2-ball *(yellow)*; the next player — the 3-ball *(green)*; the next player — the 4-ball *(brown)*; etc.

SCORING
The balls have no numerical value for scoring. The first player to follow the rules of play and legally pocket his object ball in the #6 *(side)* pocket wins the game. Players keep track of the number of fouls *(known as hickeys)* each competitor accrues throughout the game. A hickey may be assigned any value, and players must determine the differences in the totals of hickeys due at the end of each game. For example, if the winning Player A has 6 hickeys, Player B has 4 hickeys, and Player C has 10 hickeys, Player A's hickeys are irrel-

evant. Player B owes Player A the value of 4 hickeys and Player C owes Player A the value of 10 hickeys. Usually the game itself has a value and Player A receives that value from each player for winning the game.

OPENING BREAK

Starting player begins play with the cue ball on or within the D and his object ball *(for the starting player — the yellow 2-ball)* on the foot spot. His objective is to pocket his ball in pocket #1. If the first player misses, the second player takes the cue ball in hand within the D positions his object ball *(3 — the green)* on the foot spot and attempts to pocket it in pocket #1. If the second player misses, the third player takes cue ball in hand within the D, positions his object ball *(4 — the brown)* on the foot spot, and attempts to pocket it in pocket #1. Subsequent players follow the same procedure to enter the game. If a player pockets his first shot into pocket #1, his object ball is respotted on the foot spot and the player shoots again to pocket his object ball in pocket #2 from wherever the cue ball comes to rest. Once his inning is complete, the next player entering the game takes cue ball in hand within the D and starts play as described above.

SUBSEQUENT HOLES

After all players have entered the game *(unless a player runs out the game from his break)* the cue ball is played from wherever it comes to rest after each player's shot for the remainder of the game *(See below if jumped or scratched.)* Once a player pockets his object ball in pocket #1 the object ball is respotted on the foot spot, and the player continues shooting for pocket. When he misses, the next player shoots at his object ball. A player must successfully complete all six holes, playing in order, in this manner. The player who completes this pattern first wins the game.

RULES OF PLAY

1. It is a foul to pocket the object ball in any pocket other than the one in which the player is attempting to score.

2. On all shots it is necessary for the player to hit the object ball first.

3. To be a legal shot, a player is required to either send the cue ball to a rail and then hit an object ball first, hit the object ball first and pocket it, or hit the object ball first and send any ball to a cushion.

4. It's a foul to strike, touch or make contact with the cue ball in play or any object balls in play with anything *(the body, clothing, chalk, mechanical bridge, cue shaft, etc.)* except the cue tip *(while attached to the cue shaft)*, which may contact the cue ball in the execution of a legal shot.

5. It's a foul to hit another player's object ball first. If a player hits an

opponent's object ball first, the player loses his turn, is credited with a hickey, and the opponent has the choice of returning the object ball to its original position.

6. If a player has a clear shot at his full object ball and misses the entire ball, it is a foul (*hickey*), he loses his turn, and the object ball is spotted on the foot spot.

7. If a player commits a foul and the incoming player is snookered from seeing the entire ball, that player may mark the position(s) of the offending ball(s), remove the obstacle ball(s) from the table, shoot at the object ball, and replace the removed ball(s) to original position(s) immediately after the stroke.

ILLEGALLY POCKETED BALLS

All are spotted on the foot spot, unless an opponent's ball was struck first. Then the opponent may choose to return his object ball to its original position. The stroke is a foul and the offending player receives a hickey.

OBJECT BALLS JUMPED OFF THE TABLE

An object ball that jumps off the table is a foul, and the offending player loses his turn and receives a hickey. The object ball is spotted on the foot spot unless an opponent's ball was struck first. In that case the opponent may choose to return his object ball to its original position.

CUE BALL AFTER JUMPING OFF THE TABLE OR SCRATCH

The offending player fouls, loses his turn, and receives a hickey. The incoming player has cue ball in hand on or within the D, may shoot in any direction, and may shoot at his object ball if it is in the D as well. Any object balls pocketed on the foul stroke are respotted on the foot spot in numerical order unless an opponent's ball was struck first. In that case the opponent may choose to return his object ball to its original position.

SPOTTING BALLS

After each player has completed his opening break shot, if a player is required to spot a ball on the foot spot, he must do so immediately after the resulting stroke. If the ball cannot be spotted without touching another ball, the ball is spotted as close to it as possible without touching (*if the obstacle ball is the cue ball*) and frozen to the ball (*if the obstacle ball is an object ball*), and on the direct line between the foot spot and the foot rail.

GENERAL RULES
OF CAROM BILLIARDS

The rules in this section apply generally to all the specific forms and varieties of carom billiard games included in this rulebook. Certain games, however, do have exceptions that supersede or modify the General Rules; these exceptions are flagged with a parenthetical notation, referencing the particular game or variation in which the general rule might be either modified or non-applicable. Thus, unless specifically noted otherwise, the General Rules apply to all carom billiard games.

To facilitate the use and understanding of the General Rules, many terms that may require definition for some readers are set in italic in their first appearance, so that the reader may refer to the Glossary of Billiard Terms section for the exact meaning of the term.

Although most references in these rules are to a "player" or "players"; since most carom billiard games can be adapted to team play, the reader should interpret the rules as equally applicable to a team of teams when appropriate.

The United States Billiard Association today sanctions most U.S. play of the popular carom game of Three-Cushion Billiards. In the individual game rules for Three-Cushion, the U.S.B.A. official rules have been reprinted exactly as published by that group, resulting in some duplication of General Rules from this section within U.S.B.A.'s rules.

GENERAL RULES OF CAROM BILLIARDS

The Carom Table

Diagram 32

TABLES, BALL, EQUIPMENT

All games are contested on tables, and with balls and equipment, meeting the standards prescribed in the **BCA Specifications**.

BALLS DEFINED

Two white balls and a red; each player has a white ball that is a cue ball when he is shooting, while the red is never a cue ball. One of the white balls has two or three small colored spots to differentiate it from the other. (*Note: Four Ball is played with a fourth ball as well; see Four Ball rules.*)

STRIKING CUE BALL

Legal shots require that the *cue ball* only be struck with the *cue tip* only.

DETERMINING FIRST PLAYER

The player to perform the *opening break* shot is determined by either *lag for break* or lot. (*The lag-for-break procedure is required for formal competition.*) The player winning the lag or lot has the choice of performing the opening break shot or assigning it to the opposition.

LAG FOR BREAK

Red ball is spotted on *foot spot* (*except in Four-Ball*). With the *cue balls in hand behind the head string*, one player to the right and one to the left of the *head spot*, the balls are shot to the foot *cushion* and back to the head end of the table. The player whose ball ends up closest to the head cushion wins the lag, subject to the following qualifications:

The lagged ball must contact the foot cushion at least once; other cushion contacts are immaterial except as prohibited below. It is an automatic loss of the lag if:

1. the ball crosses into the opponent's half of the table, or;

2. the ball fails to contact the foot cushion, or;

3. the ball jumps the table, or;

4. the ball hits the red ball.

If both players violate automatic-loss lag rules as above, or if the referee is unable to determine which ball is closer, the lag is a tie and is replayed.

The lag for opening break is performed by both players simultaneously, although they need not stroke the lag shots in unison.

CHOICE OF CUE BALLS

The winner of the lag has the choice of cue balls, either the all-white "clear" or the color-marked "spot," which is then used throughout the game. If an odd number of players are competing, the same cue ball is not played throughout the game. Rather, the incoming player always plays the cue ball that was not used by the player who immediately preceded him *(Exception: Four-Ball Caroms)*.

BALL POSITIONS – OPENING BREAK

The red ball is spotted on the foot spot. Non-breaking player's cue ball is spotted on the *head spot*. Breaking player's cue ball is placed on the *head string* within six inches *(measured to the ball's center)* of the head spot. *(Note: Four-Ball uses a different opening break position.)*

The Break Shot

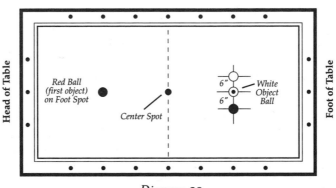

Diagram 33

RED BALL FIRST OBJECT

Player making opening break shot must contact the red ball first, rather than the opponent's cue ball. If the cue ball on the opening break strikes the other white ball first rather than the red ball, it is an *error* and ends his *inning*;

no score is valid. *(Exception: Four-Ball Caroms.)*

On all subsequent shots, players may make either the red or the white *(or "pink" in Four Ball)* ball his first object *(first ball struck by the cue ball)*. *(Exception: Red Ball.)*

FOOT ON FLOOR

It is a foul if a player shoots when at least one foot is not in contact with the floor. Foot attire must be normal in regard to size, shape and the manner in which it is worn.

SHOOTING WITH BALLS IN MOTION

It is a foul if a player shoots while the cue ball or any object ball is in motion. *(A spinning ball is in motion.)*

COMPLETION OF STROKE

A stroke is not complete *(and therefore is not counted)* until all balls on the table have become motionless after the stroke. *(A spinning ball is in motion.)*

FOULS BY TOUCHING BALLS

It is a foul to strike, touch or in any way make contact with the cue ball in play or any object balls in play with anything *(the body, clothing, chalk, mechanical bridge, cue shaft, etc.)* except the cue tip *(while attached to the cue shaft)*, which may contact the cue ball once in the execution of a shot.

FOULS BY DOUBLE HITS

It is a foul if the cue ball is struck more than once on a shot by the cue tip. If, in the referee's judgement, the cue ball has left initial contact with the cue tip and then is struck a second time in the course of the same stroke, it shall be a foul. If the referee judges, by virtue of sound, ball position and action, and stroke used, that there were two separate contacts of the cue ball by the cue tip on a stroke, the stroke is a foul and must be called.

PUSH SHOT FOULS

It is a foul if the cue ball is pushed or shoved by the cue tip, with contact being maintained for more than the momentary time necessary for a stroked shot. If the referee judges that the player put the cue tip against the cue ball and then pushed or shoved on into the shot, maintaining contact beyond the normal momentary split-second, the stroke is a foul and must be called.

JUMPED CUE BALL

When a stroke results in the cue ball being a *jumped ball*, the stroke is a foul. *(Note: jumped object balls may or may not be fouls; see specific game rules.)*

GENERAL RULE, ALL FOULS
Though the penalties for fouls differ from game to game, the following applies to all fouls:

1. player's inning ends, and

2. if on a stroke, the stroke is invalid and cannot be a scoring stroke.

ILLEGAL JUMPING OF BALL
It is a foul if a player strikes the cue ball below center *("digs under" it)* and intentionally causes it to rise off the bed of the table *(usually in an effort to clear an obstructing ball)*. Such jumping action may occur accidentally on occasion, and such "jumps" are not necessarily considered fouls. They may still be ruled foul strokes however, if for example, the ferrule or cue shaft makes contact with the cue ball in the course of the shot.

SPECIAL INTENTIONAL FOUL PENALTY
The cue ball in play shall not be intentionally struck with anything other than a cue's attached tip *(such as the ferrule, shaft, etc.)*. While such contact is automatically a foul under the provisions of "Fouls By Touching Balls," if the referee deems the contact to be intentional, he shall warn the player once during a match that a second violation during that match will result in the loss of the match by forfeiture. If a second violation does occur, the match must be forfeited.

BALLS MOVING SPONTANEOUSLY
If a ball shifts, settles, turns or otherwise moves "by itself," the ball shall remain in the position it assumed and play continues.

PLAYER RESPONSIBILITY FOULS
The player is responsible for chalk, bridges, files and any other items or equipment he brings to, uses at, or causes to approximate the table. If he drops a pen or a piece of chalk, or knocks off a mechanical bridge head, as examples, he is guilty of a foul should such an object make contact with a ball in play.

JUMPED BALLS DEFINED
Balls coming to rest other than on the bed *of the table* after a stroke *(on the cushion top, rail surface, floor, etc.)* are considered jumped balls. Balls may bounce on the cushion tops, rails or light fixtures of the table in play without being jumped balls if they return to the bed of the table under their own power and without touching anything not a part of the table equipment. The table equipment shall consist of its light fixture, and any permanent parts of the table proper. *(Balls that strike or touch anything not a part of the table equipment shall be considered jumped balls even though they might return to the bed of the table after contact with the non-equipment item[s]).*

All jumped balls are spotted when all balls have stopped moving. *(See "Spotting Jumped Balls.")*

OUTSIDE INTERFERENCE

If the balls are moved *(or a player bumped such that play is directly affected)* by a non-player during a match, the balls shall be replaced as near as possible to their original positions immediately prior to the incident, and play shall resume with no penalty on the player affected. If the match is officiated, the referee shall replace the balls. This rule shall also apply to "act of God" interference, such as earthquake, hurricane, light fixture falling, power failure, etc.

DEFINITION OF LEGAL SAFETY

Player must drive an object ball to a cushion or cause the cue ball to contact a cushion after striking an object ball. Failure to do so is a foul. *(Note: U.S.B.A. Three-Cushion rules prohibit all intentional safeties.)*

LIMIT ON SAFETY PLAY

Player may not play safety in consecutive innings. When a player's last shot was a safety, he can not play another safety on his next shot. If he does so, it is a foul. *(Note: does not apply in U.S.B.A. Three-Cushion play.)*

PLAYING FROM SAFETY

When a player has either fouled or played an intentional safety on his last shot, he comes to the table for his next shot "playing from safety."

The player must make an obvious and legal attempt to score. If he again resorts to safety play, whether or not the effort meets the requirements of a legal safety, he has fouled. *(Note: "Playing From Safety" does not apply in Three-Cushion.)*

SPOTTING JUMPED BALLS

1. If the cue ball is jumped off the table *(foul)*, is spotted on the head spot *(if occupied, the foot spot; if that is also occupied; the center spot)*.

2. If the white object ball is jumped, it is spotted on the head spot *(if occupied, the foot spot; if that is also occupied, the center spot)*.

3. If the red object ball is jumped, it is spotted on the foot spot *(if occupied, the head spot; if that is also occupied, the center spot)*. If the cue ball and an object ball are both jumped, the cue ball is spotted first, then the object ball following the appropriate spotting order above.

4. If both object balls are jumped, they are spotted as above. If the cue ball occupies either of the object balls' primary spot locations, spot first the ball that spots freely; then the other according to the appropriate alternative spotting order above.

CUSHION CAROMS

Except when clearly contradicted by these additional rules, the General Rules of Carom Billiards apply.

PLAYERS
2 or 3.

BALLS USED
Standard set of one white clear, one white spot, and one red.

OBJECT OF THE GAME
Score the predetermined number of points *(may be 30-60 in tournament play, or any agreed upon number)* for game prior to opponent(s).

SCORING
Each legal *count* is scored as one point for the shooter.

DEFINITION OF A COUNT
A shot is a count if not in violation of any "Rules of Play" or General Rules of Carom Billiards, and the cue ball contacts both object balls.

OPENING BREAK
General Rules of Carom Billiards regarding opening break apply, as well as "Rule of Play 2" below. Failure to comply is a violation; player's *inning* ends and no count can be scored.

RULES OF PLAY
1. A legal counting stroke entitles the shooter to continue at the table until failing to legally count on a shot.

2. On all shots, the player must cause the cue ball to contact one or more cushions before it contacts either of the two object balls *(red ball only on opening break)*. Failure to comply is a violation; the player's inning ends and no count can be scored on the violating stroke.

PENALTY FOR FOULS
One point is deducted from offender's score for each *foul*.

FOUR-BALL CAROMS

Except when clearly contradicted by these additional rules, the General Rules of Carom Billiards apply.

PLAYERS
2.

BALLS USED
Standard set of one white clear, one white spot and one red, plus one light red (*pink*).

OBJECT OF THE GAME
Score the predetermined number of points for game prior to opponent.

SCORING
Each legal two-ball *carom* count is scored as one point for shooter; each legal three-ball carom count is scored as two points for shooter.

DEFINITION OF A COUNT
If not in violation of any "Rules of Play" or General Rules of Carom Billiards, a shot is: a two-ball carom *count* if the *cue ball* contacts any two of the three object balls, or a three-ball carom count if the cue ball contacts all three of the object balls.

BALL POSITIONS – OPENING BREAK
The light red (*pink*) ball is spotted on the *foot spot*. The red ball is *spotted* on the head spot. Both balls are in position before the lag for break.

OPENING BREAK
The lag for break is actually part of the *opening break*. With the red and pink balls spotted as immediately above, players select cue balls and lag for break as in General Rules of Carom Billiards (*automatic loss of lag applying to contact with the pink ball as well as the red*). When lag is completed, both players' cue balls remain in position; the first shot of the game is from this position (*if cue ball[s] contacted either red and/or pink object balls – which were spotted – on lag, they are re-spotted prior to first shot of game*). Winner of lag has choice of shooting first or assigning first shot to opponent; in either case, cue ball are played from the position following lag for break, and each player's cue ball is the one used for the lag for break. The starting player (*first shooter after lag for break*) must cause the cue ball's first contact with a ball to be with the pink object ball (*on the foot spot*). Failure to comply is a violation; player's inning ends and no count can be scored.

RULES OF PLAY:
    1. On all shots subsequent to the first shot following the lag, shooter

may make his first object *(first balls contacted by the cue ball)* any of the three object balls.

2. A legal counting stroke entitles shooter to continue at the table until he fails to legally count on a shot.

SPOTTING JUMPED BALLS
(Differs from General Rules of Carom Billiards)

1. If the red ball is jumped off the table, it is spotted on the *head spot*. If the head spot is occupied *(spotting a ball on it would result in contact with another ball)*, the red ball is held off the table until the first time the head spot is vacant at the completion of a shot.

2. If the pink ball is jumped, it is spotted on the foot spot. If the foot spot is occupied *(spotting a ball on it would result in contact with another ball)*, the pink ball is held off the table until the first time the foot spot is vacant at the completion of a shot.

3. If the white object ball is jumped, it is spotted on the head spot. If the head spot is occupied, the white object ball is held off the table until the first time the head spot is vacant at the completion of a shot. Should the head spot be occupied after each shot until such time as the white object ball is required as incoming player's cue ball, that ball shall then be spotted on the foot spot; if the foot spot is also occupied, it shall be spotted on the center spot; if the center spot is also occupied, incoming player may place the ball anywhere on the head string, not *frozen* to a ball.

4. If the white cue ball is jumped, the same rule *(immediately above)* applies.

5. If the red ball and the pink balls are jumped on a shot, spot the pink ball first, then the red ball, according to spotting rules for those balls. If neither can be spotted per those rules, spot the pink ball on the center spot and continue holding the red ball off the table until the head spot is vacant per the red spotting ball rule.

6. If either one of the white balls and one or both of the red balls are jumped on a shot, first spot the white ball per appropriate rule above, then the red ball per appropriate rule *(or if both reds, the immediately preceding paragraph)*.

7. If both of the white balls and one of the red balls is jumped, spot all balls that will spot directly *(beginning with the white object ball, then the white cue ball, then the red)*. If all jumped balls cannot be spotted directly,

spot remaining balls per appropriate rule above.

8. If all four balls are jumped on a shot, the jumper's cue ball is spotted on the center spot, the red ball on the head spot, the pink on the foot spot, and the incoming player may place his cue ball anywhere on the head string not frozen to the red ball.

9. Jumped balls result in no penalty unless the player's cue ball is jumped. If a player does jump his cue ball off the table, the stroke is invalid and is a foul.

PENALTY FOR FOULS

One point is deducted from offender's score for each foul.

STRAIGHT RAIL

Except when clearly contradicted by these additional rules, the General Rules of Carom Billiards apply.

PLAYERS

2 or 3.

BALLS USED

Standard set of one white clear, one white spot and one red.

OBJECT OF THE GAME

Score the predetermined number of points for game prior to opponent(s).

SCORING

Each legal *count* is scored as one point for shooter.

DEFINITION OF A COUNT

A shot is a count if not in violation of any "Rules of Play" or General Rules of Carom Billiards and the *cue ball* contacts both object balls.

OPENING BREAK

General Rules of Carom Billiards regarding *opening break* apply. Failure to comply is a violation; player's inning ends and no count can be scored.

RULES OF PLAY

1. A legal counting stroke entitles shooter to continue at the table until he fails to legally count on a shot.

2. When the object balls are in a *crotch*, player may score no more than three successive counts with the balls remaining in the crotch. If three successive in-crotch counts are made, player must, on his next shot, drive at least one object ball out of the crotch. Failure to

do so is a violation; players's inning ends and no count can be scored.

PENALTY FOR FOULS
One point is deducted from offender's score for each foul.

UNITED STATES BILLIARD ASSOCIATION THREE-CUSHION RULES

1. USBA-sanctioned tournaments will be governed by the rules that follow. Any exception must be stated in the tournament notice, or discussed and approved by a majority of the players present before the start of any USBA tournament.

2. A three-cushion billiard is valid and is a count of one in any of the following cases:

   (a) cue ball strikes an object ball and then strikes three or more cushions before striking the second object ball;

   (b) cue ball strikes three or more cushions and then strikes the two object balls;

   (c) cue ball strikes a cushion, then strikes one object ball, and then strikes two or more cushions before striking the second object ball;

   (d) cue ball strikes two cushions, then strikes first object ball, and then strikes one or more cushions before striking the second object ball.

3. Three cushions means three impacts. The number of cushions does not mean three different ones; a valid count may be executed on one cushion, if they are the result of the overspin or underspin on the ball.

4. **LAGGING FOR THE BREAK**

   (a) The two players select a cue ball, which is placed on the table within the head string, and stroke the ball to the foot of the table and return. The side rails may be touched by the ball in lagging, though it is not required.

   (b) Player whose ball comes to rest nearest to the head rail wins the lag.

(c) The winner of the lag has the right to shoot the first shot or assign the break shot to the opponent.

(d) Winner of the lag has the choice of cue balls, which is then used for the duration of the game.

5. BREAK SHOT

(a) Opponent's ball is placed on the head spot. Starting player's cue ball is placed within eight inches to the right or left of the head spot. Red ball is placed on the foot spot.

(b) Starting player must contact red ball first. Failure to contact red ball first is an error and ends the starting player's inning.

(c) On subsequent shots, either red ball or cue ball can be the first object ball.

6. FOULS WHICH END A PLAYER'S TURN

(a) Jumped balls (Rule 11).

(b) Starting play while balls are in motion.

(c) Touching any of the balls by hand, part of clothing, cue or any other object such as chalk or pen. The balls shall remain in position to which they were thus moved.

(d) Push or shove shot (Rule 15).

(e) Double stroke (Rule 15).

(f) When, at moment of shooting, neither foot is touching the floor.

(g) Wrong ball (Rule 8).

(h) Touching ball with cue during warm-up (Rule 18).

(i) Player interference (Rule 20).

7. Any foul caused by outside interference is not to be charged as a penalty to the player with shot in progress. If the balls are displaced by the disturbance, they will be restored to their original position as precisely as possible, and the player will continue shooting.

8. WRONG BALL

(a) Shooting with a wrong ball is a foul, and ends player's inning.

(b) The opponent or the referee may call this foul; opponent may call before or after the shot, while referee calls it only after the shot.

(c) Such a foul can be called at any time during a run, but the shooter shall be entitled to all points made previous to the stroke in which error was detected.

(d) The incoming shooter shall play the balls as left after error was called.

9. FROZEN BALLS

(a) If during the course of an inning the shooter's ball comes to rest in contact with the opponent's ball, or if the shooter's ball comes to rest in contact with the red ball, the shooter has the option of playing away from the ball with which he is in contact, or elect to have the balls in contact spotted.

(b) If an inning ends with the shooter's ball in contact with the next shooter's ball, or the red ball in contact with the next shooter's ball, the incoming player has the option of playing away from the ball in contact, or may elect to have the two balls which are in contact spotted.

(c) Only those balls which are in contact are to be spotted. The loose or unfrozen ball is not to be touched. The red ball is spotted on the foot spot, the player's cue ball on the head spot, and the opponent's cue ball on the center spot.

(d) If the spot reserved for the ball to be spotted is hidden by another ball, the ball to be spotted is placed on the spot usually reserved for the hiding ball.

(e) The same rules apply when a ball or balls jump the table.

10. When a cue ball is frozen to a cushion, a player may shoot into (play against) that cushion, but the first contact shall not count. Subsequent contacts with the same cushion are valid.

11. When a player's cue ball, the opponent's ball, or the red ball jumps the table, it is a foul and the player's inning ends. Spot balls by Rule 9 (c and d).

12. No shot can be started while balls are still in motion, or are still spinning. If a player disregards this rule, it's a foul and inning ends.

13. When the cue ball bounces and rides the top of the rail and returns to the table, the ball is in play. It shall count as one cushion. If it rides two or more rails, each rail will count as a cushion. If ball remains on top of the rail, it is considered a jumped ball, which is a foul, and player's inning ends.

14. If in playing a shot the cue ball leaves the playing surface and rides the rail or cushion, regardless of the number of impacts on that cushion, only one impact will be allowed.

15. If a player has pushed or shoved the cue ball with his cue, it is a foul and player's inning ends. A push shot is one in which the cue tip remains in contact with the cue ball after cue ball strikes an object ball, or when cue tip again contacts the cue ball after cue ball strikes the object ball. Double stroke is similar and occurs when player's tip or cue shaft hits cue ball twice. If a billiard is made, it shall not count, and the player's inning ends.

16. All kiss shots are fair, whether they deprive a player of an imminent score, or whether they assist in a score.

17. Miscues shall not end the player's inning, unless it is construed that the player's ferrule or shaft also touched the cue ball. Not all miscues are fouls, and if a billiard is completed in the miscue stroke, it shall be counted and turn continues.

18. If a player during the "warm-up" stroking should touch the cue ball, it is a foul and inning ends.

19. A game is official when a player scores the number of points designated as constituting a game, even though the opponent has had one less turn at the table. If a scorekeeper is used, the game becomes official after the score sheet is signed by the players. The referee and the scorekeeper should also sign the sheet. After the losing player signs the score sheet, no protest can be made.

20. If a player at the table is responsible for interference in any manner, it is a foul, and the inning ends. Incoming player must accept balls in position. A player not at the table must not distract the opponent with undue motions or noise. The referee or tournament official may issue a warning or disqualify the player for unsportsmanlike conduct.

21. If, for reasons beyond his control, a player cannot start a game as scheduled, the game may be postponed if the tournament director so decides. If a player is unable to finish a game, he forfeits, unless the opponent waives the forfeiture and agrees to finish the game at a time convenient to the tournament management. If a player is unable to return to the tournament, all his games are nullified as they would be in disqualification.

22. If a player is disqualified in a game, he loses that game and gets no points. The opponent is credited with a game won and is given the number of points he would have scored had he won the game. If a player is disqualified from a tournament, all his games are nullified *(that is, games played and games remaining on the schedule)*. Tournament continues as though one less player started when tournament opened.

23. If, for reasons beyond his control, a player cannot start a game, he must notify the tournament manager in time to allow for a substitute player, or for another pair of players. All tournament contestants are subject to immediate call if a substitute is necessary.

24. If a referee is officiating and considers a player to be taking an abnormal amount of time between strokes or in determining the choice of shots with the intention of upsetting an opponent, the referee shall warn the player that he runs the risk of disqualification if he pursues these tactics. Continued disregard of warning shall be proper grounds to disqualify the player. If no referee is officiating, the tournament manager shall have the right to invoke this rule.

25. Deliberate safeties are not allowed. If played, the incoming player may accept balls as they are, or set up a break shot.

26. At any tournament sanctioned by the USBA, the tournament director plus some other member of the USBA who is not playing in the tournament shall constitute a grievance committee to whom unsportsmanlike conduct during the tournament may be reported. Before commencement of the tournament, the players shall designate two of the players to serve on such a committee to protect the interests of the players. The two persons representing the USBA and the two persons representing the players shall jointly consider any evidence or reports of unsportsmanlike conduct. If this grievance committee is unable to resolve the complaint, the representatives shall submit a written report to the USBA for consideration by the Board of Directors. The two player representatives may indicate their concurrence in the findings of the USBA representatives or may submit dissenting views to the Board of Directors. At the next regular meeting or special meeting of the Board of Directors, these reports shall be considered and the action recommended by a majority shall be binding on the accused member of the USBA.

THE DIAMOND SYSTEM

There are various systems in billiards which make use of the spots, or diamonds, inset in the rails. Numerical values assigned to the diamonds enable players to plan shots, particularly banks shots, with the help of simple arithmetic. Some world-class players don't use diamond systems, some use them only to check their instinct or judgment, and some use them at every opportunity. The fact is, on many shots in three-cushion billiards, diamond systems greatly reduce the need for guesswork. What follows is a description of the most widely-used system, the "Corner 5," also called "The Diamond System," or simply "The System."

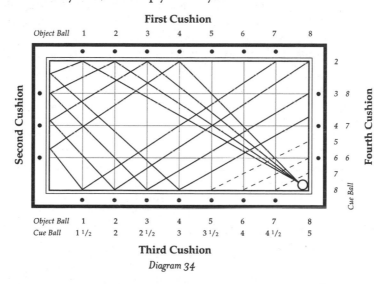

Diagram 34

A cue ball hit with slight running english that strikes the third rail at diamond No. 1 will travel back to diamond No. 7 on the first cushion. If it strikes diamond No. 2 on the third rail it will travel back to diamond No. 8 on the first rail (*or corner*). Diamond No. 3 on the third rail connects with diamond No. 3 (*object ball number*) on the lower rail. The various diamonds connect as illustrated in the diagram. A player must memorize these connections to use the diamond system, since he must know the path the ball will travel after it comes off the third rail.

Playing the diamond system, a player studies his shot backwards — that is, he must find out where he will come off the third cushion to score. Say, for example, that both object balls lie in the upper right corner of the diagram, with the cue ball in the lower right corner as shown.

The player, having memorized the connecting diamonds, knows that the cue ball must come off diamond No. 2 on the third rail to bank the shot in that corner.

Note that there are object ball markings on the third cushion. They start from No. 1 at the first diamond and go up to 8 which is the corner. If the player has to come off the second diamond, his object ball number is 2.

Note that there are cue ball numbers on the third cushion. They start with 1½ on the first diamond and go up to 5, which is the corner. The cue ball numbers also continue on the lower rail, as 6, 7, and 8. *(See diagram.)*

The player is still playing the bank shot with the two object balls in the upper right hand corner. He knows up to this time that he must come off diamond No. 2 on the third rail to count.

He must figure out where he will hit on the first cushion to bring the cue ball back to diamond No. 2 on the third cushion. In the diagram the cue ball lies at cue ball No. 5, which is the corner. Thus, knowing the object ball number (2) and the cue ball number (5), he subtracts the object ball number (2) from the cue ball number (5) and gets 3, which is the diamond he must hit on the first rail. If he wants to get to diamond No. 1 on the third rail, with the cue ball still at 5, he subtracts 1 from 5 and gets 4, the diamond he must hit on the first rail. If he wants to get to 3 on the third rail, he subtracts 3 from 5 and gets 2.

If he wants to get 2 on the third rail and finds the cue ball is at 6 on the lower rail, he subtracts 2 from 6 and gets 4, which is where he will hit on the first rail. If the cue ball lies at 3 ½ as a cue ball number and he wants to get to 2 on the third rail, he subtracts 2 from 3 ½ and gets 1 ½, which he must hit on the first rail.

Note that when a ball lies at cue ball position No. 5 *(see diagram)* and the player is playing to come off the cushion at 2 on the third rail, player must hit 3 on the first cushion. The diagram shows a line running from cue ball position 5 to the 3 diamond on the first cushion.

That line is cue ball position 5, no matter where the cue ball rests on that line. If the ball is in the corner it is 5. If the cue ball is on the line and four inches from the first cushion, it is still cue ball number 5.

Our discussion to this point covers only bank shots. The system can also be used when a ball is hit first. Consider the position in the second diagram *(diagram 35)*. In shots of this type, the first object ball gives the player his cue ball number. Suppose the first object ball lies on the line of cue ball position 5 we discussed immediately above. If the player drove the object ball on cue ball line 5 into the first cushion at diamond No. 3, he would hit the third cushion at No. 2 and travel to the lower right hand corner; assuming the second object ball is in that corner.

However, the player cannot drive the object ball with his cue. So—knowing the first object ball rests on cue ball line 5, he must drive the cue ball from the first object ball into the first cushion at diamond No. 3 to come off the third rail at diamond No. 2 and make the shot on the second object ball in the lower right hand corner. Here, the ability to make caroms reveals its importance.

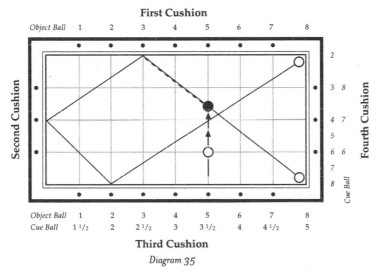

Diagram 35

The most important thing in 3-cushion billiards is being able to drive the cue ball from the first object ball into the first cushion at the point desired. In other words, unless the player can make the simple carom of driving the cue ball from the first object ball into the desired point of the first cushion, his chances of making the count are minimized.

If the first object ball lies on cue ball track (*or line*) 4 ½ and the player wants to come off diamond No. 2 on the third cushion, he subtracts 2 from 4 ½ and then proceeds to drive his cue ball off the first object ball into 2 ½ on the first cushion (*which is 2 from 4 ½*).

Many players refuse to learn the diamond system, because written explanations of it are somewhat complicated and require studious attention. However, if the player will follow the instructions above and test them out on a table, the system is comparatively simple. Oral explanations from a player who knows the system make for easier understanding, of course.

The diamond system is not infallible, but on bank shots particularly, it serves a player better than his instinct. If you watch player's in world's tournaments studies bank shots, they will determine first from what point they must come off the third rail to score.

Say a player must come off diamond 2 ½ on the third rail. He then determines his cue ball number. Say it is 4 ½. By subtracting 2 ½ from 4 ½ he knows he must hit diamond No. 2 on the first rail to get back to diamond No. 2 ½ on the third rail. The system tells him exactly where to hit. His instinct may have given him the general location of the desired point on the first cushion, but if he hit 1 ¾ or 2 ¼ on the first rail, chances are he would miss the shot.

When using the diamond system, strike the cue ball above center with running english, following through on your stroke. If you stab the cue ball with a jerky stroke you will shorten the angle. If you slam the cue ball too hard you are likely to shorten the angle. Use a stroke of medium force and follow through.

If the balls do not lie exactly on the object ball and cue ball tracks, you may parallel or figure the diamonds in fractions. For example, if the object ball number is 1 ¼ and the cue ball number is 3 ½, your subtraction gives you point 2 ¼ on the first rail. The diamond system does not apply to all shots on the table. It is confined almost entirely to natural angle shots.

You may find that in using the diamond system on a certain table that your cue ball "comes short." If this happens, you allow for it in your calculations, moving up higher on the first rail. Thus, instead of hitting 2 *(assuming your calculations tell you to hit 2)* you move down to 1 ¾ or maybe 1 ½. Make sure first, however, that you are stroking your cue ball with running english and are following through before you decide the table runs "short."

When using the diamond system, aim at the diamond through the cushion — that is, at an angle through the cushion to the diamond, which is set back on the rail. Do not aim at a point at the edge of the cushion which is directly opposite the diamond.

THREE-CUSHION PRACTICE SHOTS

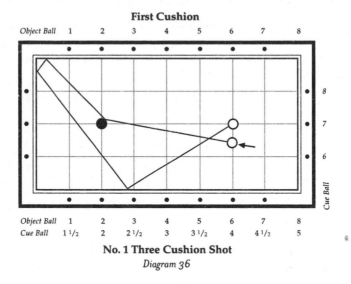

First Cushion

Object Ball	1	2	3	4	5	6	7	8

Object Ball	1	2	3	4	5	6	7	8
Cue Ball	1 1/2	2	2 1/2	3	3 1/2	4	4 1/2	5

No. 1 Three Cushion Shot

Diagram 36

Hold cue level. Hit object ball ⅓ right. Strike cue ball center, slight english left. Use 7" bridge with moderate stroke.

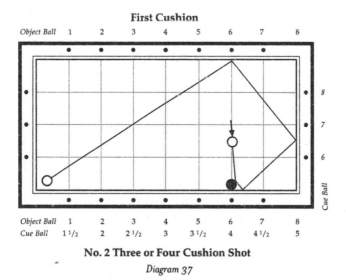

First Cushion

Object Ball	1	2	3	4	5	6	7	8

Object Ball	1	2	3	4	5	6	7	8
Cue Ball	1 1/2	2	2 1/2	3	3 1/2	4	4 1/2	5

No. 2 Three or Four Cushion Shot

Diagram 37

Hold cue level. Hit object ball ¼ left. Strike cue ball center, english left. Use 6" bridge. Use moderate stroke.

195

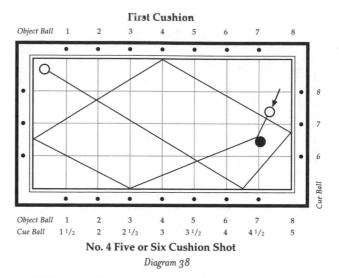

First Cushion

No. 4 Five or Six Cushion Shot

Diagram 38

Hold cue level. Hit object ball thin. Strike cue ball center, english right. Use 8"
bridge. Use hard stroke.

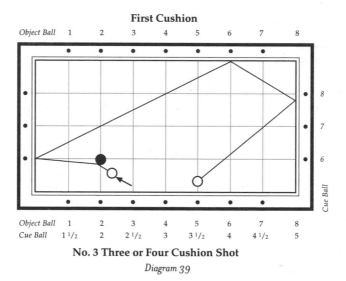

First Cushion

No. 3 Three or Four Cushion Shot

Diagram 39

Hold cue level. Hit object ball ¼ left. Strike cue ball center, english right. Use 7
inch bridge. Use moderate stroke.

BCA
HALL OF FAME

The purpose of the Hall of Fame is to honor outstanding persons who, through their skill and dedication, have enriched either the sport or the industry.

Two categories have been established in BCA's Hall of Fame. The Greatest Players category shall be reserved for outstanding players who have reached 40 years of age within the calendar year it is awarded and who have been active in national or foreign competition for at least 20 years and have won at least one national or foreign championship recognized by the BCA. At least one candidate from this category will be nominated annually. The Meritorious Service category shall be reserved for persons who have made lasting, memorable and important contributions to billiards, even though they may not have distinguished themselves as competitors.

Pictured on the following pages are those who have the distinct honor of membership in the BCA Hall of Fame.

Ralph Greenleaf
1899-1950
Inducted 1966

Fourteen-time World Pocket Billiard Champion **RALPH GREENLEAF** possessed all the flash and flair of a natural showman. With his beautiful actress wife, Princess Nai Tai Tai, the handsome Greenleaf put together a sparkling trick-shot performance and toured the Vaudeville circuit in the 20's and 30's. The audiences watched him perform his spectacular shots by looking at a huge mirror suspended on stage over the playing table.

Greenleaf won his first Pocket Billiard championship in 1919 and his last one in 1937.

William F. Hoppe
1887-1959
Inducted 1966

WILLIE HOPPE, whose brilliant career was one of the longest in the annals of the sport, is considered by many to be the greatest All-Around billiard player of any era.

In 1906, at the tender age of 18, Hoppe won his first world's title by defeating the renowned French champion, Maurice Vignaux, at 18.1 Balkline in a memorable match in Paris. He went on to win the 18.2 Balkline and Cushion Carom titles and years later, between 1936 and 1952, held the Three-Cushion title 11 times.

Charles C. Peterson
1880-1962
Inducted 1966

CHARLIE PETERSON earned the title "Missionary of Billiards" for his untiring efforts to promote the game throughout the United States.

In addition to being the world's fancy-shot champion and, for years, holder of the Red Ball title, Peterson made scores of personal appearances at colleges and universities across the country and was the guiding spirit of the Intercollegiate and Boys' Clubs of America tournaments.

Peterson died at the age of 83, after a life devoted to winning friends for the sport of billiards.

Welker Cochran
1896-1959
Inducted 1967

WELKER COCHRAN, a champion who trained for his billiard matches with the same intensity as a professional boxer, won his first of two 18.2 Balkline titles in 1927. He later went on to become the Three-Cushion champion five times in the 30's and 40's.

Like many stars of the sport, Cochran learned the game in his father's billiard establishment, and he became the protege of Frank Gotch, the wrestler, who sent young Cochran to Chicago to hone his playing talents.

Alfredo DeOro
1862-1948
Inducted 1967

The career of distinguished Spanish champion, **ALFREDO DeORO** encompassed both Three-Cushion and Pocket Billiards and spanned the closing of the 19th century and the opening of the 20th.

DeOro, who served in his country's diplomatic corps, first gained the Pocket Billiard crown in 1887. He was to repeat the achievement 16 times in the next 25 years. DeOro held the Three-Cushion title 10 times from 1908 through 1919.

In 1934, at the age of 71, DeOro came out of retirement for a Championship Tournament, winning two dramatic victories from defending champion Welker Cochran and the ultimate winner of the tournament, Johnny Layton.

Benjamin B. Nartzik
1895-1963
Inducted 1967

BEN NARTZIK will always be remembered for his tireless crusade to revive billiards from its severe doldrums in the 1950's. Nartzik deserves a lion's share of the credit for ridding the game of its "pool hall" image and reestablishing its status as a "gentleman's sport." Under his leadership, the BCA was able to help both the Boys Club of America and the Association of College Unions organize billiard programs and run successful annual tournaments. Nartzik recognized the potential of the industry and bought the National Billiard Chalk Co. of Chicago.

Willie Mosconi
1913-1993
Inducted 1968

For most people, the name **WILLIE MOSCONI** and the sport of Pocket Billiards are synonymous. And rightly so, since from 1940 to 1957 Mosconi had a near-stranglehold on the World Title, winning it 15 times in that period. Born in Philadelphia in 1913, Willie was a prodigy with the cue by the age of seven. At 20, he embarked on a hectic cross-country exhibition tour with his idol, Ralph Greenleaf, then World Champ and at the height of his game. The result, 57 wins for Greenleaf, an amazing 50 wins for the young Mosconi. One of the most astounding of Mosconi's many records is his yet-unbroken exhibition high run of 526 balls.

Jake Schaefer, Sr.
1855-1910
Inducted 1968

A player whose super-brilliance with a billiard cue won for him the sobriquet of "Wizard" so runs the lead of a 1909 newspaper article singing the praises of **JAKE SCHAEFER, SR.** From the last quarter of the 19th century through the first decade of the 20th, Schaefer, Sr. was one of the most feared names in Balkline Billiards. Derivations of the game were invented just to stymie his genius – all unsuccessfully. He traveled throughout the world winning matches and gathering fans. On March 11, 1908, though desperately ill, he successfully defended his title in his final match for the 18.1 championship against Willie Hoppe by a score of 500 to 423.

Jake Schaefer, Jr.
1894-1975
Inducted 1968

Billiard historians generally rank **JAKE SCHAEFER, JR.** as the greatest of the American Balkline players. He was the world champion at 18.2 in 1921, 1925, 1926, 1927, and 1929-1933. He held the 18.1 honors in 1926-1927 and the 28.2 title in 1937-1938. At the 18.2 game, he holds four records which have never been equalled in this country: best game average, 400 *(from the break)*; grand average, tournament, 57.14; grand average, match, 93.25; high run, match, 432.

Herman J. Rambow
1881-1967
Inducted 1969

Called the Stradivari of his trade by those who know, **HERMAN RAMBOW** crafted custom cues for the greatest players in billiards over the course of a 65-year career. Captains of industry and celebrities of the entertainment world also beat a path to his door to have the privilege of paying from $50 to $300 for one of his perfectly-balanced "Rambow Specials." It was Herman who perfected the jointed cue by inserting a countersunk screw in the recessed butt end, making an extra sturdy connection. Only death at age 86 stopped the craftsman from his labor of love. To billiard cognoscenti the world over, there will never be another Rambow.

Harold Worst
1929-1966
Inducted 1970

HAROLD WORST of Grand Rapids, MI was only 19 years old when he played the great Willie Hoppe, winner of 51 major billiard championships, in a demonstration game in Detroit in 1949. Hoppe soon took an interest in Worst's playing potential, and under his guidance, Worst won the world title for Three-Cushion billiards in Argentina in 1954, the youngest player to compete in world competition. He successfully defended this title for many years. Equally skilled at pocket billiards, Worst dominated play to win the All-Around titles in both the 1965 Johnston City, IL and 1965 Stardust Open championships.

John Wesley Hyatt
1837-1920
Inducted 1971

JOHN WESLEY HYATT, known as the father of the American plastic industry, was an inventor rather than a player, but his invention of the celluloid plastic billiard ball in 1868 revolutionized the billiard industry. Hyatt began his search for a suitable synthetic billiard ball material when a New York billiards firm offered a $10,000 prize for a substitute for ivory. Hyatt's earlier attempts involved shellacking a paper pulp sphere and a ball made of layers of cloth.

Frank Taberski
1889-1941
Inducted 1975

FRANK TABERSKI grew up in Schenectady, NY. At the age of 26, he attended a pocket billiard championship in New York City, and came home convinced he played as well as the champions. The next year, he entered and placed third behind Johnny Layton. From then on, he was almost invincible. In those days, 450-point challenge matches were the means of competition; the prize a ruby and diamond studded gold medal with the proviso that any one who won 10 consecutive challenge matches could keep it. Alfredo DeOro had come closest with five straight defenses. By 1918, Taberski had accomplished the impossible and the medal was his.

Johnny Layton
1887-1956
Inducted 1976

JOHNNY LAYTON, born in Sedalia, MO, won the world's Three-Cushion championship 12 times, defeating such champions as Willie Hoppe, Welker Cochran, Jake Schaefer, Jr. and Augie Kieckhefer in the 1920's and 1930's. Layton recorded the high Three-Cushion game mark of 50 points in 23 innings, a record which still stands today. He was credited with originating the method of using the diamond system, using table markers to indicate direction of ball rebounds, a style that he perfected through the application of his highly developed mathematical mind.

James Caras
1910-Present
Inducted 1977

JIMMY CARAS was born in Scranton, PA, and is the second living person to be elected to the Hall of Fame. Jimmy started playing billiards at the age of five. When 17, he defeated Ralph Greenleaf in an exhibition match to become known as the Boy Wonder of The World. Nine years later, in 1936, he won his first world championship. He won again in 1938, 1939 and in 1949. Eighteen years later, in 1967, he won the U.S. Open in a field of 48 players. His record of "most balls," "most games won" and "fewest innings by a champion" still stand in the record book for that size field.

Irving Crane
1913-Present
Inducted 1978

IRVING CRANE was born in Livonia, NY. His love for the game started as a child, when he was given a toy billiard table. Although he played steadily as a teenager, he did not enter tournament play until the age of 23. He won his first world title in 1942. Since then, he has won almost two dozen major championships, including the world crown in 1946, 1955, 1966, 1968, 1970, 1972, plus the International Round-Robin championship in 1968. Crane was the victor in the 1978 World Series of Billiards (*a combination of 14.1 and Nine-Ball*) against a strong field of outstanding competitors. His greatest triumph, however, was his victory in the 1966 U.S. Open, when he won the championship in a never-to-be-excelled record run of 150 and out.

Steve Mizerak
1944-Present
Inducted 1980

STEVE MIZERAK, born in Perth Amboy, NJ, was the youngest inductee to the BCA Hall of Fame. In the brief span of his career, he has been four times champion of the U.S. Open, winning the title in 1970, 1971, 1972, and 1973. Mizerak also captured the PPPA World Open title in 1982 and 1983. Mizerak continues to finish near the top in several national tournaments each year.

Dorothy Wise
1914-1995
Inducted 1981

DOROTHY WISE was born in Spokane, WA. In her early years, there were very few national tournaments for women. Since she was in many local and state tournaments, she became the self-proclaimed world champion. When the BCA staged the first national tournament for women in 1967, she immediately entered. For the next five years, she proved herself most worthy as she won five consecutive U.S. Open titles.

Joseph Balsis
1921-1995
Inducted 1982

JOE BALSIS was born in Minnersville, PA, never could resist knocking the balls around one of the pool tables at his father recreation room. By the time he was 11, Balsis was playing exhibitions against the likes of Andrew Ponzi and Erwin Rudolph. He won junior titles four consecutive years. During pool's doldrum years Balsis left the game and it wasn't until 1944 that Balsis, a boat machinist in the Coast Guard, won his next title; Armed Services Champ. In 1964 "the Meatman," as Balsis is known because of his family's meat business, returned to competitive pool. Between 1965 and 1975 Balsis competed in the finals of the U.S. Open five times, winning twice *(1968 & 1974)*. He won the prestigious Billiard Room Proprietor's Association tournament in 1965, then captured the World All-Around championship in Johnston City, IL., in 1966. He won the Jansco brothers' Stardust Open All-Around title back-to-back in 1968 and 1969.

Luther Lassiter
1919-1988
Inducted 1983

Considered by many to be the finest Nine-ball player ever, **LUTHER LASSITER** was born in Elizabeth City, NC. Lassiter earned his nickname "Wimpy," for all the hot dogs and Orange Crushes he could pack away as a youngster hanging around the local pool hall. By the time he was 17, "Wimpy" was packing away his share of opponents. Lassiter's biggest years in tournament play came in the 1960s. In the 11 years of the Jansco brothers' All-Around Championships in Johnston City, IL *(1962-1972)*, Lassiter won the straight pool title five times, the Nine-Ball title four times and the One Pocket title once. On three occasions Lassiter went on to capture the All-Around title *(1962, 1963, 1967)*. He also won the BCA U.S. Open in 1969 and the Stardust World All-Around Championship in 1971.

"Minnesota Fats"
1913-1996
Inducted 1984

Perhaps the most recognizable figure in the history of pool, **Rudolph "Minnesota Fats" Wanderone** was elected to the Hall of Fame for Meritorious Service. Although he never actually won a designated "world championship," Wanderone, the game's leading comic, orator and publicity generator, has probably done more for the game in terms of sheer exposure than any other player. Initially nicknamed "Brooklyn Fats," and "New York Fats," Wanderone dubbed himself "Minnesota Fats" after the film version of "The Hustler" hit movie screens around the country in the early 1960's. Since that time he became known around the world as pool's foremost side show. "Fats," whose exact age was a mystery, hosted a national television show, "Celebrity Billiards," during the 1960's. He stopped playing in tournaments around that time.

Jean Balukas
1959-Present
Inducted 1985

JEAN BALUKAS is the second woman inducted into the BCA Hall of Fame. She was born in Brooklyn, NY, and is the Hall's youngest member. An excellent all-around athlete, Jean competed in her first BCA U.S. Open when she was nine years old, finishing seventh. She won her first BCA crown when she was 12. Since then Jean has collected seven BCA U.S. Open 14.1 titles, six World Open titles and countless Nine-ball and straight pool crowns. She has been named Player of the Year five times.

Lou Butera
1938-Present
Inducted 1986

LOU BUTERA was born in Pittston, PA. He learned to play at his father's pool room in the small coal-mining town. After watching BCA Hall of Famer Erwin Rudolph in an exhibition, 14-year-old Lou decided to devote his life to pool. He was runner-up to Irving Crane in the 1972 World Championship in Los Angeles. In 1973 he defeated Crane in the finals of the same event to win his first World Championship. Nicknamed "Machine Gun Lou" for his rapid fire style, Lou recorded a 150-ball run against Allen Hopkins in just 21 minutes in 1973. Butera has since won numerous titles.

Erwin Rudolph
1894-1957
Inducted 1987

ERWIN RUDOLPH was born in Cleveland. Rudolph did not participate in his first world 14.1 championship until he was 24 years old. Five years later, in 1926, Rudolph gained national acclaim by ending Ralph Greenleaf's six-year reign as world champion. Rudolph's win over Greenleaf came in a challenge match. After losing his world title to Thomas Hueston, Rudolph regained the Crown by winning the 1933 World Championship. He won his third World Title in 1933, and, at age 47, captured his fourth and final world crown by defeating a young Irving Crane in the finals of the 1941 World Championship in Philadelphia. At the time of his death in 1957, he held the record for fastest game in a world tournament, scoring 125 points in just 32 minutes. *(The record has since been eclipsed.)*

Andrew Ponzi
1903-1950
Inducted 1988

ANDREW PONZI was born Andrew D'Allesandro in Philadelphia. He acquired the name Ponzi after a witness to his cue prowess compared the likelihood of beating D'Allesandro with beating the infamous "Ponzi Scheme," anearly version of the pyramid game. A dazzling offensive player, Ponzi competed in the game's Golden Era, the 1930's and 1940's, against the likes of Mosconi, Crane, Caras, Rudolph and Greenleaf. Despite that stiff competition, Ponzi captured World 14.1 titles in 1934, 1940 and 1943.

Michael Sigel
1953-Present
Inducted 1989

MIKE SIGEL., at 35, became the youngest male elected to the BCA Hall of Fame. Born in Rochester, NY, Sigel began playing pool at 13, and turned professional when he was 20. A natural right-hander who shoots left-handed, Sigel won his first major tournament, the U.S. Open Nine-Ball Championship, in 1975. His career blossomed quickly, and Sigel was perhaps the game's dominant player in the 1980's. He amassed 38 major 14.1 and Nine-Ball championships in that decade. Sigel has won three World 14.1 Crowns *(1979, 1981 and 1985)* and one World Nine-Ball title *(1985)* as well as numerous national titles.

John Brunswick
1819-1886
Inducted 1990

JOHN BRUNSWICK was a Swiss immigrant woodworker who founded what has become the Brunswick Corporation, the largest pool table manufacturer in this country. Producing his first billiard table in 1845, Brunswick went on to develop an American market for billiard equipment. He is credited with the rapid growth of billiards in the late 19th century.

Walter Tevis
1928-1984
Inducted 1991

WALTER TEVIS is best remembered as the author of two popular novels about pool, *The Hustler* and *The Color of Money*. Both books were made into enormously successful movies starring Paul Newman. *The Hustler* documented pool culture in the United States in the late 1950's and *The Color of Money* followed up on the same theme 25 years later. Both movies were directly responsible for igniting strong uptrends in pocket billiards during the years immediately following their releases. Tevis wrote numerous short stories and several other novels including *The Man Who Fell To Earth* (*a science fiction thriller*) and *The Queen's Gambit* (*a portrait of a female chess master*). He was a Milton scholar and held two masters degrees (*from the University of Kentucky and the Writers' Workshop at the University of Iowa*). He taught creative writing at Ohio University from 1965 to 1978. His works have been translated into many languages and are popular all over the world.

Nick Varner
1948-Present
Inducted 1992

Learning the basics of pool at an early age from his father in his hometown of Owensboro, Kentucky, **NICK VARNER** displayed his great overall talents in 14.1, Nine-Ball, One Pocket and Bank Pool by claiming the 1969 and 1970 national ACU-I collegiate titles, the World 14.1 Championship in 1980 and 1986 and the BCA National Eight Ball Championship in 1980. Accumulating over 20 major titles in his career, he became only the second man to earn over $100,000 in prize winnings in the memorable 1989 season in which he won eight of the sixteen major Nine-Ball events. Winner of the Player of the Year in 1980 and 1989, and the first honoree of the MPBA Sportsperson of the Year in 1991, Nick has always been an exemplary role model and has enriched the sport of pocket billiards through his many years of dedication to excellence and sportsmanship.

Michael Phelan
1817-1871
Inducted 1993

MICHAEL PHELAN is considered by many to be the Father of American Billiards. Player, inventor, manufacturer and tireless popularizer of billiards. Played in and won the first billiard stakes match in 1859. Holds many patents for table designs and cushions. Credited as being the first to put diamonds on tables. Author of "Billiards Without A Master" (1850), the first American book on billiards. Set trend for lavish billiard rooms through his New York room on Broadway.

Eddie Taylor
1918-Present
Inducted 1993

EDDIE TAYLOR is a two-time world all-around tournament champion. Defeated Hall-of-Famer Luther Lassiter in all-around finals in Johnston City, Ill., in 1964. Defeated Danny Jones and Mike Eufemia at '67 Stardust Open finals in Las Vegas. Lost to Lassiter in '63 Johnston City all-around finals. Finished 7th in '67 World 14.1 championship in New York. A Tennessee native, the "Knoxville Bear" was inducted into the Knoxville Sports Hall of Fame in 1987. Active promoter of billiards in Boys Clubs of America. Regarded as one of the greatest one-pocket and bank pool players of all time.

Ray Martin
1936-Present
Inducted 1994

RAY MARTIN: (Born in 1936) His world titles in straight pool in 1971, 1974 and 1978 make Ray Martin one of only seven players in this century to win three or more world 14.1 titles. He has many nine-ball tournament wins to his credit as well, including the 1980 Caesars Tahoe Invitational, the 1981 ESPN King of the Hill, and the 1983 Music City Open. While concentrating today more on teaching than playing, Martin is still a threat in straight pool tournaments, finishing fourth and fifth in the 1992 and 1993 BCA U.S. Opens. In collaboration with Rosser Reeves, Martin wrote "The 99 Critical Shots in Pool" (1977).

Jimmy Moore
1911-Present
Inducted 1994

JIMMY MOORE: Although Moore never won a world title, he claimed the National Pocket Billiards Championship in a 3,000 point match win over Luther Lassiter in 1958. At the National Invitational Pocket Billiards Championship in New York City in 1965 he easily outdistanced a straight-pool field which included the strongest players of the period such as Joe Balsis, Ed Kelly, Lou Butera, Luther Lassiter and Eddie Taylor. He is a five-time runner-up in world 14.1 championship play. He posted high finishes in many other major events in the '50s and '60s.

Cisero Murphy
1937-1996
Inducted 1995

CISERO MURPHY: James Cisero Murphy was the first and only African-American ever to win a world or U.S. national billiard title. He started by taking the New York City championship at age 16. While in his '20s he won the Eastern States 14.1 Championship six straight times against top competition, but because of his race was not invited to compete in world title events until 1965, when he won the Burbank World Invitational 14.1 tournament, beating Joe Balsis, Jimmy Moore and Luther Lassiter. Murphy remains the only player in the history of pocket billiard competition to win a world title on his first attempt. He continued to place near the top in straight pool events during the 1960's and, two decades later, had a winning record in the 1983 BCA U.S. Open 14.1 Championship. He posted several competitive high runs of over 250 balls.

DALLAS WEST
1941 - Present
Inducted 1996

DALLAS WEST, the only player to appear in every BCA U.S. Open straight pool championship, was born in 1941 in Rockford, Illinois. By age 13, he had run 97 balls at straight pool. The holder of several state pool titles, West was the U.S. Open champion in 1975 and 1983. An expert Nine-ball player, he earned second place in the 1995 WPA World Championship. He also plays top-level three cushions. West has shared his extensive knowledge of straight pool on video-tapes, explaining in detail how long runs are made. He has been winning tournaments for over 20 years and has earned the respect of the best players in the game for his positive attitude, gentlemanly behavior, and competitive spirit.

Arthur Cranfield
1915-Present
Inducted 1997

ARTHUR "Babe" CRANFIELD, the only person ever to win the National Junior, National Amateur and World Professional pocket billiard titles was born in 1916 to a Syracuse, New York room owner. He was giving exhibitions by the age of 10, when it was predicted he would eventually beat Ralph Greenleaf. He won the New York City and National Junior titles at age 15, breaking previous high-run records, and was the National Amateur champion in 1938 and 1940. He traveled frequently to give exhibitions for the National Billiard Program. He interrupted his promising career to enlist in the Army Air Corps in 1942. After the war, Babe appeared frequently in World Tournament ranks. He took the world straight pool title from Luther Lassiter in 1964, making him the first left-handed champion since Alfredo de Oro. Always known for being a gentleman, Babe spent his professional life as a music executive but always found time to promote the game of pocket billiards.

Ruth McGinnis
1910 - 1974
Inducted 1997

RUTH McGINNIS, who was born in 1910, began playing pool at age 7. At 14, she had defeated both Flower Sisters, then world champions at straight pool. She was acclaimed the world women's champion for the years 1932-1940 and during that time she lost only 29 out of 1,532 exhibition matches.

She entered the New York State pocket championship *(until then restricted to men)* in 1942 and was invited to compete for the world title in 1948. Her high runs were 85 on a 10' table and 128 on a 9' table. She had a tournament high run of 125 and was inducted into the WPBA Hall of Fame in 1976.

She promoted billiards by touring extensively with Willie Mosconi and appearing in several short films about pocket billiards. Her career outside of pool was as a teacher of special children. The best female player in the country from 1924 through 1960, Ruth died in 1974 in Honesdale, PA.

TOURNAMENT RESULTS AND RECORDS

For records of tournaments no longer held, check the listings at the back of this section first and then prior editions of the BCA Official Rules and Record Book.

BCA NORTH AMERICAN EIGHT-BALL INDIVIDUAL CHAMPIONS

Master Men's Singles

Date	Champion	Runner-Up
1992	David Gutierrez, Houston, TX	Marv Rapp
1993	Walter Glass, Las Vegas, NV	Jerry Prado
1994	Jeremy Jones, Baytown, TX	Dave Black
1995	Bob Vanover, Coppell, TX	David Rhodes
1996	Bernie Mikkelsen, Calgary, AB, Canada	Don McCaughey
1997	Kevin Cardinal, Edmonton, AB, Canada	Derek McMaster

Open Men's Singles

Date	Champion	Runner-Up
1977	Tom Kilburn, South Bend, IN	Dick Spitzer
1978	Mike Carella, Louisville, KY	Bob Williams
1979	Jimmy Reid, Louisville, KY	Mark Wilson
1980	Nick Varner, Owensboro, KY	Mike Massey
1981	Danny Diliberto, Buffalo, NY	Nick Varner
1982	Joe Sposit, Pittshara, MO	Gregg Fix
1983	Michael Sardelli, Detroit, MI	Tom Chapman
1984	Louie Lemke, Ft. Worth, TX	Charles Shootman
1985	Steve Matlock, Cedar Rapids, IA	Stan Fimple
1986	Jesus Rivera, Denver, CO	Mickey Leon Stone
1987	Stan Fimple, Omaha, NE	Mike Fenne
1988	Harry Sexton, Detroit, MI	Seco Varani
1989	Henry Granas, Englewood, CO	T.J. Davis
1990	Jesus Rivera, Denver, CO	Gilbert Martinez
1991	Paul Guernsey, Plano, TX	Gene Rossi
1992	Allan Jones, Porter, IN	James Hevener
1993	Mike McClain, Uniontown, PA	Jeremy Jones
1994	Ron Wiseman, Windsor, ON, Canada	Ed Castanon
1995	Steven Hayes, Kenosha, WI	Bob Pyles
1996	Kevin Cardinal, Edmonton, AB, Canada	Vince Chambers
1997	Jim Engels, Chicago, IL	Peter Laliberte

Master Women's Singles

Date	Champion	Runner-Up
1992	Linda Stepanski, Milwaukee, WI	Ellen Sellers
1993	Kathy Holman, Houston, TX	Timi Bloomberg
1994	Julie Mason, Arlington, TX	Kara Wroldson

1995 – Lori Buendorf, Minneapolis, MN	Julie Mason
1996 – Pamela Bell, Milwaukee, WI	Cindy Doty
1997 – Holly Sholes, Oklahoma City, OK	Debra Aarens

Open Women's Singles

Date Champion	Runner-Up
1978 – Catherine Stephens, Louisville, KY	Melodie Horn
1979 – Gloria Walker, Louisville, KY	Mary Kenniston
1980 – Billie Billing, Columbus, OH	Gloria Walker
1981 – Belinda Campos, Las Vegas, NV	Sherry Lively
1982 – Linda Hoffman, Kansas City, MO	Sherry Lively
1983 – Georgiana Casteel, Detroit, MI	Sherry Lively
1984 – Belinda Campos Bearden, Ft. Worth, TX	Linda Hoffman
1985 – Linda Hoffman, Arlington, TX	Diane Piercy
1986 – Linda Hoffman, Arlington, TX	Christine Glass
1987 – Linda Hoffman, Arlington, TX	Janene Hague
1988 – Timi Bloomberg, Rapid City, SD	Kathy Miao
1989 – Sherry Lively, Carmichael, CA	Christine Glass
1990 – Linda Meyer, Ponca City, OK	Janene Hague
1991 – Suzi Quall, Appleton, WI	Chris Fields
1992 – Brenda Plantz, Louisville, CO	Cindy Doty
1993 – Shelly Barnes, Albuquerque, NM	Bonita Johnson
1994 – Wendy Hill, Norman, OK	Windy Kopff
1995 – Suzanne Bosselman, Orange, NH	Laura Lo
1996 – Holly Sholes, Oklahoma City, OK	Katrina Games
1997 – Jennifer Wishinski, Surrey, BC, Canada	Dena Leath

Senior Men's Singles

Date Champion	Runner-Up
1986 – Stanley Coscia, Tampa, FL	Harold Schnormeier
1987 – Jerry Priest, Cape Girardeau, MO	Bob Keating
1988 – Seco Varani, Faribault, MN	Bob Keating
1989 – Jerry Priest, Cape Girardeau, MO	Bob Vanover
1990 – Jerry Priest, Cape Girardeau, MO	Bernard Rogoff
1991 – Bob Vanover, Dallas, TX	Beau Zimmerman
1992 – Seco Varani, Faribault, MN	Fred Guarino
1993 – John Gureckis, Brockton, MA	Bob Vanover
1994 – Bob Vanover, Coppell, TX	David Dattilo
1995 – John Abruzzo, Villa Park, IL	Pete Lewis
1996 – Ken Boam, Calgary, AB, Canada	Bernard Rogoff
1997 – Fred Guarino, Las Vegas, NV	Jim Norris

Senior Women's Singles

Date Champion	Runner-Up
1989 – Fern Reedy, Smithville, MO	Jeanne Bloomberg
1990 – Jeri Engh, Osceola, WI	Op Wheeler
1991 – Karen Wold, St. Paul, MN	Lynn Reed
1992 – Lynn Reed, New Berlin, WI	Charlene Edwards
1993 – Diane Piercy, El Dorado Hills, CA	Jeanne Bloomberg
1994 – Karen Wold, St. Paul, MN	Penni Adrian

1995 – Lynn Reed, West Allis, WI .... Sandra Chamberlain
1996 – Jean Bartholomew, Portland, OR .... Diane Piercy
1997 – Jean Bartholomew, Portland, OR .... Lorraine Lilley

BCA NA AMATEUR ARTISTIC POOL CHAMPIONS

Date Champion	Runner-Up
1993 – Craig Powers, Milwaukee, WI	Mark Dimick
1994 – Joe Shirley, Houston, TX	Rob Lundrign
1995 – Mark Dimick, Oklahoma City, OK	Dan Henley
1996 – Paul Blanchard, St. Bernard, LA	Mark Dimick
1997 – Ben Alloggio, Houston, TX	John James

BCA NA AMATEUR TARGET POOL CHALLENGE

Men's

Date Champion	Runner-Up
1993 – David Gutierrez, Houston, TX	Bernardo Chavez
1994 – Mark Buchko, Lansing, MI	Bernardo Chavez
1995 – John Abruzzo, Villa Park, IL	Andy Nikolai
1996 – Rudy Dominguez, Wyoming, MI	John Abruzzo
1997 – Mike Walker, Lewisburg, TN	Andy Nikolai

Women's

Date Champion	Runner-Up
1996 – Debra Aarens, Las Vegas, NV	Susan Mello
1997 – Debra Aarens, Las Vegas, NV	Susie Miller

BCA NA EIGHT-BALL SCOTCH-DOUBLES CHAMPIONS

Master's Division

1996 .... Paul Guernsey/June Hager-Walter (Arlington, TX)
1997 .... John Hager, Jr./June Walter (San Antonio, TX)

Open Division

1991 .... Bonnie and Mark Coats (Broken Arrow, OK)
1992 .... Maureen Finn/Pete Lewis (Clinton, IA)
1993 .... Ramona Biddle/Louie Roybal (Albuquerque, NM)
1994 .... Bonnie Arnold/Steven Hayes (Kenosha, WI)
1995 .... June Hager/Bob Vanover (Coppell, TX)
1996 .... Alex Pernas/Joanne Honeycutt (Las Vegas, NV)
1997 .... Jeff Sergent/Julie Schultz (Chicago, IL)

BCA NORTH AMERICAN EIGHT-BALL TEAM CHAMPIONS

Master Men's

1991 .... Black Sticks (Houston, TX)
1992 .... The Crunch Bunch (Dallas, TX)
1993 .... Hall of Fame Billiards (Elk Grove, IL)
1994 .... Hall of Fame Billiards (Elk Grove, IL)
1995 .... Hall of Fame Billiards (Elk Grove, IL)
1996 .... The Dream Team (AB, Canada)
1997 .... Cue Can Do (Schaumburg, IL)

Master Women's

Year	Winner
1994	Rusty's Lucky Ladies (Ft. Worth, TX)
1995	JDD's-Justice (Colorado Springs, CO)
1996	Galtier Midwest Masters (St. Paul, MN)
1997	Chix With Stix (Milwaukee, WI)

Open Women's

1979	Wheel Inn (Billings, MT)
1980	Burt's Girls (Colorado Springs, CO)
1981	Burt's Girls (Colorado Springs, CO)
1982	Richard's (Lansing, MI)
1983	Richard's (Lansing, MI)
1984	North Star (Sacramento, CA)
1985	Gold Nugget (Arlington, TX)
1986	Leisure Club (Phoenix, AZ)
1987	Leftys + (Sacramento, CA)
1988	Great American Girls (Sacramento, CA)
1989	8-Ball Express (Rapid City, SD)
1990	8-Ball Express (Rapid City, SD)
1991	Cue-T s (West Allis, WI)
1992	Lucky Ladies (Ft. Worth, TX)
1993	Lucky Ladys (Pittsburg, PA)
1994	The Lady Killers (Norman, OK)
1995	Rough Riders (Greenfield, WI)
1996	Rum Runner #2 (Las Vegas, NV)
1997	Not Bad For Girls (BC, Canada)

Open Men's/Mixed

1979	Tam O'Shanter (Colorado Springs, CO)
1980	Tam O'Shanter (Colorado Springs, CO)
1981	Tam O'Shanter (Colorado Springs, CO)
1982	The Wizards (Colorado Springs, CO)
1983	Mike's Lounge (Pittsburgh, PA)
1984	Green Acres (Ft. Worth, TX)
1985	Starlite Lounge (Arlington, TX)
1986	MeMaws (Ft. Worth, TX)
1987	Jackson All Stars (Grand Prairie, TX)
1988	Mongo Murph's (Windsor, Canada)
1989	Black Sticks (Houston, TX)
1990	Black Sticks (Houston, TX)
1991	Players (San Antonio, TX)
1992	Lassiters (Clinton, IA)
1993	Stinky's Dream Team (AB, Canada)
1994	Crown Billiards (Mpls, MN)
1995	Vegas Bound Strokers (Albuquerque, NM)
1996	Tips And Taps (Fargo, ND)
1997	Vancouver Canadians (BC, Canada)

Women's Trophy

1995	Battlin' Bitches (Oak Lawn, IL)
1996	Texas Draw (Houston, TX)
1997	Westford Whips (Thunder Bay, ON)

Men's/Mixed Trophy

Year	Winner
1995	Demmas III (Oak Lawn, IL)
1996	K&S Billiards (Evergreen Park, IL)
1997	Slims Phil (Amarillo, TX)

BCA NORTH AMERICAN AMATEUR NINE-BALL CHAMPIONS

Men's

Date	Champion	Runner-Up
1994	Glen Atwell, Aloha, OR	Jeremy Jones
1995	Don McCaughey, Des Moines, IA	Tang Hoa
1995	Brady Gollan, Vancouver, BC, Canada	Mike Bandy
1996	Paul Turner, Riverdale, GA	Ed Matusoneck
1997	Jason Kirkwood, Grand Rapids, MI	Barry Emerson

Women's

Date	Champion	Runner-Up
1994	Bonnie Coats, Tulsa, OK	Timi Bloomberg
1995	Cindy Doty, Kelso, WA	Susan Mello
1995	Sherry Ahola, Sacramento, CA	Cindy Doty
1996	Jennifer Chen, Taipei, Taiwan	Cindy Doty
1997	Julie Mason, Newton, KS	Kristi Carter

Scotch Doubles

1995	Bobby Brown/June Hager (Arlington, TX)
1995	John Abruzo (IL)/Sherry Ahola (CA)
1996	Tim Roberts/Dawn Flial (Adrian, MI)
1997	Barry Emerson/Kristi Carter (Long Beach, CA)

CANADIAN AMATEUR EIGHT-BALL CHAMPIONS

MEN'S SINGLES DIVISION
1996 Bernie Mikkelson .... Calgary, AB
1997 Stan Tourangeau ...... Vancouver, BC

WOMEN'S SINGLES DIVISION
1996 Jackie Pranteau .... Vancouver, BC
1997 Kathie MacDonald .... Calgary, AB

SCOTCH DOUBLES DIVISION
1996 Kathie MacDonald/Stan Tourangeau (Calgary, AB/Vancouver, BC)
1997 Claire Schram/Barry Mclean (Winnipeg, MB)

OPEN TEAM DIVISION
1996 The Dream Team .... Calgary, AB
1997 B.W. Special Effects ... Edmonton, AB

WOMEN'S TEAM DIVISION
1996 Indecent Proposal .... Calgary, AB
1997 Not Bad for Girls ..... Vancouver, BC

BCA NATIONAL JUNIOR EIGHT-BALL CHAMPIONS

Champion .... Runner-up
1989 – Chan Whitt, Jr., Lewisburg, WV .... Chad Duster
1990 – Nathan Haddad, Lansing, MI (15-18 division) .... Scott Marshall
     – Michael Coltrain, Raleigh, NC (14 and under) .... Chris Whitten
1991 – Max Eberle, Arlington, VA (15-18 division) .... Chan Whitt
     – Charles Williams, Newport News, VA (14 and under) .... Kelsey Jorgensen
1992 – Mike Rinella, Abington, MA (15-18 division) .... Larry Nevel, Jr.
     – Andy Quinn, St. Charles, MO (14 and under) .... Jesse Bowman

BCA NATIONAL JUNIOR NINE-BALL CHAMPIONS

Champion .... Runner-up
1993 – Michael Coltrain, Raleigh, NC (18 & Under Open) .... David Coles
     – William Lanna, N. Providence, RI (14 & Under Open) .... Brad Weast
     – Kara Wroldson, N. Adams, MA (18 & Under Girls) .... Tiffany Nelson
1994 – Denver Barger, Seymour, IN (18 & Under Open) .... Steven Golowenski
     – William Lanna, Johnston, RI (14 & Under Open) .... Jeremiah Brown
     – Kara Wroldson, Lee, MA (18 and under) Girls) .... Tiffany Nelson
1995 – Lance Salazar, Cotati, CA (18 & Under Open) .... John Paul Kinman
     – Michael Jung, Fenton, MO (14 & Under Open) .... Jesse Bowman
     – Kara Wroldson, Lee, MA (18 & Under Girls) .... Tiffany Nelson
1996 – Mike Patton, Corbin, KY (18 & Under Open) .... Dan Klemencic
     – Stephane Adam, QB, Canada (14 & Under Open) .... Wally Bentley
     – Stacee Adkins, Paducah, KY (18 & Under Girls) .... Sarah Rousey
1997 – Dan Klemencic, Terra Haute, IN (18 & Under Open) .... Mike Patton
     – Holly Sholes, Oklahoma City, OK (18 & Under Girls) .... Stacee Adkins
     – Jesse Bowman, Moline, IL (14 & Under Open) .... Shane McMinn

NATIONAL JUNIOR ARTISTIC POOL CHAMPIONSHIPS

Champion .... **Runner-up**

1993 — William Trippe, Tampa, FL (18 & Under Open) .... Aaron Johnson
 — Tom Tollardo, Taos, NM (14 & Under Open) .... Trvor Braymore
 — Stacee Adkins, Paducah, KY (18 & Under Girls) .... Kelly Monoski
1994 — Jason Roselle, Oshkosh, WI (18 & Under Open) .... Jason Hill
 — Nicholas Tedesco, Las Vegas, NV (14 & Under Open) .... Kent Montel
 — CharlaGrenz, Bismarck, ND (18 & Under Girls) .... Stacee Adkins
1995 — David Coffelt, Warren, PA (18 & Under Open) .... John Paul Kinman
 — Brandon Hallett, Holland, MI (14 & Under Open) .... Ruben Silva, Jr.
 — Stacee Adkins, Paducah, KY (18 & Under Girls) .... Jennifer Willhoff
1996 — Jamie Green, Shelbyville, IN (18 & Under Open) .... Mike Derr
 — Jennifer Willhoff, Colorado Springs, CO (18 & Under Girls) .... Jennifer Walker
 — Chris Weast, Star City, AR (14 & Under Open) .... Laura Marie Lindauer
1997 — Adam Stanton, Fairport, NY (18 & Under Opean) .... Brad Weast
 — Jennifer Walker, Glasgow, KY (18 & Under Girls) .... Martha Bays
 — Nicholas Gutierrez, Sacramento, CA (14 & Under Open) .... Chris Weast

1997 BCA LEAGUE STATE CHAMPIONS

GEORGIA
Open Singles
 Alun Champion .... Atlanta

Men's Mixed/Team
The Diamond Cutters .... Atlanta

ILLINOIS
Men's Singles
Jon Kucharo .... Moline

Women's Singles
Renee Edmiston .... Hinsdale

Men's/MixedTeam
Tastes Like Chicken .... Schaumburg

Scotch Doubles
Renee Edmiston/Jim Engels

IOWA
Eight-Ball Men's Singles
Bob McDonald .... Dubuque

Women's Singles
Kathy Christiansen .... Clinton

Men's/Mixed Teams
Cue Masters Elite .... Dubuque

Women's Team
Lassiter's Whatever .... Clinton

Nine-Ball Men's Singles
Paul Meyer .... Waterloo

LOUISIANA
Men's/Mixed Team
High Tide .... Houma

Women's Team
Bustin' Balls .... Lake Charles

Open Nine-Ball Singles
Tucker Chauvin .... Schreiver

Eight-Ball Scotch Doubles
Sharron Young/Pete Melton ... Shreveport

WASHINGTON/OREGON
Women's Nine-Ball "A" Singles
Annie Gay .... Salem, OR

Women's Nine-Ball "B" Singles
Pam Carraway .... Port Angeles, WA

Men's Nine-Ball "A" Singles
Tom Rossi .... Salem, OR

Men's Nine-Ball "B" Singles
Frank Lanaro .... Salem, OR

Men's Nine-Ball "C" Singles
Pete Walton .... Longview, WA

Women's Eight-Ball "A" Singles
Cindy Doty .... Longview, WA

Women's Eight-Ball "B" Singles
Robbin Borden .... Port Angeles, WA

Women's Eight-Ball "C" Singles
Michelle Schreiner .... Vancouver, WA

Men's Eight- Ball "A" Singles
Ivan Doty .... Longview, WA

Men's Eight-Ball "B" Singles
Steve Bartlett .... Astoria, WA

Men's Eight-Ball "C" Singles
Kevin Fong .... Port Angeles, WA

Scotch Doubles Nine-Ball "A"
Jay Collins/Jean Bartholomew

Scotch Doubles Nine-Ball "B"
Harry Peterson/Robbin Borden

Men's Team Eight-Ball "A"
John's Gang .... Portland, OR

Men's Team Eight-Ball "B"
Whoo-Whaa's .... Longview, WA

Women's Eight-Ball Team
She Strokers .... Longview, WA

BCA SANCTIONED TOURNAMENTS

UTAH EIGHT-BALL CLASSIC
1. Tim Joseph   2. Tommy Baker   3. Chris Muirbrook   4. Chris Lorenz

11TH ANNUAL ALASKA STATE STRAIGHT POOL CHAMPIONSHIPS
"A" Class
1. Don Wirtaman   2. Mike Roddy   3. Mark Tullis   4. Al Bryan

"B" Class
1. Sean Morgan   2. Ralph Butler   3. Leif Larson

"C" Class
1. Mark Lavalle   2. Mako   3. Todd Sockpick

MUSIC CITY AMATEUR BILLIARD TOUR
Tennessee Amateur Championships Men's Eight-Ball/Nine-Ball
1. Bob Halloran   2. Tommy Counts   3. Dennis Haar   4. Billy McMahan

Tennessee Amateur Championships Women's Eight-Ball/Nine-Ball
1. Michelle Head   2. Judy Kingry   3. Rodonna Woods   4. Kathy Long

B.C. PROVINCIAL INTER-LEAGUE EIGHT-BALL CHAMPIONSHIPS
Individual Results
1. Troy Richards   2. Larry Wilson   3. Tammy Korsh   4. Ken Kapalka

League Team Results
1. Victoria Eight-Ball Association   2. Fraser Valley Pool League
3. John Howard Pool League   4. Mid Island Eight-Ball Association

BCW WISCONSIN STATE POCKET BILLIARD CHAMPIONSHIPS
Master's Nine-Ball
1. Larry Nevel   2. Craig Powers   3. Mark Niver   4. Randy LaMar

Women's Eight-Ball
1. Pam Bell   2. Heather Perrigoue   3. Linda Pawelski   4. Ellen Smith

Juniors Nine-Ball
1. Chris Conrad   2. Mike Flaningham   3. Dan Llanas   4. Luke Geffers

Class "A" Nine-Ball
1. John Starr   2. P.T. Pedersen   3. Jon Lee   4. Tim Sena

Class "B" Nine-Ball

1. Dan Coppens   2. Gary Kroes   3. Kevin Meier   4. Rocko Theilman

Straight Pool

1. Craig Powers   2. Ron Dobosenski   3. Claudio Parrone   4. Larry Nevel

ARKANSAS POOL PLAYERS ASSOCIATION
2nd Annual Eight-Ball Team Championships

1. Lone Star Steak House - Springdale   2. Woodpeckers - North Little Rock
3. Happy People - Russellville   4. Slick Sticks - Conway

1997 Women's State Singles Nine-Ball Championships

1. Jana Carroll   2. Lisa Marr   3. Lisa Rathburn   4. Teresa Jones

1997 Women's State Singles Eight-Ball Championships

1. Jana Carroll   2. Lisa Marr   3. Melissa Ashe   4. Lisa Henderson

1997 Master's Division Nine-Ball Championships

1. Greg Ridenour   2. Al O'Rear   3. Brad Mc Connell   4. Calvin Harcrow

1997 Novice Division State Singles Eight-Ball Championships

1. Josh Britton   2. Thoo Douangchanh   3. Sarah Handley   4. Pick Malone

1997 Intermediate Division State Singles Eight-Ball Championships

1. Steve Matlock   2. Mike Cordell   3. Scott Adair   4. Grover Hallman

1997 Masters Division State Singles Eight-Ball Championships

1. Greg Ridenour   2. Calvin Harcrow   3. Scott Barrow   4. Brad Weast

"DR. CUE'S" NATIONAL BANK POOL TOURNAMENT

1. Milt Lewis   2. Lee Sibley   3. Steve Countryman   4. Jerry Fiehl

4TH ANNUAL NEBRASKA CHAMPION OF CHAMPIONS EIGHT-BALL TOURNAMENT

1. Al Bruha - Grand Island   2. Randy Sedlacek - Columbus
3. Greg Gasper - Columbus   4. Bill Goesch - Columbus

LINDSEY NINE-BALL TOURNAMENT

1. Jacey Hodges   2. Bill Lindsey   3. Drew Haney

NORTH AMERICAN TRICK SHOT AND ARTISTIC CHAMPIONSHIP

1. Tom Rossman   1. George Middleditch(tie)   3. Larry Grindinger   4. Brian Maiuoux

SKULSKI'S
Memorial to Jerry Cutway

1. Bill Jamieson   2. Paul Mekeel   3. Mario Seggio

Salute Jimmy and Rosalyn Carter

1. Bill Jamieson   2. Jerry Howard   3. Joey Mueller   4. Fritz Crogan

Salute to Larry Cruisdale

1. Fast Eddie Rosas   2. Mitch Dishner   3. Joey Mueller   4. Dave Wagner

Salute to Bill Jamieson
1. Mario Seggio   2. Joey Mueller   3. Fast Eddie Rosas   4. Adam Monture

Memorial to Ted Macris
1. Eddie Rosas Sr.   2. Eddie Rosas Jr.   3. Marty Lawson   4. John Schantz

St. Valentines Day Massacre
1. Jessie & Sue Szymczak   2. Gail Rytel/ Judy VanDelinder   3. Tom Gerwitz/ Terry Czaplicpi   4. Mario & Jennett Seggio

Salute to Larry "Magic" Croisdale
1. Eddie Rosas Jr.   2. Mitch Dischner   3. Joey Mueller   4. Dave Wagner

8TH ANNUAL GREATER DULUTH EIGHT-BALL OPEN
1. Louie Lemke (St. Paul, MN)   2. Vince Chambers (Thunder Bay, ONT)
3. Mike Miller (Superior, WI)   4. Rod Carr (Duluth, MN)

NORTH AMERICAN CHALLENGE-TEXAS A&M UNIVERSITY PBC
"A" Division
1. James Delgado (Univ. Of Texas)   2. Chris Gaither (Texas A&M)
3. Ryan Paxton (Sam Houston State)

"B" Division
1. Billy Tran (Univ. Of Texas)   2. John Chirico (Univ. Of W. Ontario)
3. Steve Guinn (Texas A&M)

"C" Division
1. Matt Torres (SW Texas State)   2. Josve Sotela (SW Texas State)
3. Jeremy Hayes (Texas A&M)

11TH ANNUAL WORLD OPEN "HONOLULU" POCKET BILLIARD CHAMPIONSHIP
"A" Division
1. Mark Tullis   2. "Flapper" Hamilton   3. Mike Roddy   4. Alex Varona

"B" Division
1. Ming Wong   2. Junior Jveco   3. Mike Ziegahn   4. Tom Bates

"C" Divison
1. Mark Langlie   2. Andre Rivera   3. Arnold Pyhala   4. Thomas Welte

SOUTHLAND SENIOR GAMES
60-64 Age Group
1. Jim Newton   2. Robert Hankes

65-69 Age Group
1. Robert Mook   2. Ted Allen   3. Gene Olson

70-74 Age Group
1. Robert Moorhouse   2. Robert Hughes   3. Robert Hipman

75-79 Age Group
1. Charles Whetzel   2. Bob Cunnard   3. Jim Miller

RICK LANE MEMORIAL TOURNAMENT

1. Tommy Baker   2. D. Ace Brown   3. Tim Joseph   4. Wellie Lieataua

IRVING CRANE EIGHT-BALL TOURNAMENT

1. Lyn Wechsler   2. Brian Doty   3. Tony Morrison   4. Pat Howey

4TH ANNUAL MID-WEST BAR TABLE CLASSIC

1. Larry Nevel, Jr.   2. Steve Oaks   3. Al Jones   4. Mike Vergere

INTERNET EQUAL OFFENSE RESULTS FOR 1997

Internet Equal Offense-February 1, 1997
Texas A&M Team 1 (Yesterdays), College Station, Texas, USA
540 Points, 10.80/inning
Bob Green, Jay Russell, Joe Dunn, Bob Garcia, Jeff Rogers

Internet Equal Offense - April 5, 1997
Texas A&M Team 1 (Yesterdays), College Station, Texas, USA
550 Points, 11.00/inning
Bob Garcia, Jay Russell, Jeff Rogers, Bob Green, Joe Dunn

Internet Equal Offense - August 30, 1997
Motley Cues (Carlo's Billiard Academy), Downers Grove, Illinois, USA
485 Points, 9.70/inning
Ron Shepard, Chuck Wicks, Hans Noack, Jon Fennell, Mark Kulaga

Internet Equal Offense - October 25, 1997
Texas A&M Team 1 (Yesterdays), College Station, Texas, USA
457 Points, 9.41/inning
Jeff Rogers, Marvin Harris, Bob Green, Bob Garcia, Norm Sleck

ACU-I POCKET BILLIARD CHAMPIONS
Men's

1937 – John O. Miller .... University of Wisconsin
1938 – J. L. Geiger .... University of Florida
1939 – Peter Choulas .... Colgate University
1940 – John O. Miller .... University of Wisconsin
1941 – Lloyd Green .... University of Kansas
1942 – Leo Bonimi .... Cornell University
1943 – L. Mabie .... University of Florida
1944 – J. Zvanya .... University of Indiana
1945 – 46 .... (No Tournament)
1947 – Leff Mabie .... University of Florida
1948 – Jack Brown .... University of Utah
1949 – Leroy Kinman .... Eastern Kentucky State
1950 – Leroy Kinman .... Eastern Kentucky State
1951 – Leroy Kinman .... Eastern Kentucky State
1952 – Bill Simms .... University of Georgia
1953 – John Beaudette .... Michigan State College
1954 – John Beaudette .... Michigan State College
1955 – Rodney Boyd .... Ohio State University
1956 – Joseph Sapanaro .... Suffolk University

1957 – Joseph Sapanaro .... Suffolk University
1958 – Lloyd Courter .... State University of Iowa
1959 – Donald Dull ... ,,,,,,,,,,,,,,,,,,,,,,, State College of Washington
1960 – Henry Parks .... Indiana University
1961 – Jim Finucane .... University of Notre Dame
1962 – Robert Burke .... University of Oregon
1963 – Larry Galloway .... Indiana University
1964 – William Hendricks .... Southern Illinois University
1965 – William Wells .... Tulane University
1966 – William Wells .... Tulane University
1967 – Richard Baumgarth .... Purdue University
1968 – Marshall Boelter .... Univ. of Illinois, Chicago Circle Campus
1969 – Nick Varner .... Purdue University
1970 – Nick Varner .... Purdue University
1971 – Keith Woestehoff .... Ohio University
1972 – Andrew Tennent .... University of Wisconsin
1973 – Dan Louie .... Washington State University
1974 – Dan Louie .... Washington State University
1975 – Robert Jewett .... University of California–Berkeley
1976 – John Cianflone .... Rutgers University
1977 – Jay Hungerford .... Arizona State University
1978 – Steve Cusick .... University of Illinois–Urbana
1979 – Peter Lhotka .... University of North Dakota
1980 – Rob Havick .... University of Minnesota–Duluth
1981 .... (No Tournament)
1982 – Thomas Golly .... Penn State University
1983 – Robert Madenjian .... Kansas State University
1984 – Gary French .... California State College–Stanislaus
1985 .... (No Tournament)
1986 – Gary Asbell .... Florida State University
1987 – Bill Beardsley .... University of Michigan
1988 – Nick Kucharew .... Mohawk College
1989 – Gary Asbell .... Florida State University
1990 – Marc Oelslager .... St. Cloud State University
1991 – Frank Alonso .... University of Nebraska–Lincoln
1992 – David Uwate .... University of Florida
1993 – Max Eberle .... James Madison University
1994 – Max Eberle .... James Madison University
1995 – Kevin Carlberg .... Montana State University
1996 – Anthony Piazza .... Colorado State University
1997 – Anthony Piazza .... Colorado State University

ACU-I POCKET BILLIARD CHAMPIONS
Women's

1929 – Margaret Anderson .... University of Illinois
1942 – Emily Ann Julian .... South Dakota State College
1943 – Mary Jean Noonan .... South Dakota State College
1944 – Barbara Jackson .... Colorado State College of Ed.
1948 – Jeanne Lynch .... Rhode Island State
1949 – Cora Libbey .... University of Wisconsin
1950 .... (No Tournament)

1951 – Ramona Fielder	....	South Dakota State College
1952 – Sondra Bilsky	....	Purdue University
1953 – Joanne Skonning	....	Purdue University
– Jackie Slusher	....	Oregon State College
1954 – Lee McGary	....	University of Oregon
1955 – Judy Ferles	....	University of Arizona
1956 – Judy Ferles	....	University of Arizona
1957 –	....	No Co-ed Face to Face
1958 –	....	No Co-ed Face to Face
1959 – Jan Deeter	....	Purdue University
1960 – Darlene McCabe	....	University of Oregon
1961 – Ann Sidlauskas	....	Indiana University
1962 – San Merrick	....	Bowling Green State University
1963 – Barbara Watkins	....	Bowling Green State University
1964 – Barbara Watkins	....	Bowling Green State University
1965 – Susan Sloan	....	University of Texas
1966 – Linda Randolph	....	Iowa State University
1967 – Shirley Glicen	....	University of Miami
1968 – Gail Allums	....	University of Iowa
1969 – Donna Ries	....	University of Missouri at Kansas City
1970 – Catherine Stephens	....	Western Washington State
1971 – Marcia Girolamo	....	State Univ. of New York at Oswego
1972 – Krista Hartmann	....	Santa Fe Junior College, Gainsville, Florida
1973 – Marcia Girolamo	....	State University of New York at Oswego
1974 – Janice Ogawa	....	Boise State University
1975 – Debra Weiner	....	Northern Illinois University
1976 – Melissa Rice	....	University of Wisconsin–Milwaukee
1977 – Julie Bentz	....	University of Wisconsin–Madison
1978 – Mari Dana Heydon	....	Oregon State University
1979 – Julie Bentz Fitzpatrick	....	University of Wisconsin–Madison
1980 – Shari Verrill	....	University of Wisconsin–Madison
1981	....	(No Tournament)
1982 – Jane Bartram	....	University of Colorado
1983 – Helen Yamasaki	....	California State University–LA
1984 – Shirley Weathers	....	Triton College
1985	....	(No Tournament)
1986 – Kathy Trabue	....	Ohio State University
1987 – Penny Beile	....	University of Kentucky
1988 – Janet Dordell	....	Penn State University
1989 – Cathy Petrowski	....	North Texas State University
1990 – Susan Tillotson	....	Florida State University
1991 – Leanne Okada	....	University of California–Berkeley
1992 – Laura Bendikas	....	University of Illinois–Urbana
1993 – Carla Swails	....	College of Southern Idaho
1994 – Rachel Ross	....	University of Washington
1995 – Heather Perrigoue	....	University of Wisonsin–Milwaukee
1996 – Erica Testa	....	University of New Hampshire
1997 – Heather Perrigoue	....	University of Wisonsin–Milwaukee

BCA's U.S. OPEN 14.1 POCKET BILLIARD CHAMPIONSHIP RECORDS
Men's

Champion	Runner-up
1966 – Irving Crane (Chicago, IL)	Joe Balsis
1967 – Jimmy Caras (St. Louis, MO)	Luther Lassiter
1968 – Joe Balsis (Lansing, MI)	Danny DiLiberto
1969 – Luther Lassiter (Las Vegas, NV)	Jack Breit
1970 – Steve Mizerak (Chicago, IL)	Luther Lassiter
1971 – Steve Mizerak (Chicago, IL)	Joe Balsis
1972 – Steve Mizerak (Chicago, IL)	Dan DiLiberto
1973 – Steve Mizerak (Chicago, IL)	Luther Lassiter
1974 – Joe Balsis (Chicago, IL)	Jim Rempe
1975 – Dallas West (Chicago, IL)	Pete Margo
1976 – Tom Jennings (Chicago, IL)	Joe Balsis
1977 – Tom Jennings (Dayton, OH)	Richard Lane
1983 – Dallas West (Detroit, MI)	Nick Varner
1989 – Oliver Ortmann (Chicago, IL)	Steve Mizerak
1992 – Mike Sigel (New York, NY)	Dallas West
1993 – Oliver Ortmann (New York, NY)	Chien Sheng Lee

Women's

Champion	Runner-up
1967 – Dorothy Wise (St. Louis, MO)	San Lynn Merrick
1968 – Dorothy Wise (Lansing, MI)	San Lynn Merrick
1969 – Dorothy Wise (Las Vegas, NV)	San Lynn Merrick
1970 – Dorothy Wise (Chicago, IL)	Sheila Bohm
1971 – Dorothy Wise (Chicago, IL)	Geraldine Titcomb
1972 – Jean Balukas (Chicago, IL)	Madelyn Whitlow
1973 – Jean Balukas (Chicago, IL)	Donna Ries
1974 – Jean Balukas (Chicago, IL)	Mieko Harada
1975 – Jean Balukas (Chicago, IL)	Mieko Harada
1976 – Jean Balukas (Chicago, IL)	Gloria Walker
1977 – Jean Balukas (Dayton, OH)	Gloria Walker
1983 – Jean Balukas (Detroit, MI)	Loree Jon Ogonowski
1989 – Loree Jon Jones (Chicago, IL)	Robin Bell
1992 – Loree Jon Jones (New York, NY)	Ewa Mataya
1993 – Hsin-Mei Liu (New York, NY)	Loree Jon Jones

U.S. OPEN RECORDS - 1966–1993
Men's

High run in the money: 150 by Irving Crane vs. Joe Balsis, 1966/150 by Mike Sigel vs. Jim Rempe, 1989/150 by Johnny Archer vs. Jeff Carter, 1992; 150 by Mike Sigel vs. Mike Zuglan, 1992.

High run out of the money: 116 by Rodney "Babe" Thompson, 1972.

High BPI average, career (minimum 3 Opens or 10 games): 12.47 by Steve Mizerak.

Most championships won: 4 by Steve Mizerak, (1970-1973 inclusive).

Most consecutive championships won: 4 by Steve Mizerak, (1970-1973 inclusive).

Most runner-up finishes: 3 by Balsis, (1966, 1971, 1976) and Lassiter, (1967, 1970, 1973).

Greatest victory margin (150-point match): 163 by Dick Baertsch (vs. Balsis), 1969.

Most games won, career: 58 by Dallas West, (1966-1993 inclusive).

Best winning percentage, tournament: 1.000 by Crane, 1966; Mizerak, 1971; West, 1975; Sigel, 1992.

Fewest innings by champion (32-man field): 53 by Steve Mizerak, 1972.

Most consecutive match victories: 12 by Steve Mizerak, (1970-1972 inclusive).

Most high run awards: 3 by West, (1966, 1967, 1976) and Balsis, (1968, 1969, 1973).

Best game (150 points): 1 inning by Mike Sigel (vs. Mike Zuglan), 1992

Best game (200 points): 16 innings by Joe Balsis (vs. J. Rempe), 1974.

Most appearances, career: 16 by Dallas West, (1966-1993 inclusive).

U.S. OPEN RECORDS - 1967–1993
Women's

High run in the money: 68 by Ewa Mataya (vs. Cathy Petrowski), 1992.

High run out of the money: 28 by Jean Ann (Williams) Cardwell, 1967.

High BPI average, tournament: 5.18 by Loree Jon Jones, 1989.

Most games, career: 58 by Gerry Titcomb.

Most innings, tournament (16-woman field): 373 by Madelyn Whitlow, 1972.

Most games won, career: 43 by Jean Balukas.

Best winning percentage, tournament: 1.000 by Wise, (67-68, 70-71) and Balukas, (72-83).

Best winning percentage, career (minimum 3 Opens or 10 games): .850 by Jean Balukas.

Most championships won: 7 by Jean Balukas, 1972-1983 inclusive.

Most consecutive championships won: 7 by Jean Balukas, 1972-1983 inclusive.

Most runner-up finishes: 2 by San Lynn Merrick, Gerry Titcomb, Mieko Harada, & Loree Jon Jones.

Most third place finishes: 5 by Gerry Titcomb; 1970, 1972, 1974, 1975, 1976.

Most consecutive match victories: 37 by Jean Balukas, (1972-1983 inclusive).

Most high run awards: 5 by Balukas, (1972, 1973, 1975, 1977, 1983).

Best game (75 points): 3 innings by Jean Balukas (vs. Belinda Campos), 1977.

Best game (100 points): 10 innings by Gerda Hofstatter (vs. Hsin-Mei Liu), 1993.

Best game (125 points): 13 innings by Loree Jon Jones (vs. Robin Bell), 1989.

Most appearances, career: 11 by Gerry Titcomb, (1967-1989 inclusive).

MEN'S POCKET BILLIARD CHAMPIONS 1878-1990
Compiled by Charles Ursitti, Mike Shamos and Ken Shouler

The game of pocket billiards in the United States evolved slowly beginning in the 1830s. The present competitive form, known as straight pool or 14.1 Continuous, was not invented until 1910 and did not become the official championship game until 1912, when the term "pocket billiards" was first introduced. The earliest championship game was called "61-pool," a single-rack game with 15 numbered object balls. Each ball was worth a number of points equal to its numerical value; the first player to score at least 61 points was the winner. A match consisted of a race to a certain number of games, usually 21. This was the game played for the championship from 1878 until 1888.

Because a ball in 61-pool can be worth from 1 to 15 points, it was possible to win a match by sinking far fewer balls than one's opponent. This unfairness was corrected in 1889, when the game of "continuous pool" was introduced. The players still played individual 15-ball racks without a break ball, but each ball counted for only one point and the first player to reach a pre-determined point total, usually 100, was the winner. The player who sank the last ball of a rack would break the full pack on the next rack. No ball had to be called on the break, so it was possible for long runs to occur extending over many racks. The record run at continuous pool is still 96, achieved by Alfredo De Oro in a non-championship game in 1911.

The break shot in continuous pool was very risky, since it is difficult to sink a ball in a controlled fashion when hitting a full rack of fifteen balls. Top players tended to play safety at the end of a rack rather than miss with the balls spread. This caused title games to become boring, as the audience could look forward to an exchange of safeties every 15 balls. To eliminate the problem, Jerome Keogh, the champion in 1910 and teacher of future champion Irving Crane, suggested that the last ball of each rack be left free to be used as a target on the next rack. He proposed the name, "14 racked, 1 ball free," which became 14.1 Continuous. It was adopted as the championship form for the tournament of April 1912, won by Edward Ralph, who thus became the first straight pool champion.

At first, championships were established by donors, such as the Brunswick-Balke-Collender Corporation. These expired after a certain time and a new tournament had to be held to determine the next champion. In between tournaments, the champion was obliged to defend the title against challengers, who would meet the champion in a two-man match. Until the 1940s, this was the dominant method by which the title was decided, much as in boxing. It is therefore incorrect in most cases to associate a single champion with a particular year. Not all tournaments advertised as "for the title" are listed, but only those that were sanctioned by an appropriate governing body.

The table below lists all 209 times that the pocket billiard title has changed hands or become vacant. The date listed is the month in which the title change occurred. *(In some cases, tournaments or matches took place over a period of many months lasting as long as a baseball season.)* The "Champion" is the name of the titleholder. "Runner-Up" indicates the player who lost the title match, or, in the case of a tournament, the player finishing in second place. From 1878-1888, the game was 61-pool. Continuous pool was the championship game from 1889-1911. Straight pool was the championship game from 1912-1990. Nine-Ball has been the Championship game since 1990.

Date		Champion	Runner-Up
Apr,	1878	Cyrille Dion	Samuel F. Knight
Aug,	1878	Gotthard Walhstrom	Cyrille Dion
Apr,	1879	Samuel F. Knight	Gotthard Walhstrom
Aug,	1879	Alonzo Morris	Samuel F. Knight
Oct,	1879	Gotthard Walhstrom	Alonzo Morris
Feb,	1880	Samuel F. Knight	Gotthard Walhstrom
May,	1880	Gotthard Walhstrom	Samuel F. Knight
Jan,	1881	Gotthard Walhstrom	Albert M. Frey
Jun,	1881	Gotthard Walhstrom	Albert M. Frey
Jan,	1884	James L. Malone	Albert M. Frey/Joseph T. King (tie)
Mar,	1886	Albert M. Frey	James L. Malone

Date		Champion	Runner-Up
May,	1886	Albert M. Frey	James L. Malone
Feb,	1887	Albert M. Frey	James L. Malone
Apr,	1887	Albert M. Frey	James L. Malone
May,	1887	James L. Malone	Albert M. Frey
May,	1887	Alfredo De Oro	James L. Malone
Feb,	1888	Alfredo De Oro	James L. Malone
Mar,	1889	Albert M. Frey	Alfredo De Oro
Apr,	1889		Title vacant (Frey died)
Jun,	1889	Alfredo De Oro	Charles H. Manning
Apr,	1890	Alfredo De Oro	Charles H. Manning
May,	1890	Albert G. Powers	Alfredo De Oro
Jun,	1890	Charles H. Manning	Albert G. Powers
Aug,	1890	Charles H. Manning	George N. Kuntzsch
Oct,	1890	Charles H. Manning	Albert G. Powers
Jan,	1891	Albert G. Powers	Charles H. Manning
Mar,	1891	Albert G. Powers	P. H. Walsh
May,	1891	Alfredo De Oro	Albert G. Powers
Mar,	1892	Alfredo De Oro	Albert G. Powers
Mar,	1893	Alfredo De Oro	Frank Sherman
Jun,	1893	Alfredo De Oro	P. H. Walsh
Dec,	1895	William Clearwater	Alfredo De Oro
Mar,	1896	William Clearwater	Jerome Keogh
Apr,	1896	William Clearwater	Alfredo De Oro
May,	1896	Alfredo De Oro	William Clearwater
Jun,	1896	Alfredo De Oro	Grant Eby
Fall,	1896	Herman E. Stewart	Alfredo De Oro
May,	1897	Grant Eby	Herman E. Stewart
Jun,	1897	Jerome Keogh	Grant Eby
Aug,	1897	Jerome Keogh	William Clearwater
Mar,	1898	William Clearwater	Jerome Keogh
Apr,	1898	Jerome Keogh	William Clearwater
Dec,	1898	Alfredo De Oro	Grant Eby/Frank Horgan(tie)
Jan,	1899	Alfredo De Oro	
Apr,	1899	Alfredo De Oro	Jerome Keogh
Dec,	1899	Alfredo De Oro	Fred Payton
Apr,	1900	Alfredo De Oro	Jerome Keogh
Mar,	1901	Frank Sherman	Alfredo De Oro
Apr,	1901	Alfredo De Oro	Frank Sherman
Mar,	1902	William Clearwater	Charles Weston
May,	1902	Grant Eby	William Clearwater
Dec,	1902	Grant Eby	P. H. Walsh
May,	1903		Title vacant
Nov,	1904	Alfredo De Oro	Jerome Keogh
Nov,	1904	Alfredo De Oro	Jerome Keogh
Jan,	1905	Alfredo De Oro	Grant Eby
Mar,	1905	Jerome Keogh	Alfredo De Oro
May,	1905	Alfredo De Oro	Jerome Keogh
Oct,	1905	Alfredo De Oro	William Clearwater
Dec,	1905	Thomas Hueston	Alfredo De Oro
Feb,	1906	Thomas Hueston	Charles Weston

Date		Champion	Runner-Up
Apr,	1906	Thomas Hueston	Joe W. Carney
May,	1906	John Horgan	Thomas Hueston
Oct,	1906	John Horgan	Horace D. ("Jess") Lean
Oct,	1906	Jerome Keogh	John Horgan
Nov,	1906	Jerome Keogh	Fred Tallman
Dec,	1906	Thomas Hueston	Jerome Keogh
Feb,	1907	Thomas Hueston	Edward Dawson
Apr,	1907	Thomas Hueston	Jerome Keogh
Apr,	1907	Thmas Hueston	William Clearwater
Jan,	1908	Thomas Hueston	Jerome Keogh
Jan,	1908		Title vacant
Apr,	1908	Frank Sherman	Charles Weston
May,	1908	Alfredo De Oro	Frank Sherman
Oct,	1908	Alfredo De Oro	Bennie Allen
Nov,	1908	Thomas Hueston	Alfredo De Oro
Apr,	1909	Charles Weston	Thomas Hueston
May,	1909	Charles Weston	Horace B. ("Jess") Lean
Oct,	1909	John G. Kling	Charles Weston
Nov,	1909	Thomas Hueston	John G. Kling
Dec,	1909	Thomas Hueston	Bennie Allen
Feb,	1910	Jerome Keogh	Thomas Hueston
Mar,	1910	Jerome Keogh	Charles Weston
Apr,	1910	Jerome Keogh	Thomas Safford
Sep,	1910	Jerome Keogh	Thomas Hueston
Oct,	1910	Jerome Keogh	Bennie Allen
Nov,	1910	Alfredo De Oro	Jerome Keogh
Jan,	1911	Alfredo De Oro	William Clearwater
Mar,	1911	Alfredo De Oro	Thomas Hueston
Apr,	1911	Alfredo De Oro	Jerome Keogh
May,	1911	Alfredo De Oro	Charles Weston
Nov,	1911		Title vacant
Apr,	1912	Edward Ralph	James Maturo
Jun,	1912	Alfredo De Oro	Edward Ralph
Nov,	1912	Alfredo De Oro	Frank Sherman
Jan,	1913	Alfredo De Oro	James Maturo
Feb,	1913	Alfredo De Oro	Thomas Hueston
Oct,	1913	Bennie Allen	Alfredo De Oro
Dec,	1913	Bennie Allen	Charles Weston
Jan,	1914	Bennie Allen	James Maturo
Apr,	1914	Bennie Allen	Edward Ralph
Jun,	1914	Bennie Allen	Ray R. Pratt
Dec,	1914	Bennie Allen	James Maturo
Dec,	1915		Title vacant
Mar,	1916	W. Emmett Blankenship	Johnny Layton
May,	1916	Johnny Layton	W. Emmett Blankenship
Sep,	1916	Frank Taberski	Johnny Layton
Oct,	1916	Frank Taberski	Ralph Greenleaf
Nov,	1916	Frank Taberski	Edward Ralph
Jan,	1917	Frank Taberski	James Maturo
Feb,	1917	Frank Taberski	Louis Kreuter

Date		Champion	Runner-Up
Apr,	1917	Frank Taberski	Bennie Allen
May,	1917	Frank Taberski	Larry Stoutenberg
Oct,	1917	Frank Taberski	Joe Concannon
Nov,	1917	Frank Taberski	Louis Kreuter
Jan,	1918	Frank Taberski	Ralph Greenleaf
Jan,	1918		Title vacant
Dec,	1919	Ralph Greenleaf	Bennie Allen
Nov,	1920	Ralph Greenleaf	Arthur Woods
Oct,	1921	Ralph Greenleaf	Arthur Woods
Dec,	1921	Ralph Greenleaf	Arthur Woods
Feb,	1922	Ralph Greenleaf	Thomas Hueston
May,	1922	Ralph Greenleaf	Walter Franklin
Oct,	1922	Ralph Greenleaf	Bennie Allen
Dec,	1922	Ralph Greenleaf	Arthur Church
Jan,	1923	Ralph Greenleaf	Thomas Huestonm
Apr,	1924	Ralph Greenleaf	Bennie Allen
Apr,	1925	Frank Taberski	Ralph Greenleaf
Apr,	1926		Title vacant
Nov,	1926	Ralph Greenleaf	Erwin Rudolph
Jan,	1927	Erwin Rudolph	Ralph Greenleaf
Mar,	1927	Erwin Rudolph	Harry Oswald
May,	1927	Thomas Hueston	Erwin Rudolph
Sep,	1927	Frank Taberski	Thomas Hueston
Nov,	1927	Frank Taberski	Pasquale Natalie
Jan,	1928	Frank Taberski	Arthur Woods
Mar,	1928	Ralph Greenleaf	Frank Taberski
May,	1928	Ralph Greenleaf	Andrew St. Jean
Dec,	1928	Frank Taberski	Ralph Greenleaf
Dec,	1929	Ralph Greenleaf	Erwin Rudolph
Dec,	1930	Erwin Rudolph	Ralph Greenleaf
Dec,	1931	Ralph Greenleaf	George Kelly
Dec,	1932	Ralph Greenleaf	Jimmy Caras
May,	1933	Ralph Greenleaf	Andrew Ponzi
Dec,	1933	Erwin Rudolph	Andrew Ponzi
Feb,	1934	Andrew Ponzi	Erwin Rudolph
	1934		Title vacant
Dec,	1935	Jimmy Caras	Erwin Rudolph
Apr,	1936	Jimmy Caras	Erwin Rudolph
Apr,	1937	Ralph Greenleaf	Andrew Ponzi
Nov,	1937	Ralph Greenleaf	Irving Crane
Dec,	1937	Ralph Greenleaf	Irving Crane
Mar,	1938	Jimmy Caras	Andrew Ponzi
Apr,	1938	Jimmy Caras	Andrew Ponzi
Apr,	1940	Andrew Ponzi	Jimmy Caras
May,	1941	Willie Mosconi	Andrew Ponzi
Nov,	1941	Erwin Rudolph	Irving Crane
May,	1942	Irving Crane	Erwin Rudolph
Dec,	1942	Willie Mosconi	Andrew Ponzi
Apr,	1943	Andrew Ponzi	Willie Mosconi
Dec,	1943	Andrew Ponzi	Irving Crane

Date		Champion	Runner-Up
Mar,	1944	Willie Mosconi	Andrew Ponzi
Feb,	1945	Willie Mosconi	Ralph Greenleaf
Mar,	1946	Willie Mosconi	Jimmy Caras
Nov,	1946	Willie Mosconi	Irving Crane
Dec,	1946	Irving Crane	Willie Mosconi
May,	1947	Willie Mosconi	Irving Crane
Nov,	1947	Willie Mosconi	Jimmy Caras
Mar,	1948	Willie Mosconi	Andrew Ponzi
Feb,	1949	Jimmy Caras	Willie Mosconi
Feb,	1950	Willie Mosconi	Irving Crane
Jan,	1951	Willie Mosconi	Irving Crane
Feb,	1951	Willie Mosconi	Irving Crane
Apr,	1952	Willie Mosconi	Irving Crane
Mar,	1953	Willie Mosconi	Joe Procita
Mar,	1955	Willie Mosconi	Joe Procita
Apr,	1955	Irving Crane	Willie Mosconi
Dec,	1955	Willie Mosconi	Irving Crane
Feb,	1956	Willie Mosconi	Jimmy Caras
Mar,	1956	Willie Mosconi	Jimmy Moore
Apr,	1956	Willie Mosconi	Irving Crane
Apr,	1963	Luther Lassiter	Jimmy Moore
Aug,	1963	Luther Lassiter	Jimmy Moore
Mar,	1964	Luther Lassiter	Arthur Cranfield
Sep,	1964	Arthur Cranfield	Luther Lassiter
Mar,	1965	Joe Balsis	Jimmy Moore
Mar,	1965	Joe Balsis	Jimmy Moore
Mar,	1966	Luther Lassiter	Cisero Murphy
Dec,	1966	Luther Lassiter	Cisero Murphy
Apr,	1967	Luther Lassiter	Jack Breit
Dec,	1967	Luther Lassiter	Jack Breit
Apr,	1968	Irving Crane	Luther Lassiter
Feb,	1969	Ed Kelly	Cisero Murphy
Feb,	1970	Irving Crane	Steve Mizerak
Feb,	1971	Ray Martin	Joe Balsis
Feb,	1972	Irving Crane	Lou Butera
Feb,	1973	Lou Butera	Irving Crane
Feb,	1974	Ray Martin	Allen Hopkins
Aug,	1976	Larry Lisciotti	Steve Mizerak
Aug,	1977	Allen Hopkins	Pete Margo
Aug,	1978	Ray Martin	Allen Hopkins
Aug,	1979	Mike Sigel	Joe Balsis
Aug,	1980	Nick Varner	Mike Sigel
Aug,	1981	Mike Sigel	Nick Varner
Aug,	1982	Steve Mizerak	Danny DiLiberto
Aug,	1983	Steve Mizerak	Jimmy Fusco
Aug,	1985	Mike Sigel	Jim Rempe
Aug,	1986	Nick Varner	Allen Hopkins
Jan,	1990	Bobby Hunter	Ray Martin

WOMEN'S POCKET BILLIARD CHAMPIONSHIPS
WORLD 14.1 CHAMPIONS

Date		Champion	Runner-Up
Feb,	1974	Meiko Harada	Jean Balukas
Aug,	1977	Jean Balukas	Gloria Walker
Aug,	1978	Jean Balukas	Billie Billing
Dec,	1979	Jean Balukas	Mary Kenniston (WPBA Natl's)
Aug,	1980	Jean Balukas	Billie Billing
Aug,	1981	Loree Jon Ogonowski	Vicki Frechen
Aug,	1982	Jean Balukas	Loree Jon Ogonowski
Aug,	1983	Jean Balukas	Loree Jon Ogonowski
Aug,	1985	Belinda Bearden	Mary Kenniston
Aug,	1986	Loree Jon Jones	Mary Kenniston

WPBA NATIONAL CHAMPIONS

Date	Champion	Runner-Up
1978	Jean Balukas	Billie Billing (14.1)
1979	Jean Balukas	Mary Kenniston (14.1)
1980	Gloria Walker	Sabra MacArthur (Nine-Ball)
1983	Jean Balukas	Belinda Bearden (Nine-Ball)
1984	Jean Balukas	Mary Kenniston (Nine-Ball)
1985	Belinda Bearden	Linda Haywood (Nine-Ball)
1986	Jean Balukas	Mary Kenniston (Nine-Ball)
1987	Mary Kenniston	Loree Jon Jones (Nine-Ball)
1988	Loree Jon Jones	Robin Bell (Nine-Ball)
1989	Robin Bell	Loree Jon Jones (Nine-Ball)
1990	Loree Jon Jones	Ewa Mataya (Nine-Ball)
1991	Ewa Mataya	Belinda Bearden (Nine-Ball)
1992	Vivian Villarreal	Ewa Mataya (Nine-Ball)
1993	Loree Jon Jones	Dawn Meurin (Nine-Ball)
1994	Jeanette Lee	Loree Jon Jones (Nine-Ball)
1995	Allison Fisher	Loree Jon Jones (Nine Ball)
1996	Allison Fisher	Loree Jon Jones (Nine-Ball)
1997	Gerda Hofstatter	Allison Fisher (Nine-Ball)

WORLD POOL BILLIARD ASSOC. WORLD NINE-BALL CHAMPIONS
Men's

Date	Champion	Runner-Up
1990	Earl Strickland (USA)	Jeff Carter (USA)
1991	Earl Strickland (USA)	Nick Varner (USA)
1992	Johnny Archer (USA)	Bobby Hunter (USA)
1993	Fong-Pang Chao (Taiwan)	Thomas Hasch (Germany)
1994	Takeshi Okumuru (Japan)	Yasunari Itsuzaki (Japan)
1995	Oliver Ortmann (Germany)	Dallas West (USA)
1996	Ralf Souquet (Germany)	Tom Storm (Sweden)
1997	Johnny Archer (USA)	Kun Fang Lee (Taiwan)

Women's

Date	Champion	Runner-Up
1990	Robin Bell (USA)	Loree Jon Jones (USA)
1991	Robin Bell (USA)	Joann Mason (USA)

1992	Franziska Stark (Germany)	Vivian Villarreal (USA)
1993	Loree Jon Jones (USA)	Jeanette Lee (USA)
1994	Ewa Mataya-Laurance (USA)	Jeanette Lee (USA)
1995	Gerda Hofstatter (Austria)	Vivian Villarreal (USA)
1996	Allison Fisher (England)	Helena Thornfeldt (Sweden)
1997	Allison Fisher (England)	Chun Chen Chen(Taiwan)

Junior's

Date	Champion	Runner-Up
1992	Hui-Kai Hsia (Taiwan)	Michael Coltrain (USA)
1993	Hui-Kai Hsia (Taiwan)	Hsieh-Chun Wang (Taiwan)
1994	Jorn Kjolaas (Norway)	Andreas Rindler (Austria)
1995	Kung-Chang Huang (ROC)	Alexander Dremsizis (Germany)
1996	Kung-Chang Huang (ROC)	Andreas Rindler (Austria)
1997	Christian Goteman (Germany)	Chi Hsiang Chuang (Taiwan)

1997 PROFESSIONIAL TOUR CHAMPIONS

1997 WOMEN'S PROFESSIONIAL BILLIARD ASSOC. CLASSIC TOUR

P & B Mag/St. Croix Press, Twin Cities Classic	Allison Fisher
Connelly Philadelphia Classic	Allison Fisher
Huebler Cues Nashville Classic	Jeanette Lee
Olhausen San Diego Classic	Jeanette Lee
Imperial International Detroit Classic	Allison Fisher
Brunswick New York Classic	Allison Fisher
McDermott Los Angeles Classic	Allison Fisher
Gentleman Jack Great Dallas Shoot Out	Helena Thornfeldt
Billiard Congress of America Phoenix Classic	Allison Fisher
Leisure Bay New Orleans Classic	Gerda Hofstatter

1997 PROFESSIONIAL CUESPORTS ASSOCIATION TOUR
Men's

World One Pocket Challenge	Jose Parica
Sands Regency Challenge	Kim Davenport
Dallas Viking Challenge	Johnny Archer
Shooter's Nine-Ball Open	Efren Reyes
Sharkey's Nine-Ball Open	Jose Parica
Treasure Island Resort & Casino	Efren Reyes

1997 FINAL RANKINGS

WPBA RANKINGS			PRO CUESPORTS RANKINGS		
1st	Allison Fisher	1905	1st	CJ Wiley	1115
2nd	Jeanette Lee	1470	2nd	Roger Griffis	980
3rd	Vivian Villareal	1080	3rd	Earl Strickland	840
4th	Ewa Mataya Laurance	1005	4th	Efren Reyes	840
5th	Gerda Hofstatter	935	5th	Allen Hopkins	735
6th	Helena Thornfeldt	775	6th	Johnny Archer	710
7th	Robin Dodson	735	7th	Dave Matlock	695
8th	Nikki Benish	725	8th	George Breedlove	635
9th	Loree Jon Jones	725	9th	Jose Parica	615
10th	Jennifer Chen	680	10th	Mike Immonen	520

1997 SENIOR TOUR

Magoo's - Tulsa, OK .... Buddy Hall
Romine's - Milwaukee,WI .... Paul Thornley
Cue Can Do - Schaumburg, IL.. Billy Incardona
J.O.B.'s - Nashville, TN .... Mike Massey

1997 MEN'S CAMEL PRO SERIES

Riviera HotelProfessional Eight-Ball Open .... Danny Medina
US Open Nine-Ball, Holiday Inn .... Earl Strickland
JOB Open, J.O.B. Billiards .... Francisco Bustamante
Boston Open, Country Club USA .... Jose Parica
South Jersey Open, Expo Center .... Jose Parica
Tulsa Open, Magoo's .... Jim Rempe
Denver Open, Merchandise Mart Expo .... Francisco Bustamante

1997 FINAL RANKINGS

SENIOR TOUR RANKINGS

1st	Bob Vanover	740
2nd	Claude Bernatchez	695
3th	Danny DiLiberto	625
4th	Paul Thornley	580
5th	Dave Bollman	450
6th	Mike Lebron	445
7th	Steve Mizerak	430
8th	Dallas West	400
9th	Buddy Hall	385
10th	Willie Munson	340

CAMEL PRO SERIES RANKINGS

1st	Jose Parica	630
2nd	Buddy Hall	625
3rd	Francisco Bustamante	470
4th	Rudolfo Luat	430
5th	Efren Reyes	420
6th	Earl Strickland	400
7th	Jim Rempe	400
8th	Danny Medina	380
9th	Kim Davenport	355
10th	Johnny Archer	325

NATIONAL CHAMPIONS-U.S. BILLIARD ASSOCIATION

1989 ...... Carlos Hallon (*grand average* 1.103)
1990 ..... Sang Chun Lee (*grand average* 1.471)
1991 .... Sang Chun Lee (*grand average* 1.416)
1992 .... Sang Chun Lee (*grand average* 1.476)
1993 .... Sang Chun Lee (*grand average* 1.596)
1994 ... Sang Chun Lee (*grand average* 1.422)
1995 ... Sang Chun Lee (*grand average* 1.665)
1996 ... Sang Chun Lee (*grand average* 1.552)
1997 ... Sang Chun Lee (*grand average* 1.492)

NATIONAL CHAMPIONS-BILLIARD FEDERATION OF U.S.A.

1968	Allen Gilbert	1979	Eddie Robbin
1969	Bill Hynes	1980	Harry Sims
1970	Allen Gilbert	1981	George Ashby
1971	Allen Gilbert	1982	Carlos Hallon
1972	Eddie Robin	1983	Harry Sims
1973	John Bonner	1984	George Ashby
1974	Frank Torres	1985	Frank Torres
1975	John Bonner	1986	Carlos Hallon
1976	George Ashby	1987	Allen Gilbert
1977	Allen Gilbert	1988	Allen Gilbert
1978	Frank Torres		

NATIONAL CHAMPIONS-AMERICAN BILLIARDS ASSOCIATION

1969	Bud Harris	1975	George Ashby
1970	Bud Harris	1976	Allen Gilbert
1971	Jim Cattrano	1977	Allen Gilbert
1972	Jim Cattrano	1978	George Ashby
1973	Allen Gilbert	1979	George Ashby
1974	not held	1980	George Ashby

Regional Tournaments only were held in 1981-1988

1981	Carlos Hallon	Eastern	1985	Bill Maloney	Eastern*
	George Ashby	Central		Dick Reid	Eastern*
	Allen Gilbert	Western		George Ashby	Central
1982	Chris Bartzos	Eastern		Rick Bryck	Western
	Bill Hawkins	Central	1986	Dick Reid	Eastern
	Allen Gilbert	Western		Bill Smith	Central
1983	Dick Reid	Eastern		Nahib Yousri	Western
	George Ashby	Central	1987	Dick Reid	Eastern
	Allen Gilbert	Western		George Ashby	Central
1984	Carlos Hallon	Eastern		Harry Sims	Western
	George Ashby	Central	1988	Carols Hallon	Eastern
	not held	Western		Mike Donnelly	Central
1985	Ira Goldberg	Eastern*		Allen Gilbert	Western

In September 1988, the BFUSA and ABA merged to form The United States Billiard Association.
*3 Way tie for first place

WORLD THREE-CUSHION CHAMPIONS (PROFESSIONAL)

1878	Leon Magnus	1916	George Moore
1899	W. H. Catton	1917	Charles McCourt
1900	Eugene Carter	1917	Robert L. Cannefax
1900	Lloyd Jevne	1917	Alfredo De Oro
1907	Harry P. Cline	1918	Augie Kieckhefer
1908	John W. Daly	1919	Alfredo De Oro
1908	Thomas Hueston	1919	Robert L. Cannefax
1908	Alfredo De Oro	1920	John Layton
1909	Alfredo De Oro	1921	Augie Kieckhefer
1910	Fred Eames	1921-22	John Layton
1910	Thomas Hueston	1923	Tiff Denton
1910	Alfredo De Oro	1924-25	Robert L. Cannefax
1910	John W. Daly	1926	Otto Reiselt
1911	Alfredo De Oro	1927	Augie Kieckhefer
1912	Joseph W. Carney	1927	Otto Reiselt
1912	John Horgan	1928-30	John Layton
1913-14	Alfredo De Oro	1931	Arthur Thurnblad
1915	George Moore	1932	Augie Kieckhefer
1915	William H. Huey	1933	Welker Cochran
1915	Alfredo De Oro	1934	John Layton
1916	Charles Ellis	1935	Welker Cochran
1916	Charles McCourt	1936	William Hoppe
1916	Hugh Heal		

1936-37	Welker Cochran	1969	Juan Navarra
1938	Roger Conti*	1972	Juan Navarra
1939	Joseph Chamaco	1984	Ludo Dielis
1940-43	William F. Hoppe	1988	Ludo Dielis
1944-46	Welker Cochran	1989	Torbjorn Blomdahl
1947-52	William F. Hoppe	1990	Raymond Ceulemans
1953	Raymond Kilgore	1991	Torbjorn Blomdahl
1954	Harold Worst	1992	Torbjorn Blomdahl
1964	Arthur Rubin	1997	Torbjorn Blomdahl**

*Tournament held in Paris, France, with Welker Cochran and Jake Schaefer in the field.

**The Billiard World Cup Champion was regarded as the World Champion from 1993-1996, when the Union Mondiale de Billard reestablished the World Championship Tournament in 1997.

WORLD THREE-CUSHION CHAMPIONS (AMATEUR)

1928-29	Edmond Soussas, Egypt	1960	Rene Vingerhoedt, Belgium
1930	H. J. Robyns, Holland	1961	Adolfo Suarez, Peru
1931	Enrique Miro, Spain	1963-73	Raymond Ceulemans, Belgium
1932-33	H. J. Robyns, Holland	1974	Nobuaki Kobayashi, Japan
1934	Claudio Puigvert, Spain	1975-80	Raymond Ceulemans, Belgium
1935	Alfredo Lagache, France	1981	Ludo Dielis, Belgium
1936	Edward L. Lee, U.S.A.	1982	Rini Van Bracht, Holland
1937	Alfredo Lagache, France	1983	Raymond Ceulemans, Belgium
1938	Augusto Vergez, Argentina	1984	Nabuaki Kobayashi, Japan
1948	Rene Vingerhoedt, Belgium	1985	Raymond Ceulemans, Belgium
1952	Pedro L. Carrera, Argentina	1986	Avelino Rico, Spain
1953 & 58	Enrique Navarra, Argentina	1987	Torbjorn Blomdahl, Sweden

*World amateur tournament discontinued.

BILLIARD WORLD CUP THREE-CUSHION CHAMPIONS
(Professional)

Champion determined by results of 4 to 7 tournaments. Matches are best 3 out of 5 (15-point games, single elimination format.)

1986	Raymond Ceulemans, Belgium
1987	Raymond Ceulemans, Belgium
1988	Torbjorn Blomdahl, Sweden
1989	Ludo Dielis, Belgium
1990	Raymond Ceulemans, Belgium
1991	Torbjorn Blomdahl, Sweden
1992	Torbjorn Blomdahl, Sweden
1993	Sang Chun Lee, USA
1994	Torbjorn Blomdahl, Sweden
1995	Torbjorn Blomdahl, Sweden
1996	Torbjorn Blomdahl, Sweden

THREE-CUSHION RECORDS

CLASSIC ERA (BEFORE 1960) - IVORY BALLS
Best Tournament Grand Average

1950 — Willie Hoppe 1.333

Best League Game

1926 — Otto Reiselt .... 50 pts. in 16 innings

Best Tournament Game

1949 — Jay Bozeman .... 50 pts. in 23 innings
1958 — Jay Bozeman .... 50 pts. in 98 innings

High Run, Exhibition

1918 — Willie Hoppe 25
1926 — John Layton 18
1939 — Joe Chamaco 18

High Run, Tournament

1915 — Charles Morin 18
1930 — Gus Copulus 17
1940 — Tiff Denton 17

High Run, Match

1945 — Willie Hoppe 20

High Run, Practice Games

Gus Copulos & Welker Cochran 22

MODERN ERA (AFTER 1960) - CAST PHENOLIC BALLS

Best Tournament Grand Average

1995 — Torbjorn Blomdahl, Zundert, Netherlands 2.506
1995 — Torbjorn Blomdahl, Monte Carlo, Monaco 2.324
1995 — Torbjorn Blomdahl, Istanbul, Turkey 2.308
1993 — Torbjorn Blomdahl, Rotterdam, Netherlands 2.252
1994 — Torbjorn Blomdahl, Oosterhout, Netherlands 2.250
1992 — Torbjorn Blomdahl, Tokyo, Japan 2.250

Best Tournament Games

1996 — Torbjorn Blomdahl (vs. Tay Quoc Co) .... 5.000 (50 pts. in 10 inns.)
1996 — Frederic Caudron (vs. Semih Sayginer) .... 5.000 (45 in 9)
1995 — Torbjorn Blomdahl .... 4.167 (50 in 12)
1994 — Semih Sayginer .... 4.091 (45 in 11)
1985 — Raymond Ceulemans .... 4.000 (40 in 10)
1996 — Raymond Ceulemans (vs. Ralf Kostner) .... 4.000 (40 in 10)
1990 — Christ van der Smissen .... 4.000 (40 in 10)
1996 — Eddy Merckx .... 4.000 (40 in 10)
1996 — Torbjorn Blomdahl (vs. Raymond Ceulemans) .... 4.000 (60 in 15)
1994 — Torbjorn Blomdahl (vs. Dick Jaspers) .... 3.846 (50 in 13)
1995 — Raymond Ceulemans (vs. Mark Donvil) .... 3.636 (40 in 11)
1995 — Torbjorn Blomdahl (vs. Richard Bitalis) .... 3.571 (50 in 14)
1994 — Semih Sayginer (vs. Sang Lee) .... 3.571 (50 in 14)
1994 — Torbjorn Blomdahl (vs. Sang Lee) .... 3.333 (60 in 18)
1995 — Sang Chun Lee (vs. Michael Garcia) .... 3.333 (50 in 15)
1994 — Torbjorn Blomdahl (vs. Tonny Carlsen) .... 3.214 (45 in 14)
1994 — Dick Jaspers (vs. Tonny Carlsen) .... 3.214 (45 in 14)
1992 — Sang Lee (vs. Torbjorn Blomdahl) .... 3.125 (50 in 16)
1992 — Raymond Ceulemans (vs. Frederic Caudron) .... 3.125 (50 in 16)
1995 — Sang Lee (vs. Tommy Thomsen) .... 3.076 (40 in 13)
1994 — Sang Lee (vs. Fredric Caudron) .... 2.812 (45 in 16)
1992 — Torbjorn Blomdahl .... 2.812 (45 in 16)
1992 — Torbjorn Blomdahl .... 2.812 (45 in 16)

1991 – Torbjorn Blomdahl .... 2.812 (45 in 16)
1988 – Nobuaki Kobayashi .... 2.812 (45 in 16)

High Run, Tournament

1968 – Raymond Ceulemans in Simonis Cup 26

High Run, League

1993 – Junichi Komori, Dutch League 28

High Run, Inter-Club Match

1969 – Raymond Ceulemans 23

High Run, USA Regional Tournament

1977 – Bill Hawkins 19

High Run, Exhibition

1992 – Torbjorn Blomdahl (vs. Sang Lee) 22

High Runs, Not Scored In Major Tournament Or Exhibitions

Raymond Ceulemans (Belgium) 32
Yoshio Yoshihara (Japan) 31
Torbjorn Blomdahl (Sweden) 24
Allen Gilbert (USA) 22

WORLD PROFESSIONAL BILLIARD AND SNOOKER ASSOCIATION WORLD CHAMPIONS

1927-40	Joe Davis	1973	Ray Reardon
1941-45	Not held	1974	Ray Reardon
1946	Joe Davis	1975	Ray Reardon
1947	Walter Donaldson	1976	Ray Reardon
1948	Fred Davis	1977	John Spencer
1949	Fred Davis	1978	Ray Reardon
1950	Walter Donaldson	1979	Terry Griffiths
1951	Fred Davis	1980	Cliff Thorburn
1952	Fred Davis	1981	Steve Davis
1953	Fred Davis	1982	Alex Higgins
1954	Fred Davis	1983	Steve Davis
1955	Fred Davis	1984	Steve Davis
1956	Fred Davis	1985	Dennis Taylor
1957	John Pulman	1986	Joe Johnson
1958-63	Not held	1987	Steve Davis
1964	John Pulman	1988	Steve Davis
1965	John Pulman	1989	Steve Davis
1966	John Pulman	1990	Stephen Hendry
1967	Not held	1991	John Parrot
1968	John Pulman	1992	Stephen Hendry
1969	John Spencer	1993	Stephen Hendry
1970	Ray Spencer	1994	Stephen Hendry
1971 ... (Played in Nov. 1970)	John Spencer	1995	Stephen Hendry
1971	Not held	1996	Stephen Hendry
1972	Alex Higgins	1997	Ken Doherty

U. S. SNOOKER ASSOCIATION NATIONAL CHAMPIONS

1991	Tom Kollins	1995	Tang Hoa
1992	Tom Kollins	1996	Peter Ong
1993	David Yao	1997	George Lai
1994	David Yao		

INTERNATIONAL BILLIARD & SNOOKER FEDERATION
WORLD AMATEUR CHAMPIONS

1963	Gary Owen (England)
1966	Gary Owen (England)
1968	David Taylor (England)
1970	Jonathan Barron (England)
1972	Ray Edmonds (England)
1974	Ray Edmonds (England)
1976	Doug Mountjoy (Wales)
1978	Cliff Wilson (Wales)
1980	Jimmy White (England)
1982	Terry Parsons (Wales)
1984	O.B. Agarwal (India)
1985	Paul Mifsud (Malta)
1987	Darren Morgan (Wales)
1988	James Wattana (Thailand)
1989	Ken Doherty (Republic of Ireland)
1990	Stephen O'Connor (Republic of Ireland)
1991	Noppadon Noppachorn (Thailand)
1992	Neil Mosley (England)
1993	Tai Pichit (Thailand)
1994	Mohammed Yusuf (Pakistan)
1995	Sakchai Sim-Ngam (Thailand)
1996	Stuart Bingham (England)
1997	Marco Fu (Hong Kong)

WORLD LADIES BILLIARD AND SNOOKER
ASSOCIATION WORLD CHAMPIONS

1976	Vera Selby
1977-1979	Not held
1980	Lesley McIlrath
1981	Vera Selby
1982	Not held
1983	Sue Foster
1984	Not held
1985-1986	Allison Fisher
1987	Ann-Marie Farren
1988-1989	Allison Fisher
1990	Karen Corr
1991	Allison Fisher
1992	Not held
1993-1994	Allison Fisher
1995	Karen Corr
1996	Not Held
1997	Karen Corr

BCA SANCTIONING OF
BILLIARD TOURNAMENTS

The BCA offers tournament sanctioning for amateur and professional tournaments for a nominal fee. This official sanction signifies the tournament's authenticity.

With each sanction, the sponsor shall receive the following:

- Official Rules & Record Book
- Double Elimination pairing charts
- Official Tournament Report Forms
- Official Tournament Sanction Certificate
- BCA Logo Sheet
- Advance listing in the BCA BREAK newsletter
- Recognition of the tournament and winner in the next BCA Official Rules and Record Book

PLEASE SEND US A SANCTION APPLICATION FOR:

Type of Tournament

Name

Company

Address

City   State   Zip

Daytime Phone   Fax

Return to: BCA, 910 23rd Avenue, Coralville, IA 52241-1221

Searching for something to improve your game?
Look no more!

BECOME A BCA
SANCTIONED PLAYER MEMBER

- As a sanctioned player member you will be eligible to participate in the $31,000 added BCA North American Amateur 9-Ball Championships and the singles division of the BCA North American 8-Ball Championships in which over $500,000 will be awarded this year.

- When you join BCA as a sanctioned player member, you will receive complimentary copies of the Official Rules & Records Book and the "How to Play Pool Right" instruc tional booklet.

- In addition, you will also receive member discounts, the *BCA BREAK* newsletter and much, much more. And all this for only $25.

   ❏ YES, I want to reap the benefits of BCA membership. Enroll me as a member today. My check for $25 is enclosed.

   ❏ YES, I am interested in joining BCA. Please send me additional information.

Name

Address

City   State   Zip

Daytime Phone   Date

Return to: BCA, 910 23rd Avenue, Coralville, IA 52241-1221

BECOME A BCA MEMBER

Together, We can make billiards the sport of the new millineum.
By becoming a member of BCA, you will become part of the industry-
wide movement to promote pool and billiards.

BUSSINESS MEMBERSHIPS

Voting Member $1,000
(Manufacturers, Distributors, Importers, etc. represented by 12 members on the board)
Associate Member *(has 1/2 vote)* $500
Retail Member *(rep. by 2 board members)* $250
Room Proprietor Member *(rep. by 2 board members)* $100
Prof. and Trade Association Member $100
Amusement Operator Member... $100
Affiliate Member $100
Non-Profit/Recreation Center Member $60

Note: Business Memberships (above) run Jan. 1–Dec. 31.

Sanctioned Player Member *(rep. by 3 board members)* $25

❏   YES, I would like to become a member of the BCA.

Type of Membership

Name

Company

Address

City   State   Zip

Business Phone   Fax

Web Site   e-mail

Signature

❏ My check for $ ———— is enclosed.

Return to: BCA, 910 23rd Avenue, Coralville, IA 52241-1221

239

BCA PRESIDENTS

William Gunklach
1966 & 1968

Bud Hobbs
1967

James F. Wilhem
1969-71 & 1980-81

Charles L. Bailey
1972-1973

Michael Geiger
1974-1975

Kim Gandy
1976-1977

Paul Lucchesi
1978

No Picture
Available

Darrell Lawless
1979

Paul Huebler
1983-1984

David Maidment
1985 & 1991

Charles Robertson
1986-1988

James Bakula
1989-1990

Daniel Gauci
1992-1993

Raoul Rubalcava
1994-1995

Don Shimel
1996-1998